Shift

Shift

Let Go of Fear and Get Your Life in Gear

JEFFREY W. HULL, PhD

Guilford, Connecticut

An imprint of Globe Pequot Press

To

Toni, Lucille, and Judy:
My mother, my mom, and my muse

GPP Life is an imprint of Globe Pequot Press

The following poem, which appears on pages 226–27, has been reprinted by permission: "The Mess in the Middle," from Toni Stone Wonder Works Studio, copyright © 1995 by Toni Stone. www.wonderworks.org

Text design by Sheryl P. Kober

Library of Congress Cataloging-in-Publication Data is available on file.

ISBN 978-0-7627-5662-9

Printed in the United States of America

10 9 8 7 6 5 4 3 2 1

The material in this book is intended to provide accurate and authoritative information, but should not be used as a substitute for professional care. The author and publisher urge you to consult with your mental health care provider or seek other professional advice in the event that you require expert assistance.

CONTENTS

INTRODUCTION

Welcome to the crossroads of fear and change. If you're holding this book in your hands having already purchased it, or are perusing the bookshelves in your local bookstore, or—more likely these days—scanning the online "stacks" in an Internet shopping mall, I have two questions for you:

- *Have you experienced any changes in your life lately?*

- *Have you experienced anything you might call fear (or maybe stress, anxiety, worry, guilt, anger, or irritability)?*

If not, if no big change has happened to you recently and everything is happily status quo, if you are relaxed, serene, and vivaciously optimistic—happily in the flow of life—well, this book is probably NOT for you.

On the other hand, if you can look over your shoulder and see huge change in the recent past, or gaze out toward a major shift on the not-too-distant horizon, if the thought of "smooth sailing" feels alien and out of reach, well, it may be time to grab a cappuccino and join me on the good ship Life-Shifting! Of course, I'm being a bit tongue-in-cheek here, because the truth is, I don't know anyone who is not feeling the heat of change these days. As the billboard I saw recently on the New York Thruway triumphantly proclaims, "Change Is the New Black!"

As I sit here in the midst of a forty-five-degree, overcast New York City July day (speaking of upheaval, can I hear anyone say "climate change"?), I'm struck by how "normal" it feels to most of us to almost always be in the midst of endless change. It is simply an understatement to say that we live in turbulent times.

The world is in the midst of an economic recession deeper than at any time since the Great Depression, there are innumerable "hot spots" fraught with terrorism and political fragmentation all over the globe, and historically stable industries such as automobile manufacturing and finance have literally come apart at the seams. Climate change, with its tiny, incremental shifts in temperature that may prove to have a monumental impact on the entire planet's livability, has become a ubiquitous presence in our lives.

Perhaps I have an overly rosy rearview-mirror sense of the past, but I do think there used to be periods of calm, even relative stability. Today, everywhere I look people are in mental, physical, and emotional meltdown. With the blessings of the Internet, CNN, and emerging social media technologies such as Facebook and Twitter, we now witness the tragedy of terrorist attacks in Mumbai moments after they occur. We know as much about famine in North Korea, refugee camps in Sudan, and terrorists in Afghanistan as we do about job losses, swine flu, and child abuse tragedies that occur in our own backyard. Everything, and I mean everything, feels up close and personal.

The pace of change in the world—and in our lives—may not have actually increased that much. Yet, with moment-by-moment interactive access to the global community, not just the neighbors and folks down the block, it feels like everything is changing faster, with greater intensity—and we're freaked. On the other hand, human beings are surprisingly adaptable. Given that we are the least physically protected of all the animals on the planet, it is our amazing ability to adapt—to migrate, learn, and manipulate the world around us—that has helped us survive, and thrive, in ever greater numbers across the globe. As I reflect on what I hope to accomplish with this book, I can't help but wonder if we're losing ground—evolutionary ground. We've become an anxious lot.

Let's look at a few real-life examples where having a program to support you through the throes of major change—and help to release the fear that accompanies it—can really make a difference. See if you recognize a bit of yourself in these vignettes, all of which—as with every story in this book—are based on real people (some identifying information has been changed to protect their anonymity):

> *Frank, a thirty-five-year-old investment adviser, climbed the corporate ladder with agility and speed for fifteen years when he suddenly hit a wall. When accepting his promotion to executive vice president, he was quietly warned by a friendly human resource manager that he would be reporting to a "tough guy"—a business euphemism for an abusive, autocratic boss. Within six months, Frank, who had always been optimistic and politically astute, found himself in a deep rut—hating his job, dreading coming to work, and fearful of doing anything that might result in losing his job.*

When Frank arrived at my office complaining of anxiety and insomnia, I recognized the real enemy he was fighting immediately, and it wasn't his boss: It was his own fear. Within a few short months, armed with an understanding of the nature of change and a set of practices customized for his particular brand of self-induced terror, Frank was able to shift his fear—which was not really about his boss, but a deep-seated fear of authority figures stemming from his relationship with his father—and get back on track.

He left me having accomplished his goal—learning how to not just survive but thrive under his abusive boss. Yet in the wake of our work together, I was not in the least bit surprised when, just two years later, I heard that he had waved good-bye to abusive bosses forever and started his own investment advisory firm. As you might imagine, he is a great boss to his growing staff.

Sylvia, a forty-five-year-old mother of two and senior sales executive for a global technology firm, was hit simultaneously with two of life's most difficult events: She was "downsized" from her job through no fault of her own (thanks to a new boss who suddenly appeared six thousand miles and one whole continent away), while in the midst of a painful divorce. Experiencing an (understandable) emotional meltdown, Sylvia arrived at my door bereft of energy, anxious, angry, and confused about where to turn next.

With the help of her own customized Life-Shifting Program, she was ultimately able to retreat, regroup, and rediscover her own innate sense of power and strength. It wasn't an easy process and although she recognized that major change was afoot, it took awhile for Sylvia to realize that her biggest foe wasn't the former boss, the nasty corporate world, the unrepentant ex, but her own fear of change. Today, with two blossoming teenagers, a new man in her life, and an even higher-powered job, she returns to the Life-Shifting techniques over and over again—to shift out of fear and into the flow of her life.

At sixty, Paula should have been excited to see retirement on the horizon. But she was terrified. With her having been a successful professional, mother, and wife for thirty years, the prospects of an empty nest, no job, and playing bingo with girlfriends for the next twenty years left her feeling lost and, frankly, old. The Life-Shifting Program we created together helped Paula realize that it was actually her deep-seated fear of being a beginner again that was holding her back. When she shifted her focus—from endings to beginnings—she was able to replace the dread of aging with delight in her strength and wisdom. This realization gave her the courage to rediscover her long-buried inner child, to become playful and re-energized by life. Today, retirement is far from Paula's mind as she pursues her new career as a high school guidance counselor and yoga instructor.

All of the above illustrate one point: Shift happens. Change is a basic part of life. Jobs change, lovers change, ideas change, people change. No matter how much money we've stashed away for a rainy day, or how well thought out our "life plan" might be, life inevitably throws us a curve. But too often, when faced with a new direction in life, we become overwhelmed by fear; we become stuck. It seems to me that if the cycle of life always includes an inevitable rupture—and subsequent release and renewal—our goal in becoming facile as a "life-shifter" is simple: We need to get better at it. We need to become more adept at spotting and moving through the cycles of life. This is the goal of the Life-Shifting Program—and the focus of this book.

BIRTH OF A PROGRAM

What is immediately evident, as I reflect on how the Life-Shifting Program came into existence, is that it was—and still is—a group effort. Many friends, workshop leaders, shamans, therapists, healers, and even corporate executives have offered me their wisdom and knowledge over the years in which this program has been developed. I have been fortunate to find myself, when in the throes of my own *life shift*s, or in a quandary about how to help a client, in front of just the right teacher at the right time. You will become acquainted with many of them as you read the book.

Though there have been, and continue to be, many teachers who cross my path and enrich my perspective (in fact, that pretty much includes everyone I meet), three are most responsible for the birth of the Life-Shifting Program: S. N. Goenka, Carl Jung, and Sadie Nardini. As a foundation, I'd like to introduce you to them.

VIPASSANA MEDITATION

In the spring of 1995, I had my first major career shift. As a human resources director with a global management consulting firm headquartered in New York City, the view from the outside was success. I had a corner office (with a view!), a management job with worldwide responsibilities, a sizable paycheck, a corporate American Express card, and all the requisite trappings of corporate achievement. But toiling away under a workaholic boss, who kept me "drinking from the fire hose" (as he summarily called it) at all hours of the day and night, I was miserable. Stress, anxiety—and fear that I was arriving at mid-career materially successful but way off track from my earlier aspirations—were my constant companions.

When it became virtually impossible to sit at my desk for more than fifteen minutes without experiencing excruciating lower back pain, I found myself wandering the streets of Manhattan looking futilely for an ergonomic desk chair. I remember my boss giving me permission to buy one of those kneeling-style chairs that keep your back straight and knees bent—supposedly a tension reliever. Not very helpful when people would wander into my office and casually ask, "Are you praying?" (The truth is: I was! Praying for someone or something to come along and get me out of there!)

One morning, after a particularly arduous overnight flight from São Paulo, Brazil, to New York City (during which my boss snored happily away in first class as I sat bolt upright, many rows behind, plotting how to murder him without getting caught), I escaped his 6:00 a.m. roll call by running to Starbucks. Flopping down exhaustedly on a stool, sighing into my latte, I thought to myself: Something has got to give! Change was afoot. So when a good friend and mentor suggested that I start meditating—to reground, get centered, and calm my overwrought back and mind, I took up his suggestion, and attended my first Buddhist meditation retreat.

Venturing off to the resplendent Berkshire Mountains in western Massachusetts, I discovered the teachings of S. N. Goenka, Vipassana meditation, and, most important, silence. For ten days I spoke not a word, spending eight hours a day sitting cross-legged, eyes closed, trying desperately not to move. Goenka, our Buddhist teacher flown in on wings of DVDs from central India, taught me to focus on my breath, to calmly observe my own internal sensations, to gently—and compassionately, without judgment—watch the endless swirl of thoughts that raced through my mind like the Daytona 500. Throughout the ten-day ordeal and the onslaught of back pain, sexual fantasies, mosquito bites, and bouts of severe loneliness (even though I was surrounded by people!), one question kept rising to the fore: WHO is doing the watching?

I learned many things on that first foray into Buddhist practice: that pain and pleasure are two sides of the same coin; they are simply physical sensations, always in motion, never static. I learned that the mind constantly regurgitates an endless litany of fantasies, stories, and complaints about everyone and everything; and I learned that the small resplendent details of life—a blade of grass, a passing cloud, the taste of a raisin—can bring tears of ecstasy. But most important, I learned that there is no such thing as a "self."

Just as the Buddha pointed out thousands of years ago, I discovered this truth by employing what Goenka describes as the ultimate empirical experiment: self-observation. Wherever I looked for "myself" during those ten days in silence, I never found much there. I never heard the "real" voice called "mine"; I never got to the root of my essential being; I never figured out anything essential about who I am or where I am going. What a revelation and, ultimately, a relief!

Thanks to this powerful Buddhist practice and the gentle, compassionate disciples who taught me to meditate, I learned a key principle that undergirds the work of the Life-Shifting Program: There's no there there. Everything, including all of my physical, emotional, and mental "systems," is always changing, always shifting, never complete, never finished, always arriving, and then, just as quickly, leaving again. Today, I am a committed meditator and devotee of the Vipassana style of Buddhist practice. As we go through the Life-Shifting Program together, you will learn more about how the Eastern perspective on change, fear, and the self can serve to break us out of our false attachments to the so-called real world of material objects. The truth is that we are all constructed—made up—and therefore immeasurably more free to reinvent ourselves than we ever thought possible.

JUNGIAN PSYCHOLOGY

Like many devotees of Carl Jung, I got my first introduction to the famous man by reading his autobiography, *Memories, Dreams, Reflections*, as an undergrad. Jung wasn't taught in the psychology department, which at that time was a fundamentalist shop of cognitive-behaviorism, replete with endless experimentation with rats in cages. (I remember thinking that the main thing that really connected the rats and the students was that they were both stuck, at least metaphorically, in cages!) Jung, viewed with skepticism by the psychological community (even though he was a dedicated empiricist who along with Freud is clearly a key progenitor of all the so-called Western healing modalities that are currently in vogue, including neuroscience and psycho-pharmacology), was taught in the religion department.

Jung describes a theory of individual development that he calls "individuation." He believed that the earliest sense of self that we develop, what he called the "ego," or personality, is constructed through environmental influences—parents, siblings, and the community. By early adulthood, however, he noticed, many, if not most, people are confronted with painful emotional upheaval—life shifts—some caused by outer circumstances, some not, under which the ego seems to come under attack. In supporting his clients through these personal ruptures, he came to understand that their real story, the breakthroughs they achieved and the anxiety they felt, was all developmental; it was personal growth in the guise of pain.

Jung came to declare that throughout adulthood, continued personal growth requires that the ego soften, break open, and become permeable; that our personalities, in some sense, get shunted aside to make room for a more fundamental psychological wholeness to emerge. It became Jung's contention that all of life's evolutionary thrust is toward the individual and collective emergence of this deeper self, which he also called the soul, and that our attachment to "ego identities" along the way, although necessary to build our capacity to function in the world, ultimately must be shed, dissolved, and transcended. Only then may the deeper voice, the call of the soul, be heard.

In many ways, Jung is the West's version of an Eastern mystic, a shamanic counterpoint to the Western biomedical model of healing and personal growth. He understood, long before the neuroscientists who are coming around to validate him, that our emotional pain in the face of change is born of fear, fear that emanates from an overwrought personality (our ego) that is being asked to step aside so that something deeper, richer, and more essentially human may emerge: our soul.

Most, if not all, of our major life shifts are a result of this yearning, this deep desire we have to constantly grow. As you will discover in the unfolding of the Life-Shifting Program, the changes you most resist and defend against actually happen *for* you and not *to* you. They are designed to unleash your true potential. It is in the ongoing dance between ego and soul that we find the lesson that I learned and understood from Jung: All of life's shifts, however fearsome, painful, and apparently destructive, provide an opportunity for reinvention, rebirth, and renewal.

VINYASA YOGA

I am a reluctant yogi. As an intuitive-feeler type on the Myers-Briggs Type test and many other personality assessments, I've never been particularly drawn to or adept at physical programs for fitness, or for that matter, fun. What can I say, I'm a nerd. So when a few years ago my back pain re-emerged—and I recognized the signpost that a shift was in the works—I took the advice of a good friend who is a picture of physical and emotional alignment, and stepped gingerly onto the mat. It wasn't an easy transition.

When I first encountered Sadie, a youthful, lithe sprite of a yoga teacher, I was less than thrilled. She was much too young, much too beautiful, and much too wise for my taste. I—or I should say my "confronted ego"—disliked her immediately. My first forays into "downward dog" and "crow pose" were excruciatingly painful and, surrounded as I was by Sadie's mostly young, mostly female devotees, embarrassing. Nevertheless, I forced myself to return week after week, and soon the self-critical voice diminished and the fluidity, flexibility, and balance began to return to my back and body.

One day I had a profound "awakening," as I listened to Sadie describe the teachings of yoga—with their focus on alignment, centering, and flow—and the gentle *shift* that occurs as the body reaches a crucial point of resistance (fear) and then releases: Yoga itself is a metaphor for my life-shifting work with clients. The body itself goes through the exact same stages of change—and fear in the form of resistance—as it forms and solidifies, breaks down, and remakes itself anew every day, in each moment. I understood then, as I listened to Sadie seamlessly weave together the physical, emotional, and mental threads that bind us together into the miracle of "me," that no impactful change, no transformation or true reinvention of the self could occur unless the body was part of the plan—full stop.

Today, as a certified teacher under Sadie's tutelage, it is my contention that the body is a crucial leg in the three-legged stool of the evolving self. Many of us—especially in the West—are particularly adept at thinking our way through problems. Many of today's popular self-help books advocate a simple approach to change: Change your mind and you will change your life. Yoga has taught me that they are only half right. Ignoring the body—or treating it as a vehicle just along for the ride—is a recipe for disaster. As another of my spiritual teachers, Tom Lutes, often states, "Human beings are much more than brains on a stick." The body must not only come along for the ride, it must be a true partner in any process of self-renewal. Otherwise, with symptoms like malaise, anxiety, lack of vitality, and even full-on disease, it will fight you. All transformation requires that the body—the container of fuel that makes change possible—be right up in the front seat, firmly situated next to head and heart.

These three teachings represent a synthesis of Eastern philosophy and Western science. As you read the book, you will hear much more about them, and others that have informed my path in the evolution and development of the Life-Shifting Program. Born in far-flung corners of the globe—India, Thailand, Switzerland—these teachings share a clear, unclouded through line: Your full physical, emotional, and mental powers must be aligned and called forth in order to tackle your fears and dance with change. Nothing can be left out. This principle lies at the heart of all the exercises, diagnostics, and practices that I will share with you throughout this book. Self-renewal requires that we play full out with everything we have to offer: body, mind, and heart.

MY PERSONAL STORY

Holding the faded green book in my hands today, forty-two years later, I can instantly recall the day I received it. I was seven years old and about to have my first major life shift. My parents called me into the family room, which we had just painted this garish, glowing orange color that Mother loved and Father hated. I remember that just the night before they had fought about whether to paint the piano the same color. No, really. It was the sixties.

They brought me to the sofa, a rough, beige corduroy affair, and I remember squirming with anticipation. It was not my birthday, but they had said they had a "present" for me. Presents, for a seven-year-old, are usually a good thing. They handed me a book. I remember thinking that it wasn't wrapped, which wasn't a good sign (good presents came wrapped!).

It was called *The Chosen Baby* by Valentina Wasson, and it tells the story of a happily married couple who have just one thing missing from their lives: a baby. So they go to "Mrs. White," who helps people find "lost babies," and they bring home a baby boy, whom they name Peter. They are now a happy family, with love and joy and a baby they can call their own.

I can't say that I really understood what this little green book was trying to tell me back then. I do remember that Mom and Dad "wanted me to know" that I was adopted, but that I was loved and "chosen" . . . and that I never had to mention the story ever again if I didn't want to (and I feel fairly sure that they didn't want me to). As a good, compliant little boy, I got the message.

I didn't speak about it again for twenty-eight years. Yet, I also know, deep in my heart, that what tiny burgeoning sense of identity I had amassed to that point—the seven-year-old me—was shattered completely that day. Who was I? Who were these people who called themselves "mom" and "dad"? Were they just "borrowing" me from my real parents? Why didn't *they* (my real parents) come for me? Was I a pure-blood Hull from the New England Hulls? Or was I a store-bought phony whose real parents had ditched him? Maybe a little bit of both.

THE CHANGING SELF

Many years later, I would start to see a pattern in my clients, my patients, even my friends and family: We all struggle with issues of identity. It seems that just when we get comfortable with some semblance of "self," there comes a shift in the landscape—the "wife" becomes a "divorcée," the "student" becomes the "unemployed," the "professional" becomes the "laid-off," the "playboy" becomes "the dad"—and who we know ourselves to be gets torn right out from under us.

I sometimes wonder why it took me twenty-eight years to "come out" to a close friend, and soon thereafter, a therapist, about being adopted. Now I think it was because it took me that many years to face down the shame of being "given up," to grieve, let go, and release the loss—the death—of the "Jeff" I thought I was. At thirty-five years old, it was time for the "real" Jeff to be born anew. No wonder I've dedicated my life to helping people move through issues of identity, to slough off outdated labels, to reinvent themselves with a deeper, more grounded sense of self.

Life is a series of cycles of birth, growth, death, and rebirth. I'd even go so far as to claim—rather unscientifically, I admit—that most of our "cycles of identity" seem to occur in five- to eight-year patterns. Somewhere around the seventh, fourteenth, twenty-first, twenty-eighth years, and so on, most of my clients—and it is certainly true in my own life—have undergone a major life shift: a shift that involves the dissolution of a role, an identifying marker of who we thought our "self" to be.

The goal of this book is to make this change and evolutionary process—the birth, death, and rebirth of identity—easier, more accessible, and less daunting. We are all changing constantly. In fact, psychologists' admonition that there is an "authentic self" notwithstanding, I believe that key to our progress as humans in this time of global, ecological, and political peril is to wake up to the fact that what we consider "solid" or "authentic" or "real" in terms of ourselves—and our labels, identities, and roles—is all constructed.

We are all made up. And this is GOOD NEWS. If we are all constantly "under construction," then we can be less terrified of change, less attached to our overwrought sense of self, and open to the possibilities that lay before us: A new self is always waiting just over the horizon. But, all along the way, we need to learn to let go of outdated attachments to *whom we think ourselves to be.*

THE PATTERN OF CHANGE

Although the birth of this book can be traced all the way back to that fateful day when I was seven, when my life shifted in a seismic way, it more practically emerged from watching hundreds of my clients go through their own life shifts—divorce, career change, family loss, illness, and so on—and my recognition, about fourteen years ago, of a pattern in these processes of change. The content was different, each case unique, yet the cycle—the stages, the fears, the movement—was always similar. In fact, it was startlingly similar.

We all know about books on change and transition that describe a three-stage process—a beginning, middle, and end—to most major change events. But if we look closer—and over the years I've started to look much closer—we discover that the onset of change always includes two key shifts, what I call the "rupture" and the "release." Likewise, if we look deeper at what we all recognize as the "mess in the middle," we see that there are major shifts that occur here too, which I call the "retreat" and the "revival." And finally, when we move toward the culmination of a cycle—achieving a pinnacle moment, experiencing a new level of personal or professional success, or perhaps reaching a period of tranquility and contentment—even here are two clearly identifiable stages: the "rehearsal" and the "realization."

In this book, you will learn how to navigate these six inevitable stages or steps that we all move through in the process of change. It is my contention that many of our classic symptoms of malaise—anxiety, stress, depression, anger—are a result of our resistance to and lack of awareness of *how things change.* My goal with this book is to make it easier for us to navigate these shifts, by becoming aware of how the change process unfolds and by learning to utilize specific practices that help keep us moving, even flowing, through the change instead of getting stuck. Shifts are inevitable but stalling, becoming mired interminably in mud along the road, resisting future curves, and sticking rigidly to tried and true pathways—the all too common side effects of change—are not.

And there is more. What about our fear? Fear is the great partner in change. Nothing new in hearing this perhaps, yet if we look at most of the books on change, they don't include a whole lot on fear. And if we look at the books on fear—and there are many, on how to conquer, overcome, or even embrace our fears—they usually don't talk about change. Yet, again I say: They go together.

THE FOUNDATION

With this in mind, we can outline the six basic premises upon which this book stands:

1. There is no such thing as an "authentic self." The self is a story—a narrative—that we construct and deconstruct throughout all of life.

2. Life shifts are points along the way when our sense of self becomes outdated and worn out, and no longer serves us.

3. Personal growth is NOT a linear process. Life, like nature itself, moves through a constant, yet shifting, pattern of cycles that are clearly identifiable if you know where to look.

4. The cycles of self-renewal are more complex than the typical three-stage process with a beginning, middle, and end. Life shifts occur in a six-stage cycle: rupture, release, retreat, revival, rehearsal, and realization.

5. Anxiety, worry, stress, anger, illness, and even depression are

common symptoms that appear to mark the arrival of change. Yet, more often than not, fear is the real culprit.

6. Fear, once recognized and understood, becomes a natural partner—a trainer, a coach, a motivator—in the process of change.

Twenty-eight years after being told that I wasn't really, at least genetically, a Hull, I began the process of rediscovering the story of my unfolding identity. I started working with a wonderful therapist, who understood intuitively that deep interconnection between my fear—and desire—of knowing the truth and my shame at being abandoned. Judy Fox was my first true "life-shifting" coach, and the person without whom this book would not exist. She was the first to use the "life-shifting" method (although she didn't call it that) and I was the first patient to go "through the program." To say that the program works is the ultimate understatement.

Seven years later, after moving, sometimes quite painfully, through each of the six stages of change—and vanquishing my associated fears and anxieties along the way, I sought and found my birth mother, and was fortunate to be "welcomed home" by my genetic family. It has been an amazing journey, one that has afforded me the opportunity to access a deeper version of my self-identity. (I won't use the word "true" because that would imply that some sort of final self emerged in discovering my roots, which is far from the case. It is, in fact, just another plateau moment in the ongoing evolution of the self.) Yet, even now, as I face the recent loss of my adoptive mother and deepen the connection to my birth family, I am aware of how the cycles of change remain alive and active. We are never finished.

A LEARNING SPACE

As a manual for handling life's inevitable shifts, this book is designed to be more than just a good read. It is structured to create a "learning space" for the reader, by interweaving the following: a clear and accessible guide that can be read in chunks or as one continuous thread; theoretical foundations; self-tests for diagnosis; ongoing exercises and practices that engage the mind, the heart, and the body; and further reflections and support. My intention is simple but key: to encourage the reader to move beyond the purely mental activity of reading, to literally bring heart—and skin—into the game.

Current research into brain chemistry and physical evolution demonstrates that real change—truly breaking bad habits, learning new skills, developing an expanded sense of self—can happen at any time in life (remember my sixty-year-old client who became a yoga instructor!), but it requires engaging *the whole person*. Throughout this book, the reader will find exercises and ways to utilize the tools offered to engage the heart (working with feelings and intuition) and the body, as well as the mind. To accelerate and move more seamlessly through any life shift, learning must be embodied.

One very large evolutionary shift occurring in scientific and psychological circles is the shift away from the false Cartesian split between the mind, heart, and body. They are all one integrated mechanism, and to become a master of self-renewal (discussed in part three of the book), we must all take up the mantle of what my yoga teacher, Sadie, a spiritual fitness instructor if there ever was one, calls "embodied wisdom."

There are three major sections in the book, each of which may be read and reread in standalone format. The first section is a "primer" for the program that follows, with background information on the major themes outlined above. Right from the start, however, you will find life-shifting action steps that are designed to shift your perspective from observer to participant. You may simply read through each of the three sections of the book, but if you happen to have chosen, or been given, this book as a tool for helping you through some major (or minor) transition occurring in your life, I recommend that you "jump in" and start doing the accompanying exercises right away. Shifting from observer to player, you will feel the impact of the book immediately as you make the first major leap on the road to mastery: self-awareness.

Just as I didn't even know—with all my psychology training—that my deep fear surrounding my birth identity was shame-based until someone gently pointed it out to me, you may very well be unaware of how fear is stalling you on the road to self-renewal and making your life shift a living hell. Doing the exercises as you read section one in the book will help you begin to "wake up"—to reflect deeply on where you are on the trajectory of change.

Part two of *Shift* describes your program for working through fear. Here you will discover six key tools for transforming your relationship with the fear that always accompanies any major change. As you move through the six stages of the cycle, starting wherever your current life shift is occurring, the program provides exercises and ways to utilize the tool set within each domain of learning: thinking, feeling, and sensing/physical. You will begin this program by completing a simple diagnostic that will help you clarify whether you are, fundamentally, a "thinker," a "feeler," or a "doer." The key to accelerating your change process and mitigating the stalling effects of fear is to choose practices that reinforce your natural tendencies, but also push your edge into the less comfortable domains.

Part three of *Shift* will take you on a journey, complete with driving companions, through the six stages of every life shift. You begin by taking a simple diagnostic exam that will help you discover where you are on the road map of change. Then I will introduce you to three companions for the journey: clients of mine who, although they come from very different backgrounds and are facing different shifts in their own lives, have each moved through the six stages themselves, reinventing, rediscovering, and reclaiming new aspects of their ever-evolving sense of self.

One of your life-shifting companions is a "thinker"—someone who tends to utilize her intellect and capacities for rational and deductive reasoning in order to move through change. Another is body-focused, and finally one is a "feeler"—an individual who leans on her emotional, felt sense of the world around her. Each of these clients has used the Life-Shifting Progam and the tools provided to become more balanced in using all three learning capacities. There is no *right* way to learn. Each of us has a predisposition toward one of the three modes of learning, yet each of us also needs to tend to those parts of our core essence that we might choose to ignore or dismiss.

I encourage you to watch yourself closely as you arrive at a new stage in the cycle, asking: What practices do you find appealing? Which do you ignore, dismiss, or avoid? If you tend toward the cerebral mode of learning—and many of us in the Western culture are acculturated to "think our way out of problems"—take up the gauntlet and jump into a yoga practice or make a leap of faith and do creative explorations using visualizations or poetry—something you might initially dismiss as irrational or even kooky. You'll be glad you did. The goal here is to finely tune the instrument called "self"—to move through our resistance and our fears by bringing to bear all the fruits of our uniquely human capacity for learning, by doing, thinking, moving, and creating. It is all in there . . . in all of us.

MASTERY

In the final section of the book, I share with you some closing thoughts on my own journey through life's endless shifts and discuss the theme of mastery. In the context of our broader cultural, political, and economic upheavals—change is clearly accelerating on every level—we each need to take steps to become masters at handling change at a local level. By local, I mean only this: We must learn first to successfully navigate the road toward opening and manifesting our own soul's desires, to heal and integrate the wounds of our fragmented ego-self, before we can take up the banner to change the world. Only then, as role models for others along the accident-prone highway of self-realization, may we step up and offer ourselves in service to our communities, our cities, and our planet. As the Native American adage reminds us, "We are the ones we have been waiting for."

It is my fondest hope that this book serves as a tool for shifting readers into a more loving, fluid, flexible, and permeable operating mode; that we learn to understand the roots of our fear and work to unearth and embrace the gifts of soul—compassion, creativity, empathy, tolerance, and understanding: the essence of our humanity—all of which are constantly pushing to break through to the light of day.

That said, there is much work to do. So get ready, get in gear, and let's go!

Part I:
Life-Shifting 101

A Primer: Rules of the Road

INTRODUCTION

"Being able to shift perspectives is like having a freely functioning vehicle. If a car is stuck in any gear, what you've got is a dysfunctional car. Even if it's a Maserati, if you're stuck in first gear, or you're stuck in reverse, no matter what gear you're stuck in, it's dysfunctional. But the moment you have fluidity and movement and you're able to shift up or down or into reverse, or whatever you need to do, you've got a functional vehicle."

—Zen Master Dennis Genpo Merzel

Imagine you are driving on the highway. There are small curves in the road that you automatically adjust your steering to accommodate. You cruise along calmly, enjoying the scenery, when suddenly you are shocked out of your reverie by an abrupt change: The gas meter's "empty" light goes on, or the "next exit" sign displays a town that is clearly *past* the one where you were supposed to turn off. We've all been there: forced to make a U-turn, searching for gas in a strange town, stuck changing a flat in the middle of the night.

Just three nights ago I set out for a late-night trip up the East River highway, along the eastern flank of Manhattan, otherwise known as the infamous FDR Drive. All was well until about two miles up the still mostly bumper-to-bumper highway, somewhere around Ninety-Sixth Street, I heard a horrible clunking sound coming from under the car—right rear—and sensed that something was very much amiss. Loathe to stop in the midst of a high-speed, traffic-choked freeway, I clunked along a bit longer, until it was safe to pull into the emergency lane at the off-ramp.

I got out of the car and in the dim, eerie light zooming past from the onslaught of headlights, I saw immediately that I had a very flat tire. Fortunately, I have one of those "emergency roadside" service contracts that come with car insurance, and with a cell phone that worked, I had a service guy at my side within minutes. The guy who fixed my tire made it known to me gently—like a dull hammer—that the tire under question was "extremely bald," and that if I had just taken the time to look under the car and examine the tire more closely, I would have seen that a disaster was just waiting to happen. I actually take fairly regular care to service my car, but what I don't do, I now reluctantly admit, is *look* at the car—inside or out—very often myself. I tend to assume that my "car doc" will let me know when to take care of things—like a tune-up, lubricant, and tires.

The moral of the story? If I had more awareness of how tires wear (turns out that they don't wear evenly and that one can go bald while the others still look new—it's called, ironically, being "out of alignment"!), I might have avoided an hourlong anxiety attack on a crowded city highway. As an analogy for "better driving" across a changing landscape, it brought home the importance of understanding the basics of vehicular operations—and points the way toward why it is crucial that we understand the basic workings of the "machine" we get up and drive out of the bedroom each morning.

Most of us spend more time shopping for a car than we do investigating the inner and outer workings of what we call the self—that complex, seemingly impenetrable bundle of mystery in which we drive through life—and the real trouble starts when we motor along, without ever getting a license, an inspection, or even regular checkups. Then when the machinery breaks down, the connections get severed, the "check engine" light goes on—all of which are inevitable—we fall apart and reach for the Prozac. It doesn't have to be that way.

In this primer section, you will learn the basic principles that form the foundation of the Life-Shifting Program, so that when we hit the road in parts two and three, you will be ready to master the cycles of change and release the debilitating impact of fear. Armed with a basic understanding of how the self is designed, you can face down the challenge of change and move through the accompanying fear with greater flexibility, adaptability, and equanimity.

Chapter One

THE LANDSCAPE OF THE SELF

"When you are present in this moment, you break the continuity of your story, of past and future. Then true intelligence arises, and also love."

—ECKHART TOLLE

Just as you don't drive one car for a lifetime, you are not the same person for a lifetime; you are constantly shifting with age and changing desires, needs, and interests. When I was just out of college I drove a beat-up Chevy Vega; in my mid-thirties I went through a Volvo station wagon phase. Today as a mid-lifer I drive a black coupe. Perhaps it is not an accident that our vehicles tend to have built-in obsolescence, since the human body itself appears to be in a constant process of growth, decay, and rebirth. Scientists tell us that every single cell in the human body dies and is replaced over a seven-year period (incidentally, *Consumer Reports* magazine reports that 6.8 years is about the average length of time most people own a car). The point is this: Change is inevitable.

So just as the vehicle we choose to drive over many different periods of our lives varies according to our needs, our desires, and our life circumstances at the moment, our sense of self, our identity, is also never static. The pace of change may at times feel glacial, but we are always changing, always growing and evolving.

In fact, despite attempts by some self-help gurus to get us to discover our authentic or "true" self, there may very well be no such thing. Ask yourself this question: How much of who you are as a person today—your roles and responsibilities, your hobbies, your beliefs—resembles who you were five, ten, even twenty years ago? It can be startling how much we change over time without really even noticing it.

See if this example sounds familiar: Over the past twenty years, my friend Susan has gone from being single to married, from a corporate executive in New York City to a grade-school teacher in the suburbs, from a swinging single nightclubber to a soccer mom, from an empty refrigerator (she always ordered takeout when I visited!) to gourmet chef. She is clearly not the same Susan I met in graduate school many years ago, yet at some deep level she is still the same: witty, generous, philosophical, and strong-willed.

LETTING GO

When we look back at our lives and who we were then and who we are now, we discover that the self is as often in the process of deconstruction as construction. As we journey through life, we need to stop, rest, and cut away some of the older deadwood weighing us down. To make room for something new, some aspects of who we think we are and how we see ourselves need to be pruned and snipped away. When change is afoot in the lives of my clients—and in my own life—I've often noticed that the most difficult part of the transition is the "letting go" phase, that time when you have to hit the "delete" button on some aspect of who you have known yourself to be. Some part of the "story of me" no longer serves what wants to be born going forward, and this can bring on what we often call a "crisis of identity."

As we will see when we explore the nature of a six-stage Life-Shifting cycle of change, the first half of any life shift is this "cutting away" process—the pruning, releasing, and dying of some aspect of ourselves—that is required for the second half of the journey (the reconstruction phase) to unfold with less fear, and more energy and joy. This can be a painful process—yet it is necessary if we are to remain vital, alive, and ready to be born anew.

THE BURDEN OF IDENTITY

Have you ever heard the phrase "That's my story and I'm sticking to it"? Of course you have. You may have even said it a few times in the course of your life, and you certainly have thought it. I know I have, more times than I like to admit. What I'm talking about is inconvenient but true: Over the years, as we build up a personal history, a web of relationships and experiences, we literally *become our stories*. We invest a great deal of time and energy in creating a sense of self—our identity—and for the most part, we are loathe to alter it, give it up, or *shift* it, even though it may be killing us!

What exactly do we mean by our "sense of identity"? Perhaps we reach into our wallets, pull out our driver's license or identity card, and begin telling a story: of height, weight, age, skin color, eye color, family origin, homeland, religion, nationality, education level. The list, or more accurately, the

Life-Shifting Action Step:
The Self—A Vehicle in Motion

Reflect on the cycles of your own life story. No matter how old you happen to be at this moment, go back seven years and ask yourself these questions:

- What roles, responsibilities, and defining characteristics did you have then that you still have today? What is different?

- What about your life circumstances has changed?

- How has your body changed? Your finances? Are you surrounded by the same people? New people? How are they different?

Subtract seven more years from the number, and seven more years from that. Keep going back in your reflections until you reach adolescence and late childhood. Keep on asking yourself the questions outlined above. Can you sense the evolution of the self?

labels we assign ourselves—like a mishmash of patches in a hand-me-down quilt—are seemingly endless.

Yet, not every identifying "patch" has the same or equal importance. Very quickly, as we run down that lengthy list, we find that our sense of self evolves into a clear hierarchy of values. What we hold as most valuable, and care about passionately, tends to show up higher on the list of affiliation. For example, if we are particularly career-oriented, such that our profession is top-most on our list of identity markers, "I am an architect," or "I am a surgeon" will trump "I'm from Arkansas" or "I'm an only child."

Likewise, our sense of self will often revolve around a tribal affiliation, based on religion, race, homeland, or other key moniker that defines who we are. Sadly, we are all too familiar with what this can lead to, when we draw imaginary—or sometimes real—boundaries around who is "in" our affiliated circle and who is "out." Unfortunately, we rarely ask ourselves how or why we get so attached to this or that identifying story and become so protective of it. We toss off our heritage or background as if we literally woke up one day, rolled out of bed, and *became* a highbrow Bostonian, or a staunch Republican, or a born-again Christian. But is it really that simple?

Our Wounds Become Our Stories

As fragile beings we enter the world in a deeply vulnerable state. We develop strong attachments to tribe and family in order to create a sense of belonging—to carve out a "homeland" where we feel safe. Yet, when we become overly attached to these affiliations or come to believe that they represent *who we are* at some fundamental level, the story may devolve into a toxic and potentially dangerous tale, detrimental to our health and the health of others.

Through the long delicate cycles of change that constitute childhood, adolescence, and emergent adulthood, we bury, repress, and push aside hurts that may be just too painful to experience within the thin, underdeveloped *skin* of the child. Yet, the wounds remain. There is a reason why most traditional psychotherapy will, at some point, take us backward into dark corners of memory to uncover, and retell, stories of abandonment, hurt, or humiliation that we suffered as children. Those stories, deeply etched in our hearts—even if hidden from the world or ourselves at a conscious level—very often define and run the show called "me." Unfortunately, stories we carry with us from last week and last decade then become fraught with paradox. That same patchwork quilt of identity, which could be lightweight and "mix and match," flexible and adaptable, becomes a heavy overcoat—a suit of armor—to be worn perpetually, as protective gear, in summer or winter.

I will always remember the day my therapist gently suggested that I was carrying a deeply held story of shame, self-loathing, and pain at the core of my identity as an adopted child. I was shocked. It seems that as a young child, I had unconsciously convinced myself that being adopted was a taboo subject, a family secret that if brought into the light of day would betray my adoptive mother by unmasking her as an impostor. If I wasn't careful, the story line goes, I would be sent back (to the orphanage). That I had spoken about being adopted to only one or two people in thirty-five years, that I had held it as my own personal scar, hidden from view, was obvious to the therapist as an unspoken symbol of pain, of humiliation—a core wound around which I had attempted to carve a life. It was painful to move through this "rupture" into awareness of how I had held this simple fact, to learn how my hurt had become my story, but it was a necessary "pruning"—a death of sorts—that ultimately freed me to be more open, honest, and connected, able to have more compassion for myself and others.

Somewhere along the way, we seem to decide consciously or unconsciously that this story of the self is *real*, that our identity is not simply a story we tell ourselves—subject to change and reevaluation—but a tried and true *fact*. In this context I think becoming a "self" is less a gift at times and more of a burden, even a curse. Just as I had to release the weight I had attached to being adopted, a code word in my childhood story meaning "unlovable," we all must wake up to the stories that bind us; the shame, fear, and resistance that often hold our fragile identity story together. What drives the wounded self at the deepest level is always the same: our fear of being discovered as unworthy and flawed in some way.

The Self: Fluid Not Fact

Every day in the midst of this difficult economic recession, I see individuals who, when faced with job loss or a sudden change in economic circumstances, act as if they have had the cloak of identity torn from their backs. I recently watched a television special on the lives of American autoworkers, whose livelihoods have been severely jeopardized by the downfall of these manufacturing behemoths.

One individual, who had worked for General Motors for many years and faced either job loss or at the very least a major job change (she was still employed), spoke of "feeling lost and empty at the prospect of not being a GM employee," going so far as to declare, "I'm not sure who I would be without GM."

Now don't get me wrong, I have a great deal of compassion for people who are struggling financially and economically in the aftermath of the great recession of 2008–2009. Yet, what is particularly striking about these situations is not just how challenging it may be to find another job, but rather how fearful, lost, depressed, and empty people feel when their sense of self gets disrupted.

What is it about identity that when some integral component of the story line is interrupted, we hold on tight in fear, and struggle so deeply with letting go, in many cases unable to move on, to reinvent our self anew? The truth is that if we stop, breathe, and take a close look "under the hood" of the vehicle of self, we would realize that there is no "there" there. The quilt of identity is sewn together with patches of influence, experiences, and roles that are constantly shifting, evolving, and changing. Nothing stays the same.

We Americans pride ourselves on being flexible and adaptable, able to assimilate strangers into our homeland and retool for a changing job market. Yet, we struggle with issues of identity, of not knowing who we are when our attachment to a particular job or role or tribe comes under the fire of change. Seeking safe places to hang our hats, where "everyone knows your name," may be a worthwhile and thoroughly human pursuit, for it creates a sense of worth, belonging, and comfort. But making the story of "me" and all that surrounds it unyielding and solid winds up contributing to our wearing a different and much less helpful badge: fear.

Life-Shifting Action Step:
The Cloak of Identity

Take out a blank sheet of paper and very quickly, without censoring yourself, complete the following five sentences:

1. I would describe myself as_____

2. The things I value most in life are_____

3. I feel strongly about _____

4. One thing that will never change about me is_____

5. I care about _____

Then reflect on these questions: Where did these descriptions and values that you ascribe to yourself come from? Have you always felt this way? Have your values and passions evolved over time? What would happen if a new description of "you" appeared on the horizon? How would you adjust to the change? Is your story of identity fixed, permeable, or fluid? Fiction or fact?

The key to Life-Shifting in times when change seems afoot with a capital "C" (like now) is to remember that our identity is fundamentally a story, a narrative that is constantly being written and never complete or final. Like those wonderful moments as toddlers, when we were allowed to run around naked on the beach, we all need to disrobe and hang out in our birthday suit occasionally, allowing the sun's rays—and their life-giving energy of rejuvenation—to penetrate down to the bone.

THE QUANTUM SELF

How do you feel about this image: running naked on the beach, not wearing anything, least of all the "cloak" of identity? My guess is that many will be horrified at the thought of actually being naked at all, let alone consider the idea of dismantling the key elements or labels that make up the apparel of your identity. I also imagine that some of you might feel relieved, enthused, even a bit excited at the prospect of untethering the mantle of self and running around free and unadorned. Of course, our response to the idea of being naked—a vulnerable, yet freeing space—gets to the crux of the matter when it comes to the self, change, and *fear*. The in-between space from release to rebirth can be scary.

Of course, the rub about running naked on the beach is that it is fundamentally not allowed within the purview of our adult, single-file universe. Running around naked, especially on beaches in broad daylight, is a child's domain; the younger the better.

This makes perfect sense if we go back to the idea of self as a story—a narrative of traditions, roles, affiliations, and ties—that gets written and built up over time, becoming, in effect, solid and real. When we are young children and the story has yet to be written, we are free to roam the world naked. But soon enough the unadorned becomes the adorned, and once we've started bundling up in the accoutrement of "self," we are never again encouraged to disrobe, or for that matter, to disarm.

What we have to accept—and what we will explore together throughout this book—is that my suggestion that we learn to "wear" the story of identity more lightly, not becoming so attached that we become rigid, brittle, and ultimately burdened by it, is fundamentally a paradox. It appears to ask that we regress developmentally, to actually become more childlike in order to grow flexible and remain adaptable in a world that is constantly in flux.

How do we reconcile this dilemma? Well, one place to look is in the most sophisticated and mature realm of the physical sciences: the quantum world.

Quantum physics is the study of the infinitesimally small, fundamental particles of the universe, which, it turns out, operate more like a free-flowing world of possibility than the staunchly solid material world that most of us think of as "adult," or "real." Proven over a hundred years ago in experiments with photons, neutrons, and electrons, the identity of the universe is anything but solid. At the subatomic level, things settle down to become "things" only in the exact moment in which they are observed. It turns out that the universe is like a wide-open playing field with no boundaries or borders. The bottom line on the quantum world is that it "proves" that the universe is more childlike than adult—less rigid and structured in its sense of self than we have thought for hundreds of years.

The nature of selfhood—that is, the story we come to accept about who we are at any given moment in time—seems to depend entirely on *how we observe, label, and interact* with the very thing we are trying to name. It is in direct observation of the self in action where the fabric of identity gets woven, such that it is impossible to separate the cloth of self from the thing itself. We are, it turns out, exactly what we wear, and what we wear is constantly evolving. Think of it this way: On the one hand you see yourself as having a "skin" that feels, appears, and seems solid—in fact, not only does it seem to be solid but it actually appears to hold us together. Without it, we believe that we would come apart into a bloody, messy mishmash of bones, nerves, and organs. Yet, we also know the opposite to be true: Skin is made up of cells—and ultimately subatomic particles—that are alive, breathing, shifting, growing, and dying, composed mostly of water (which in turn is mostly empty space); it is not, in fact, "solid." No wonder we often feel "uncomfortable in our own skin."

What becomes crystal clear is that what matters most in the defining of self, other, and everything else is this: the relationship, the event, and the moment of choice. The self literally gets created, defined, and made real in the moment that it gets spoken, written, and interpreted. *We make it all up.* How we settle into any sense of grounding whatsoever, in a universe that is multiple and parallel and in constant motion, may seem like an irreconcilable paradox, but it is actually quite straightforward: Self is born and developed through an ongoing dialogue that we conduct with others, with nature, and within ourselves. It is both an inner and outer dialogue. Consciousness, and the field of infinite energy that makes up reality, is everywhere.

Even though the idea of any sort of "authentic" or "true" self may be false, *the way we choose to speak about it matters.* Our words, our language, as a reflection of a perspective—an observational moment, you might say—becomes the creative "event" that brings the self into focus. What we say, think, and feel about the self, in effect, *becomes* the self.

What is interesting and important to note is that as we begin to accept that the nature of reality is event-driven and self-constructed through dialogue, we must become more aware of the *power of language.* It is language that is the purveyor of dialogue, the vehicle for conversation, and hence, the building block, however tenuous and ephemeral, of the self.

Life-Shifting Action Step: The Story of "You"

Learn to pay close attention to how you tell yourself, and others, the story of "you." Take out a blank piece of paper and complete the following sentences by writing as much as you can—a few lines or a paragraph—without censoring yourself.

1. When I was born, I was _____

2. When I was a teenager, I was _____

3. When I became an adult, I was _____

4. Today, I am _____

Now reflect on these questions:

- Does this accurately describe who you really are?

- If you were to answer these questions again tomorrow or five years from now, would the answers be the same?

Now ask a close friend or relative to complete the sentences above (focused on his or her perception of you). How do you feel about the answers? Are the answers congruent with yours? How "solid" is your sense of self? Does your feeling about this bring on excitement and desire and feelings of possibility? Or do you feel anxious, worried, and fearful?

THE GHOST IN THE MACHINE

Plato was right. And not just about conversation (dialogue or "dialectic," as he would have described it) being the fuel of human knowledge. He was right about the soul, or *psyche* in the Greek. It really does exist. We human beings really do have souls, and the experts finally—almost—agree on it! It is such a relief to get this puzzle solved during my lifetime.

As a multi-majored liberal arts undergrad, I always enjoyed reading a wide variety of books on philosophy, science, psychology, and Eastern thought. Throughout my learning journey, however, I would always get bogged down when trying to reconcile scientific literature with self-help or spiritually oriented books that take such subjects as the soul and spirit simply for granted, as if everyone agrees they exist. The truth is that until recently most scientists, medical doctors, even psychiatrists (whose field is based on the word "psyche," or soul!) have dismissed soul, spirit, even intuition pretty much out of hand, as lacking empirical evidence. Behavioral psychologists who have embraced an entire field of human developmental theory based originally on how dogs and rats behaved when reinforced or punished (remember Pavlov's dogs and Skinner's rats?) still shake their heads at the notion that human beings might be more than just a pile of flesh, bone, and reflexes.

If it weren't for the works of Carl Jung and more recent spiritually oriented scientists from the East, such as Amit Goswami and Deepak Chopra, who have used the latest advances in quantum theory to reconcile the science versus spirit conundrum, I might never have healed this schism between head, heart, and mind within myself—and this book would never have come to be. It was, in fact, Jung's autobiography, *Memories, Dreams, Reflections*, which I had read as a college student many years before, that echoed in my head and reverberated in my heart during my first "breakdown," while toiling away in the corporate world. In many ways, Jung's personal story and the history-making theory that grew out of it supported me through the first major life shift of my adult life. It was this very rupture that led me to exit my corporate career and veer instead on to the path to become a psychologist, a coach, and a psychotherapist. In essence, Jung saved my soul.

In his reflections, Jung writes of having powerful dreams from as early as twelve years old, in which vivid characters would "come to life" and speak to him from a deep, unfathomable place that he knew, even then, however unexplainable, was real. Later in life, at the time of his break with Freud around the age of thirty-eight, he would make a leap of faith and begin paying closer attention to the images and voices of his "inner guides" and those of his patients, especially as they appeared in dreams.

Distinct images, symbols, and stories seemed to emanate from a place beyond the so-called identity of personality—a deep, mysterious realm in the psyche that came to hold the key, for Jung, to the entire opus of his work. His theory of the unconscious—wherein lies not simply the repressed instincts of sexual energy Freud called the "id," but a mysterious drive toward wholeness that he called the archetypal self, or soul—became the crucial building block of his understanding of how human potential unfolds.

The Corporate Conflict: My Boss or My Soul

Jung's work, which I had found mysterious and moving and yet impractical, came alive again when I ran up against the hard, unyielding force of my own ego/personality, when the corporate identity I had forged over ten years as a human resource manager for a series of major corporations came apart at the seams. As is often the case, breakdown—and life shifts—first appear in the guise of conflict with significant others. My case was no different. The story of "me" fragmented and broke apart in a showdown with my boss.

He was the ultimate authority figure, with a powerful, direct, and forceful sense of his own identity as a "master of the universe." Harvard Business School–trained to be logical, rational, and data-driven to a fault, he didn't believe in the "soft side" of life, declaring that showing emotion in the corporate arena is a sure way to "get you fired." As a boss, he was a caricature to be sure, but he was also very real.

One evening at a corporate dinner event, I found myself, under the influence of a bit too much white wine, inadvertently pushing his buttons, confronting him directly on his oft-spoken thesis that "data is the key to solving every problem," that logical analysis was all that mattered in facing the complex mystery of life. I remember swallowing hard, feeling my heart beating loudly, and bursting forth rather inelegantly, "Well, then, if everything can be analyzed and measured, how did you decide to marry your wife? How do you 'measure' falling in love?" He looked at me quite directly, not appreciating this challenge to his structured and rigid worldview, and said very simply, "I just did a data analysis of her good points and bad points, and she came out ahead on the plus side . . . so I married her. Love had nothing to do with it."

I knew then that I was not long for the corporate world. I knew that the voice stirring inside me that yearned to break out of the box called "corporate life," the voice that taunted me to toss all the data in the garbage and go running naked on a beach, was a real, separate, *knowing*—even wise—part of my self. I didn't want to become my boss. Two weeks later, rereading about Jung's break with Freud and his need to follow the voice of his own inner guide, I made the decision to leave my job—and thus the shift, the "rupture" as we will explore in detail in part three of this book—was under way.

Jung's theory of individuation, a fancy word for unfolding human potential, identifies two aspects of the human psyche that can be understood distinctly: the ego and the self (or soul). This theory unfortunately, but accurately, paints the psyche as naturally split, explaining human development as a dynamic point-counterpoint evolution between the ego and the soul that inevitably entails conflict.

It seems that as the personality, that sense of identity we talked about earlier, becomes more solid and unyielding, with its practical assimilation into the day-to-day, bill-paying, nine-to-five world, the voice of soul gets relegated to the sidelines—submerged in the unconscious. The problem, however, is that as much as we might like the fantastical, dreamy, imaginative, childlike voice of soul to disappear, it just goes underground. It waits. It pops through in our dreams both day and night. One day, perhaps when we least expect it, the voice gets so loud that it breaks through the walls of our exalted identity— and the *shift* happens.

If we follow recent developments in neuroscience, at least at a layman's cursory level, it turns out that Jung was on the right track: The very field of inquiry that would banish the concepts of soul or spirit as products of a flaky New Age spirituality is coming full circle to embrace them. Somehow the soul is getting reinserted in the equation, as the powers of imagination, metaphor, and as yet unnamed "representations of subjective experience" (e.g., symbols) turn out to be crucial building blocks of the human consciousness. Gone forever, it seems, are the unquestioning days of dualism, where mind and body were viewed as separate entities and the exalted nation-state of science never crossed into the province of poets.

The Neuroscience of Soul

With the emergence of technologies that allow us to observe the deeper functioning of the brain, psychiatrists and neuroscientists have opened a window and begun to peer into the inner landscape of human consciousness. Brain researchers and neuroanatomists, focusing on recent discoveries in the area of brain plasticity, have found that the brain is constantly developing and changing throughout the human lifespan and that, in fact, the continuous development of new neural pathways linking the left and right hemispheres is known to be commonplace. What is especially fascinating is that scientists have determined, through neural mapping of the brain centers at times of key relational development (infancy and early childhood), that metaphor and mirroring are the source code, the learning language, for emotional intelligence. Just days after birth, a human baby is able to assimilate and process empathy, warmth, and safety through the symbolic mirroring of facial expressions, eye movement, and touch. The mother speaks to the child in ways—without words—that we all understand, and she learns.

The shifting, fluid movement of consciousness, as interpreted through the symbolic mapping of neural activity along the trillions of pathways that compose the brain, seems to be most engaged, flexible, and open when the mirroring we receive from loved ones—primarily Mom—is poetic, empathic, musical, and symbolic. It turns out that the human brain, the core material home of the self, responds best to the symbolic language of the imagination. The brain loves soul.

And so we come full circle. The three-way, or tripartite, split between mind, body, and soul postulated by Plato over two thousand years ago is very real; it exists literally within the human brain at a subatomic level. But it is not, as it turns out, a split at all; it is rather a dynamic, sometimes contentious conversation. The soul—or spirit—is very much alive and engaged in the human drama.

Rather than a ghost in the machine, it turns out that soul or spirit is a mysterious energy force emanating from an infinite field of consciousness, capable of bursting forth as an idea, a fantasy, an image in a dream, an emotion, and, ultimately, birthing the tangible reality that we see, know, and touch. It is the soul that stirs the imagination, builds bridges, writes books, drafts laws, and creates businesses: It is life's creative principle. It may be hard for us to imagine how we might capture with "evidence" the emergent voice of soul, yet think of it this way: Do you ever catch that moment in time when a flower reaches full bloom?

We see and smell and touch the flower; we can measure the result—we can even destroy it—but the exact moment of flowering confounds us still. Despite our grand scientific exactitude, we have only the one experience to grasp—being moved and touched by its beauty. No matter how we choose to describe it, one thing is for certain: The soul is real.

Healing the Self through Listening, Not Fixing

Unfortunately, this self-soul/spirit split is one area where we in the West are still conditioned to function with a true machine mentality. Like good car mechanics, most medical doctors in the West would be very reluctant to *treat* the spirit or tend to the soul of a patient. On the contrary, if the machinery is broken, the approach they take is to simply replace the part, cut out the infection, or attempt to kill off the intruder. What's worse—or better, depending upon how you view this conundrum—is that science and technology are often quite successful at fixing the body, keeping the identity intact, and returning the machine to work.

Herein lies the problem: The soul does not need to be *fixed*. It needs to be heard. Many, if not most, of the life shifts I encounter in my practice with corporate and private clients alike are the result of the stirrings of soul, the push into awareness of a long repressed or suffocated voice of yearning, not to have more material success, but to live more deeply—to find meaning, purpose, and love: the province of soul. Much of what we will explore together in parts two and three of this book, the tools for transforming fear and the stages of change we all go through in the process of reinvention, are designed to soften the rigidity of ego and welcome the voice of soul.

A Story of Soul and Corporate America: Sophia's Lament

Consider my client Sophia, whose inner voice of judgment recently reached a fever pitch of self-recrimination against her long-suppressed soul's desire—to simply quit her job. In her mid-forties, Sophia is a successful senior executive with a large technology company. A no-nonsense, practical businessperson, she has very nimbly been climbing the corporate ladder for eighteen years. A couple of years ago, in the wake of Hurricane Katrina, she got a loud call from somewhere inside (not comfortable with words like "soul" or "spirit," Sophia describes it as a megaphone in her head) telling her to "go and help." So, with my support and encouragement, despite her strong instinct not to leave her job even for a moment, she decided to heed the inner call by taking a three-month leave of absence to volunteer with the Red Cross and help out victims in New Orleans. It was a profound experience for Sophia, and one that has, according to her traumatized ego, essentially ruined her life!

Ever since returning from her stint as a volunteer, she has been unable to muster up any passion, energy, or commitment for her old job. A strong sense of yearning has taken her over, a need to do something more meaningful in the world, to quit her job altogether and find a way, as she puts it, "to

make a difference for people." Yet, the voice of practicality, gui
recrimination, emanating from the all-powerful internal authority
corporate identity writ large—has been winning the war.

She even managed to get promoted in the midst of her misery at work.
And yet, as a newly minted senior vice president, with all the consumer gadgets and fancy cars and mortgages that this level of American success brings,
she lives in terror of the day that her inner voice wins the final battle and, as
she puts it, "I quit my job and become a bag lady." Of course, quitting her job
is exactly what her soul desires, and becoming a bag lady, however dramatic
and unlikely, is what her brittle self most fears. This painful internal conflict,
what we know all too well as a "crisis of identity," lies at the core of most of
our seemingly unwelcome life shifts.

No wonder we hesitate to dive below the surface and listen to the voice of
soul stirring within us. No wonder the pundits of culture—political, science,
and business leaders—would choose to marginalize the voice of the human
spirit, relegating soul to the province of music or poetry. Yet, living constantly
with the terror of inner (and imagined outer) reprisal, ignoring or denying the
voice that makes us essentially human—our yearning for meaning, depth, and
connection—may be the most dangerous thing we do.

○　　○　　○

The scientists finally agree: Jung was right. Life unfolds toward wholeness
in the guise of a dynamic and sometimes painfully conflicted conversation
between two apparent adversaries, the ego and soul. Personal growth, it
would seem, like the grinding necessary for a grain of sand to transform into
a diamond, is born of conflict; life shifts are a necessary, if painful, way for our
deepest desires to be made known—and manifest in the world. If we hope to
master these inevitable cycles of self-renewal, we must learn to break down
the walls that cordon off our fragile sense of identity, and welcome the arrival
of soul. In a word, we need to master the art of change.

But before we switch gears and move beyond the landscape of the self
and into the territory of change, let's recap the key road rules for navigating
the self:

1.　There is no such thing as an "authentic" self. The self is a story
constructed through the assimilation of life experience. We can
remake it at any time.

2.   The story of the self unfolds in a quantum field of possibility. The self is made and remade through the symbolic conversation between words, feelings, and acts. Life shifts are opportunities for growth born of the inherent conflict between ego and soul.

3.   The soul is real, vibrant, and alive. It is the creative principle that provides the energy for growth and renewal. The soul never needs to be fixed, only heard. It is almost always a behind-the-scenes provocateur when *shift happens.*

Chapter Two

THE DANCE OF CHANGE

"When we are no longer able to change a situation, we are challenged to change ourselves."

—VIKTOR FRANKL

My friend and spiritual teacher, Tom Lutes, is a silver-haired, muscular pillar of strength. Still bursting with energy, he just turned sixty-five and, never being one for following convention, he celebrated by becoming the oldest aikido practitioner in the United States to achieve black-belt status. What's more, he started practicing aikido only five years ago, when he was a youthful sixty. It is an impressive accomplishment. Achieving the black-belt level in aikido is usually reserved for only a tiny percentage of practitioners; most are barely out of their teens and early twenties. Aikido is as much a mental as a physical art; it demands that one stay centered in the face of an attack, while simultaneously remaining fluid, open, instantly able to move in on an opponent or retreat. Aikido is a for-midable martial art to learn at any age: a mental and physical dance of agility, stamina, and strength that seeks to overpower an opponent by usurping, block-ing, and redirecting the energy of the attack. It is all about energy.

What is particularly noteworthy about Tom's story is not that he is driven to fight off aging, but that he is living out a different story, one of his own making. He chooses to live at what he would call the "growth edge"—a mental, emotional, and physical space in which he continually pushes against any "story" of limitation or lack that emerges to keep him stuck. Ask Tom what he means by the "edge" and he would say something like this: "We all live in self-constructed 'boxes' that circumscribe our lives. Especially in our consumer-driven Western culture, our box typically shows up as a lifestyle of comfort and security, with a focus on the trappings of material wealth—homes, cars, stock portfolios—all designed to keep us safe from the inevitable ravages of time. There is nothing inherently wrong with material success, but if we are not constantly seeking to extend the boundaries of our boxes, to learn and to grow, then the trappings of success become a trap—a self-imposed prison."

The edge is that place where we bump up against the walls of the box of complacency in which we have set up our lives. It shows up in that moment when we have a desire or fantasy or a thought of possibility but quickly feel the heat of fear rise up in protest. Words like "I can't" or "that's impossible" will swirl through our minds. Sensations of anxiety take over as our hearts beat faster, our breath becomes shallow. The box, however, is not real but manufactured, and the walls of the box are not solid or finite. The goal of living at the edge is to recognize that the box is a permeable structure, one whose walls are not solidified by any intrinsic reality, but by our choice to shut down the metaphorical—or literal—windows and doors through which the energy of life constantly streams. Tom's achievement in aikido is not focused on "showing up the youth" but about staying connected to the energy of growth and possibility that is always available to everyone at any age and any time.

INFINITE ENERGY—PHYSICAL, MENTAL, AND EMOTIONAL

The key to life-shifting, as you will discover as you work the program in parts two and three of this book, is to raise our awareness of how the two apparently competing energies—of fear and change—show up at specific moments in our lives, jolting us out of our complacency and forcing us to recognize that we are living in a self-imposed box of limitation. The boxes in which we craft our stories of identity are not any more or less permeable depending upon our age or circumstances. It is another well-worn myth in our culture that it is easier for us to change when we are younger, or that by the time we reach retirement, we are too old to change. As we will discover when we move through the six stages of change and put to work the tool set for releasing fear, the energy to make the shift is always available to us, at any age. Life-force energy is infinitely abundant at all times and in all places, but it appears in different forms—thoughts, feelings, and physical symptoms—depending upon the dynamics of the "box" into which it is corralled. If we want to break down the walls in our heads or our hearts that keep us stuck—when our energy flow is stanched—we must work with the energy on all three levels.

Recently, I had two clients show up on my doorstep at around the same time. One was twenty-two years old, the other sixty-three. They were both frustrated and depressed. Mike, the younger of the two, believed his career as an entrepreneur was over due to the extreme anxiety he felt whenever he was required to fly. Fear of flying is fairly common and can hit at any age. It was especially debilitating for this young man, as he lived in New York City but planned to work for an online marketing company based in California. When confronted with the need to fly regularly to the West Coast, he shut down in fear, arriving at my office with the self-imposed box fully formed: "I can't fly." Bill was a recently retired schoolteacher who for the past thirty years put a great deal of his life energy into his work with disabled children. Now bereft of that "box" of accomplishment and meaning, he was also depressed and feeling fearful about the future, which he described as a life of "being alone, lonely, unable to change."

Both of these situations were difficult and painful for the individuals involved, and their choice to seek help was actually the first major step in casting light through the walls of their respective boxes. On the surface, the situations look starkly different. We might think a fear of flying at twenty-two and a fear of retirement at age sixty-three are worlds apart, but in many ways, the energy of fear that was blocking the movement of change was the same. With no pun intended, I can declare that they both had a "fear of flying," whether it was literally for the former who feared "taking off" from his home turf and winging west, where his career dreams lay waiting, or metaphorically for the retiree, whose "fear of flying" kept him locked up in his apartment, grieving the loss of his career and resistant to future happiness. In both cases, the energy of fear was winning the battle over the energy of possibility. Both the youth and the elder came up against the edge of their defined "locus of control"—the box of their identity. As the young man set forth on the tarmac toward his dream career or the retiree stepped out his door and on to an unknown future, the burden of their past stories of self and their self-imposed limiting beliefs clamped down in fear.

The courses of treatment that my work has taken with these individuals may look quite different because the flow of energy we will seek to unblock may be different, but the steps for working through their fear and making the shift into a new story of possibility—of flying, of reinventing the self—are fundamentally the same. The key starting point, after recognizing that the box that limits them is one of their own making, is for them to release the blocked energy of fear and reconnect with the flow of energy that generates possibility. That they are living at two distinct ends of what we might call the "developmental" spectrum of life is quite irrelevant.

I'm often struck by the cultural story that says that our progression as humans is linear and that our needs, hopes, and fears at twenty are substantially different than at forty or fifty and beyond. Surely we do go through a series of developmental physical and psychological growth stages as we emerge from childhood into adults, yet life's evolution, as we know from nature, can be equally described as a series of cycles—of seasons. The need to reinvent oneself at twenty as we emerge from the identity of "youth" and "student" and "underling" is not fundamentally different from the renewal of our sense of self as we shed adult roles of teacher, parent, or provider. The process of life-shifting at twenty or sixty is only different insofar as the type of energy resources available to support us in making the shift may vary.

The younger of the two has abundant physical energy, but a limited ability to express his thoughts and feelings in words. Thoughts and emotions are energy forms that can be blocked and cut off just as easily as physical energy. It is interesting to note that with severe phobias like fear of flying or agoraphobia, the therapeutic method that tends to work best—according to recent research—involves cognitive-behavioral techniques. But what are "cognitive" or "behavioral" practices in psychotherapy? For the most part, these support mechanisms are designed to help a patient to become aware of the habituated thoughts and repetitive behavior patterns the ego employs to quell the onslaught of fear. Cognitive practices seek to offer the patient new "stories" to counter the running negative narrative that overwhelms the mind. Behavioral practices seek to provide the patient with alternative paths of mobility—shifts in perspective and action—that promote the forward momentum of blocked energy: becoming aware of destructive habits, engaging in self-talk that helps to reframe the story, and putting in place new practices that channel the body toward positive action. With its focus on rewards and celebration—positive reinforcement—when a patient takes incremental strides into new territory, behavioral therapy seeks to break apart the closed loop pattern of self-criticism that typically keeps the patient stuck. In each case, making the shift out of a negative pattern and into a trajectory of possibility requires an unblocking of energy—mental, emotional, and physical—so the patient can redirect the vehicle of self.

In Mike's case, his ability to express his story in thoughts and words that reinforce a sense of self-esteem and empowerment has been "shut off"—as evidenced by his difficulty articulating the nature of his fear of flying except in the most rudimentary language and self-critical tone. Our work together will involve my helping him to access and nurture his ability to articulate his feelings and needs in words—to "find his voice." His physical energy of youth and vitality will support him greatly during the change process, but his work to recover the lost language of feeling and to replace the self-critical thoughts with supportive mental models that spur him onto that plane, will still require a great deal of energy. Despite his youth, he still needs to tune in to the buried voice of inherent wisdom that lies beneath the loud roar of his rigid and defended ego—to heed the call of soul.

Likewise, the retired client, whose richly nuanced and storied life overflows with a deeply resonant language and fully articulated narrative about who he is, where he comes from, and how he has lived, also needs to "find his voice"—but a new one. This voice of reinvention and exuberance lies submerged in a torrent of negative self-talk, buried deeply in a physical body that he, for the most part, has ignored, preferring to live a life, as he would say, "of the mind." Unblocking his energy and releasing his fears may actually require him to quiet the loud voice in his head and reconnect to the language of vitality and possibility that has been buried in his neglected body. His growing "edge" will be to reclaim his lost physical vitality—to re-engage with the somatic life force that pumps through his veins—and reconnect with the youth within.

The energy of change is always flowing—it depends on how we understand energy as a resource. Earlier in life we may have more physical energy; later we may have more energy in the mental domain in the form of wisdom, cognitive skills, and the ability to reflect. Emotional energy, as described by the quantum physicists, "appears" throughout our lives naturally, abundantly, and effortlessly, showing up at the intersection of thoughts, feelings, and physical sensations. These three forms of energy come together and entwine to form the lifeline of change, and no successful shift can occur without bringing all three into alignment. This is why self-help books that focus exclusively on "changing your thoughts" to change your life are providing only a partial solution. The energy of feeling, of emotional and physical vitality, must also be harnessed, explored, and employed in the dance of change. The key to living on the edge, as Tom demonstrates, is to engage in practices that help us break apart the cultural story about energy, to see through to the truth of the matter: Energy is infinite. It can be neither made nor destroyed. It is always available to us so long as the sun rises each day, keeping a supply of photons, neutrons, and electrons streaming toward the earth.

LEARNING TO DANCE: SURRENDERING CONTROL

Early on the morning of August 7, 1974, a young Frenchman named Philippe Petit did something that was not only not "petite," despite his name, but that would inspire and ignite the human imagination—and our sense of possibility—for decades to come: He walked across a high wire between the twin towers of New York City's World Trade Center, at the time the world's tallest buildings. As those who witnessed the spectacle would forever recall, he didn't just walk out on a wire 1,368 feet above the ground without a net, he *danced* on it! One of the police officers, Sgt. Charles Daniels, who later arrested Petit for "sky trespassing," stated, "I observed the tightrope 'dancer'—because you couldn't call him a 'walker'—approximately halfway between the two towers. And upon seeing us he started to smile and laugh and he started going into a dancing routine on the high wire. . . . And when he got to the building we asked him to get off the high wire but instead he turned around and ran back out into the middle. . . . He was bouncing up and down. His feet were actually leaving the wire and then he would resettle back on the wire again. . . . Unbelievable really. . . ."

Yes, unbelievable. I mean it's difficult enough to dance well, with balance, grace, and aplomb, on the ground, let alone on a 3/4-inch-wide cable slung between two skyscrapers. When asked why he did it, he simply stated, "When I see three oranges, I juggle; when I see two towers, I walk." What about you? When you feel the winds of change about to throw you off course, do you grab hold of the wire, hold on for dear life, and pray for clear skies? Or do you smile, tiptoe out over the abyss, and spring sure-footed into the gale? The answer, at least for me, is pretty simple: It depends. I might like to fantasize that I'm an aerial ballet dancer, skipping with glee across the high wire of change, but the truth is more banal: I spend most of my time with my feet firmly planted on terra firma, thank you very much.

As fanciful as it might seem to be able to dance across a high wire, without a safety net, the truth of the matter is quite serious; otherwise, it would potentially be deadly. For his high wire act to be successful, Petit had to find that crucial, elusive balance between total control and total release. Petit was playing at the edge between dread and delight, always in full control of himself—mind, body, and spirit—and yet in the moment he left the wire to dance in midair, he had to surrender, to let go. His smile, in the face of huge danger, was a true leap of faith.

I think this image of our gallant Frenchman out there on the wire, high above the ground but still tethered to it, is a beautiful metaphor for our relationship with change, and fear. If you think about it, our relationship with life itself is a high-wire act of sorts—a constant balancing act between two opposing forces: control and surrender. As you move through any major change, whether you follow my road map of six stages or simply stick with the well-worn beginning, middle, and end, this tension of opposites, a dynamic relationship between fear and desire, freedom and attachment, holds sway, on the ground or in midair. Our walk across the abyss of change is made up of a moment-by-moment series of choices, to either cling tightly to what we "know" and think we can control, or to lighten up, and go with the flow.

If we step back and look at this conundrum of control and surrender through a wide-angle lens, we see that the high wire of life is actually a spectrum of possibilities, with total control on one side and total release on the other. The goal of life-shifting, in following Petit's lead, is to find our way into the middle—and learn to dance.

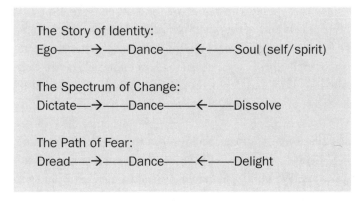

The Story of Identity:
Ego———→——Dance———←——Soul (self/spirit)

The Spectrum of Change:
Dictate——→——Dance———←——Dissolve

The Path of Fear:
Dread——→——Dance———←——Delight

In the box above, we begin to unravel the parallel tracks on which our life-shifting journey unfolds. As I described in chapter one, the first point/counterpoint dance we learn to navigate is between the personal sense of self that most psychologists call the ego or the personality—our story of identity—and the mysterious, yet very potent energy of creativity and possibility that I call the soul. As we will see repeatedly in parts two and three of this book, the essential nature of every cycle of self-renewal, whether at sixteen or sixty, involves the disruption of our attachment to a current ego-state, a movement toward surrendering our story, and welcoming into the dance a new partner—a new idea, a new belief about our selves, a new way of walking in the world—that is the mark of soul.

THE THREE D'S OF CHANGE

The second track on which we can lay out the process of change delineates how the flow of emotional, mental, and physical energy moves. The spectrum of change, as I call it, involves our coming to recognize that even in the midst of periods of relative calm, no matter what stage we may be in, we can always find ourselves positioned somewhere along a path denoted by what I call the three D's of change: Dictate, Dance, and Dissolve.

The Dictator

On the far left side of the spectrum, we live in the energy field of the "dictator"—that is, the ego identity is fully in charge, running the show called "me." I have designated this far end of the spectrum as a place of "dictatorship," because in effect that is what we become: Our sense of living in a fully formed "I" coalesces into a life of comfort, defined boundaries, and clear definitions of the way the world operates and how we—and others—should think, behave, and act. Life at this end of the spectrum is anything but democratic; there is little room for the cacophony of competing narratives when the seemingly solid self or ego or "I" is in charge. Given that our cultural legacy is born on wings of so-called freedom and democracy, the irony is that the walled-off self-state of dictatorship is where most of us, most of the time, seek to arrive and settle.

In basic terms, this comfort zone is the tried and true result of discipline, a solid upbringing, a good education—all the developmental steps our culture lauds and approves: We build a name for ourselves, a career, a family, a business, perhaps a profession. In the energetic space of the dictator, however, there is little room for change to occur with ease. The paradox of "settling down" into our defined roles and responsibilities, as our parents, our boss, our spouse, and our culture might dictate, is that as we fortify the walls of the box called "me," change becomes an unwelcome visitor.

There is a reason why I choose to call this end of the change spectrum the "dictator." It is unfortunately an almost fascistic stance toward life: We carve out our day-to-day existence in stark black-and-white terms, making lists of what we need to do, what we should do, what money we need, what material comforts we require, what accomplishments we aspire to achieve. In so doing, for the most part we are trying to force our way through life, demanding that changes, when we must engage with them, be incremental and workable. We strive to be in control.

Of course, there is nothing inherently wrong with focusing on goals, educating ourselves, or living life with a sense of discipline and commitment to finding happiness—and success. In fact, the practices we will explore together in parts two and three of this book do require effort and focus and a concerted effort to interweave the energies of feeling, thought, and sensation into a force that enables greater flexibility and agility, allowing us to make a shift out of fear—and adjust more gracefully to change. But the nature of this dynamic is paradoxical, for like Philippe Petit, as much as we may need to harness our energy in order to relax and dance with change, our cultural and developmental legacy in the West would have us not so much embrace, play, and dance with creative energy so much as clamp down on it, attempt to define, limit, and hold it hostage to the demands of a fearful ego. The dictator state of mind does not countenance change.

We all know what resistance to change looks like; we see it every day on the six o'clock news when any kind of "reform" is introduced into the hardened capitalist system of economics and governance that we have come to claim as the "best." This black-and-white view of the world—where anything reform-minded is dubbed a conspiracy and change is considered dangerous—operates on the individual level as well. When the identity state of "me, my, and mine" is fully formed into a role, takes on the onerous weight of tradition, and gets subsumed into a community of like-minded personalities, the energy of change is quite unwelcome. The "box" I referred to earlier becomes solidified around "me" and encompasses others like me, such that an external "other" or an internal "other" in the form of a voice from within—the whisperings of soul—causes us to erupt in fear.

The Dissolve

At the other end of the spectrum, which I have named the "dissolve," we find the enlightened ones, those revered teachers whose words we admire but whose lives seem unattainable to us. I describe this end of the spectrum as the land of dissolution, because this is the place where, if we were to fully transcend or discard our sense of identity—allowing the ego to literally or figuratively dissolve—we would enter a selfless state of non-being. A faraway land of no conceivable reality for most of us, we might find here the great sages of spiritual wisdom, teachers like Buddha or Gandhi or Christ, who have released their demands on life, dissolved their attachments, and surrendered their very need for a self. It is a laudable goal to want to dissolve, to let go of all egotistical "claims," to release our demands on the world, and relax. But it would mean no more high-wire walks, no more flights to the moon, no more best-selling spiritual tomes. The truth is that I doubt many of us really want to be enlightened; the price is too high.

The Space Between—The Dance

Most of us, including most spiritual teachers, don't live at the extremes of either end of this spectrum. If you think about spiritual teachers whom you admire today, perhaps Deepak Chopra or Pema Chödrön, or if your spirituality has a religious orientation, the preachers or religious leaders you follow, you may discern that they have surrendered some of the trappings of their need for ego control, yet in most cases, even they fully embrace their identities as "teachers" and want to get paid well for their efforts. Few are immune to the pull of a cultural story that applauds clear role definitions, material prosperity, and most of all, the comfort and pleasure of "things."

Where do you live on this spectrum? Most of us live somewhere in the middle, moving back and forth along the spectrum, buffeted along by the winds of change, making demands of ourselves and others at times, and on occasion, in moments of awareness of the fruitlessness of that endeavor, allowing ourselves to relax, to surrender, to dissolve into the free space of play, of possibility, of the unknown, but only for a moment.

And what about our fears? Do they not follow us as we move back and forth on the spectrum of change, joining us hand-in-glove on the high wire of life? I submit that fear, a constant companion all along the road, intersects most poignantly with us at the far left, on the "dictate" side. It lives in our pocket when we feel that strong need to control, to have life unfold on our terms. It is at this intersection in the road, where our ego-state plants itself firmly in the terra firma of the dictator, that fear is most likely driving the bus. The goal of this book is to help you become better at floating in the "dance" of the middle way, moving back and forth across the spectrum with less fear and more joy, able to upshift to control and downshift to release, as needed.

So how do we break free from the chains that envelop our inner dictator? Returning to the spectacular example provided by our ace midair dancer Petit, the goal is simple: We need to learn to dance. We need to learn to work with the energy of change and find the middle path between the two extremes of dictatorship and dissolution. All the exercises in part two of this book are designed to facilitate this shift from a fear-based need to control, to a more present-focused, relaxed, and dynamic dance between the energies of the ego and the soul. Fundamentally, the shift occurs in a dance that can be summed up quite simply: It is a two-step; a ride in the vehicle of self in which we take turns playing passenger one moment and driver the next.

The Two-Step

There are two components involved in any two-step dance: attention and intention. As any Texas two-stepper would likely corroborate, the key to dancing without stepping on your partner's toes (e.g., being the dictator) is becoming aware of your footing: learning to watch, witness, and observe yourself in action. Stepping out of the ego-story and taking on the perspective of observer, you gain access to a different energy source—one that is not born or bred on fear, but emerges from a place of compassion and curiosity. It shows up mentally as the energy of inquiry, where you stop, breathe, reflect, and become aware of the present moment, asking yourself: Who am I? Where am I? How did I get here? What am I trying to accomplish? It shows up physically as bodily sensations that you experience in the moment of "now"—as a grounded, centered, focused attention on the energy system in which your thoughts are contained: the body. By shifting your perspective and taking the stance of observer, while simultaneously becoming present in the moment to the physical sensations of being alive, we are capable of "getting out of our story."

If you think about the presence of mind Petit must have had, along with the sharp focus on his physical body and its exact movements and the flow of its energy at the moment he landed on the high wire and then lifted into the air, you can perhaps imagine how he danced, literally, with the flow of his thoughts and sensations. In a split second, he would be "dictating" his role on the wire—in total control of his thoughts and sensations—yet also surrendering to the unknown and unknowable, allowing his sense of self to dissolve and flow, trusting that he would "hold together" in midair, high above the ground, and that the delicate interplay between his need to control his movement and his desire to "fly" would flow together into a seamless dance.

So the first step in the two-step dance is to become aware that the dance exists at all: to let go of the controlling story just long enough to catch a glimpse of the other end of the spectrum and witness the possibility that there is another story holding everything together, even your ego. The second step in the dance—once you have encountered your inner observer and recognized that there really are two stories available to you at any given moment, one authored by the ego, the other sourced from a mysterious, deep, unfathomable place that I call soul but that you might just as easily label God, or spirit, or essence—is to bring to consciousness your *intention to dance.*

It may once again smack of paradox, but the two-step dance of life-shifting requires that you not only get out of the driver's seat but still hold on to the steering wheel and give the vehicle gas. You do this by harnessing the energy that is always available and giving it a focus, a direction, away from a fear-based stance of protection and clinging, over toward the creation of something new, eyeing the future but grounded in the present moment. The energy of intention is crucial because we have to have some semblance of where we are headed, while at the same time we relinquish control over the outcome.

Petit knew where he was—on a wire high above the streets of Manhattan—and when he shifted into dance mode, trusting his body to flow seamlessly within the confines (the box) of his well-tuned physicality, his thinking mind was hard at work as well, holding the intention to play, have fun, and enjoy his moment in midair. It is a delicate and deliberate operation, this two-step dance that would keep us on the road to realizing our deepest dreams, yet allow us to flow in partnership with the high wire on whose underpinnings we depend. The constant interplay between attention and intention demands that we become awake to the present flow of energy within and outside of us—to recognize that the story we are telling ourselves, in any given moment, is always subject to change; in fact, it *is* always changing.

The "middle way" along the spectrum of change—the place of the dance—unfolds in a constant series of practices whereby we become aware of the tendency of our ego-state to shut down, to cling to a story in fear, and to utilize our capabilities of attention (our focal point) and intention (the force of desire) to come together in alignment and, bringing us out of fear and into a state of relaxation, letting go and going with the flow.

As you will discover, as you begin to play at the edge of your box by putting down this book and getting into the dance through the life-shifting action steps, change is always occurring and you are always, whether in the act of reading or breathing or stretching or talking, moving back and forth between the two partners in the dance: attention and intention. In this sense we can come to see a deep truth about the story of self and the nature of fear: Fear is a story. Accompanying the story of identity, the fear body is dissolvable at any moment in time, but it requires a shift in the way we view energy—and energy includes mental, emotional, and physical sensations, not just thoughts—and the creation of a new conversation within ourselves and with the world.

VITAL SIGNS

In case you've missed the latest in the "Healthy Living" series on Oprah Winfrey's television show, she's recently done a series focused on life extension—that is, how, with the aid of a diet loaded with vitamins, minerals, and vegetables, and a tightly restricted intake of calories, we may soon be able to live to the advanced age of 120 or beyond. Her medical expert, Dr. Mehmet Oz, studies the intersection between nutrition, diet, and longevity. What I struggle with, however, in addition to wondering whether the assumption that we all want to live to be 120 is accurate, is the casual way the experts toss out such terms as "vitality"—as in, "He was 110 years old and filled with vitality and a zest for life."

What exactly do we mean when we label someone "filled with vitality"? Like happiness, "vitality" is one of those words we bandy about as if we all know exactly what we mean by it, but do we? Clearly, vitality has to do with feeling good and having energy, motivation, and enthusiasm for life. It is one of those descriptors of life experience that we recognize when we see it in others, and can sense when it is missing, but pinpointing where we get it or how to generate, hold on to, and keep it is easier said than done.

The trouble starts when we become aware that just having a good diet, average weight, and a regimen of regular or semi-regular exercise does not always produce vitality. I have had a number of svelte clients, some of whom ate really well and exercised, some of whom did not, but even when they all focused on becoming super-healthy and started eating vegetables and working out, they did not necessarily become a whole lot more vital in their experience of the world. Vitality, in the form of enthusiasm, high energy, joy, and passion, can and surprisingly often does remain elusive, hidden, locked up inside even the healthiest bodies. Equally untenable, yet not surprising given our cultural tendency toward overachievement, vitality can also become an obsession, a dis-ease of manic proportions.

Dawn was a client who arrived on my doorstep looking vibrant and energized—on the surface. She was so committed to her diet and exercise program that she talked of nothing else. She was always doing a "cleanse"—not just dieting but doing regular "fasts" to wash out the endless supply of toxins with which our mucked-up society was supposedly degrading her body and soul. To the outside world, Dawn appeared to have "vitality"—she was thin (extreme but not quite anorexic), vivacious, and chatty, always willing to share her latest saga with nutritional supplements, Chinese mushroom tea concoctions, and the like. Yet, as "vital" as she seemed, there was always an energy of desperation about her. She seemed to want to live forever, but it wasn't clear what was really driving her frenetic focus on physical health.

At one point, in a rare, calm moment of deep conversation, she shared with me her sadness about a simple, biological fact over which she had no control: She was not able to have children. In that moment of candor, my heart broke open for her with compassion. Suddenly, I understood her almost maniacal attempts to perfect her body. Although she might not be directly aware of how the two stories interrelated, it was clear to me that her commitment to being "vital" was an attempt to make up for this "loss" by being hyper-vigilant with her body.

It was a laudable goal to build up her physical system with loads of veggies and limited calories, but the motivating story behind it was based on fear—and self-criticism—not self-love or compassion. In the annals of paradox in which I often find my clients, she was an extreme case: She overflowed with vitality according to the culturally defined story, but her emotional and mental energy flowed in the opposite direction, caught in a doom loop of disappointment that bordered on self-hatred. She blamed herself for the biological flaw that had disrupted her plans for a family, and no matter how thin, how beautiful, and how "vital" she appeared on the surface, the energy of fear—of being discovered as imperfect, flawed, and broken—ruled her life.

On the complete opposite side of the vitality coin, my client Mary had an equally fascinating and frustrating dynamic: She ate well, exercised fairly regularly, took in fewer than two thousand calories a day, and still remained more than fifty pounds overweight. Her vitality, in terms of energy level and enthusiasm, was extremely low, and no amount of green-leafed vegetables, supplements, or disciplined treadmill action seemed to help. She went to a number of doctors about her weight, all of whom told her there was nothing wrong with her—at least in terms of thyroid or hormones or genetics—and that she should be able to lose weight by just "sticking to your diet."

Unfortunately, none of these medical practitioners took the time, nor did they likely have the time, to conduct a true dialogue with Mary about her situation. If they had, they would have learned that Mary's physical condition, and the energy that held it in place, was only partially responsible for how she showed up in the world. Her emotional and mental story—a profoundly solid box of identity in which she saw herself as always being overweight—actually held sway over the body. Mary, in truth, was terrified of being thin.

When the story of her fear of change—and the emotional attachment she had to her weight—began to emerge within the safe container of our conversation, I immediately thought back to how she had described herself on her very first visit. She plodded in to my office, sprawled on the sofa, and simply declared, with little emotion (which in retrospect reinforced the deeply etched belief system that underpinned her assertion—the solidity of her box):

"I don't want to work on my weight issues. I've always been fat. That is not why I'm here. I hope you'll be able to just ignore it." Of course, the proverbial "elephant in the room" was difficult to ignore, and the fact that she brought it up immediately was a covert cry for help.

Over time, without prompting from me, she returned to the story of her weight herself and allowed it to slowly unravel. She knew, perhaps initially unconsciously but later actively, that the blocked energy of fear and self-criticism was directly linked to her weight, her vitality, and her lack of career motivation (which is what she believed she had come to me for in the first place). By engaging in a new conversation around her physical state, one not focused so much on diets or exercise but on her emotional relationship with her body, I helped her to crack the box of identity called "fat." Today, Mary is forty pounds lighter, but that, as she would be the first to point out, really isn't the issue: Her newly compassionate relationship with her self, her story, and her energy—physical, mental, and emotional—is what matters.

As far apart as these two cases seem to be, in terms of what the Oprah watchers are thinking about vitality, they are very similar. They are both missing the key ingredient that ultimately generates what we might call "healthy vitality"—a healthy emotional relationship with themselves. The real key to turning on vitality—a sense of self-worth, empowerment, an energy of enthusiasm for life—is found through the exploration of one's inner dialogue, the energetic conversation, which manifests on more than just a physical level, that we have with ourselves.

The two clients described here are doing well. Dawn's life shift occurred when she became aware of her deep sadness about not having children. Keeping herself going at full throttle with diets and exercise regiments and fasts, she had denied her fear of feeling the depth of self-loathing and recrimination (as if it were her fault that she was unable to have children) that was eating away, literally, at her life force.

When she finally felt safe enough to slow down, engage in dialogue with me, and ultimately herself, about her feelings of pain and loss, she was able to release her fear, disengage from the story of self-loathing, and grieve. In time she moved, physical, mentally, and emotionally, back into her life in a more grounded, centered, and vital way, gaining weight, exercising less, liking herself more. Surely, with her remaining focus on diet and nutrition, she may live to be 100, but that hardly matters: It is her life NOW that counts.

Mary is also doing well. She started to lose weight when she shifted into conscious awareness of how her mental picture of herself was holding the body stuck, and she consciously decided to *want* to lose weight. The internal story that had remained firmly intact and hidden from view, that no amount of vegetables or exercise or doctor's exams had been able to dismantle or reframe, was the story she had told herself: that she needed to be obese. The weight protected her from the world, from intimacy, from success. It kept her story about her self, as a failure, intact. Only when she was able to bring the story up to the surface of consciousness, to engage in a true dialogue with her emotional body and mind, was Mary finally able to release her fear of the outer world and begin to source, once again, her true vitality.

It may seem crazy and irrational, but it is true: Our emotional and thought stories are more powerful than food, diet, exercise, or any supplement. They run the show called self. Surely, exercise, diet, and nutrition are important, even essential, elements of health and success in the world. But only when coupled with a narrative of self-worth and self-acceptance can the vitality of the soul be embodied. It is through the dynamic relationship between the underlying story of our soul's longing and the energy of the machine called self that the power of true vitality can be found.

I do think that Dr. Oz and Oprah are onto something important. Even if I don't want to live to be 120, I do want to understand the components of good health and become more aware of the key sources of well-being and vitality, of which diet, nutrition, and exercise are surely critical factors. What frustrates me is that the mainstream media still tend to focus on the mechanical aspects of dealing with life change. We focus on food items, caloric intake, and tuning up the machine with high-octane fuels, but we rarely bring into the mix the conversation about how the individuals *feel* about life, how they feel about themselves, what kind of inner conversation they are having with the three energy streams that flow through their life: emotions, thoughts, and physical sensations. At the end of the day, vitality is an emotional process and the recipe for its arrival on the landscape of self *must* include a dialogue between the physical, mental, and feeling components of self.

THE SUBTLE AND NOT-SO-SUBTLE BODY

"I am beginning to get a charge out of our conversations, Jeff. I think I'm finally seeing the light of possibility. Maybe it really will be possible for me and my wife to start our own business one day."

"Not 'one day,'" I replied. "How about next year?"

Life-Shifting Action Step:
Test Your Vital Signs

Test yourself for the key elements of vitality by answering True or False on the following list. Be honest with yourself. If you check False more than once or twice in any one domain, ask yourself these questions: Do I have a tendency to avoid focusing on one or more areas of life energy? What blocks me from running on all cylinders and scoring 100 percent "True"? What story am I telling myself about my vitality? How long have I believed this story? Is it still accurate? What am I afraid of changing?

Physical System Check

1. I have no trouble falling asleep without sleep aids, TV, or alcohol   ❏ T   ❏ F

2. My sleep pattern is consistent: I get between seven and nine hours of sleep each night   ❏ T   ❏ F

3. I generally awaken feeling refreshed and energized for the day ahead   ❏ T   ❏ F

4. I exercise at least three times a week, including stretching (e.g., yoga) and aerobics   ❏ T   ❏ F

5. I eat a balanced diet that includes lots of fruits and vegetables   ❏ T   ❏ F

Emotional System Check

1. I get angry or irritable occasionally but it dissipates quickly   ❏ T   ❏ F

2. I don't stop myself from feeling sadness or grief; I am OK with tears   ❏ T   ❏ F

3. I regularly share my feelings with friends and loved ones   ❏ T   ❏ F

4. I experience happiness and joy on a
   regular basis   ❏ T   ❏ F

5. My emotional system is generally relaxed with
   only intermittent highs/lows   ❏ T   ❏ F

Mental System Check

1. I am intellectually curious and open to new
   and different ideas   ❏ T   ❏ F

2. I enjoy debating different sides of issues that
   I care about   ❏ T   ❏ F

3. When I get stuck in "thinking mode," I gently
   bring myself to the present   ❏ T   ❏ F

4. I spend at least half my time listening instead
   of talking   ❏ T   ❏ F

5. I try to avoid either/or, black/white, or right/wrong
   kinds of thinking   ❏ T   ❏ F

Spiritual System Check

1. I take time to experience and reflect on the
   mystery of nature   ❏ T   ❏ F

2. I take time to nurture and tend to the longings
   of my soul/spirit   ❏ T   ❏ F

3. I regularly experience gratitude for the blessings
   of my life   ❏ T   ❏ F

4. I look for the humor in life—always ready
   for a good laugh   ❏ T   ❏ F

5. I look for the goodness, the divine nature,
   in myself and in everyone I meet   ❏ T   ❏ F

"Well," he responded hesitantly, "that feels like a stretch . . . but the prospect sure excites me."

"Then let's set a date," I came forth with a bit of a push.

"OK, OK, I know where you're going with this . . . but what about my work on losing weight . . . and as you like to put it . . . building up my vitality. I'm frustrated in that department . . . just can't seem to get the weight to budge. It is really a pain in the neck!"

After four months of regular sessions, George was making great progress toward redesigning his career and changing his life. He had formulated an exciting vision of leaving his job as a hotel manager and starting a new business with his wife running a "pet resort"—a hotel/spa type resort that catered to pets and their owners. It was literally a dream for George, to step off the corporate ladder and become an entrepreneur in a way that would bring together his two great loves: his wife and animals, especially dogs.

Yet, after the conversation above, three weeks went by without a word from him. Finally, I reached out to George only to hear that he had been laid up with severe pain in his head and shoulders, supposedly caused by a pinched nerve or disc that had come "out of alignment" in his neck. After a few months of working together, he was clearly on the verge of a breakthrough—shifting from the rupture stage into a full release—of his fears that the "box" he lived in was "coming apart" (as he put it). I was sorry to hear about the onset of his debilitating pain and discomfort, but not entirely surprised.

Over the years of working with hundreds of individuals in private and corporate settings, I've come to almost expect that at some point along the roadway of change, we will hear directly from the body. In short order, I have had a client who, soon after making the life-changing decision to move into the city, give up his job, and set forth on the adventure of becoming an actor (at forty-two!), promptly had a car accident and wound up laid up for six weeks in leg traction. Another client, a world-class tennis player, hit with feedback from his boss that he "might not make it around here" due to worsening economic circumstances and his seeming inability to get his salespeople to perform, wound up having a motorcycle accident in which he shattered his elbow—almost ending his tennis career and forcing him to spend three weeks at home. The irony, of course, is that just the day before the accident, I had suggested to him that some "time away" from the office might be just what he needed to work through his anxiety, reflect on the situation, and come to grips with his desire for change.

I could go on with examples like this, but the point is simple: The body doesn't lie. When the flow of life energy that runs the vehicle called self gets blocked or depleted, flooded with fear-driven energy from the mind—in the form of swirling thoughts and fantasies of disaster—the body will respond, literally. The language of the body is always available to us, in subtle forms and signals, but the trouble is that in our intellectually focused culture, where the prefrontal lobe of cognition generally rules the roost and calls the shots—most of my clients call it the "monkey mind," due to its endless chatter—the message from the body gets ignored. Then, at a moment when a shift occurs, and the internal box of fear breaks open, the body may speak—loud and clear. When the back pain descends, or you get hit with the flu, or the car careens out of control, the body, reminding you who is ultimately in charge, is anything but subtle.

What is your relationship with the vehicle that carries you through the day? Do you consider the body to be a key component in your overall energy system? Do you tend to the stirrings in the body, listening for the subtle cues, the signals it sends to support you in loving and nurturing ways—to rest, to sleep more, to exercise, to refuel with healthy foods, to get out in nature, to play? Do you listen when the body needs a hug, wants to stretch, implores you to move, urges you to be strong? In a world where a large percentage of the population is overweight, and most of that extra poundage shows up right smack in our midsections, my teacher Tom once again notes the direct body-mind connection that keeps the energy of fear expanding in us (like added pounds) and the energy of change so hard to bear: We just don't have the stomach for it!

At any given moment, if I were to take a quick scan of my current clients both private and corporate, I'm quite sure I'd discover that very few of them are what I would call "body-oriented" or somatically inclined in their relationship with the world. We tend to the body mostly as an afterthought, not as a beacon of internal communication, which is why when major change is afoot, the call of alarm, asking us to pay attention, to pause, and to slow down, may be, unfortunately, dramatic, even life threatening. Most of us are oriented toward judging and confirming the story of self—our identity—by tending not to the body but to the thoughts we generate in our minds and the words we hear reflected back to us from the external world. But our thoughts constitute just one form of energy that informs our sense of reality, and even thoughts, as we are discovering from the burgeoning field of neuroscience, have a biological source. Everything we think, feel, and do ultimately is sourced through the body.

In this context, the body is like a tuning fork; it speaks to us as we move through change—and discharge fear—always ready and available to help gauge our progress, indicate when a shift is about to occur, and support us through the transition. So how do we learn to listen with more depth and sensitivity to the subtle messages from our bodies? How do we avoid having to respond to the body only when it screams at us, with a total lack of subtlety, "Stop, look, listen"?

First, we need to shift our perspective on the relationship we have with our body, to wake up to the truth that the body is our partner in the journey of life. In a word, we need to befriend the body again, welcoming it back into the house of self as a companion that, like a trusted friend, is truthful, consistent, and reliable in its attempts to support us in moving seamlessly and effortlessly through life. For many of us—and I was included in this category until I discovered yoga—the body is either an afterthought (a heavy, burdensome passenger best kept in the backseat) or worse: the enemy.

If you doubt the extremely conflicted relationship many of us have with the body, think about the mind-set that many medical professionals bring to the symptoms that present themselves in their offices. It is certainly not unusual to hear things like, "Don't worry. We're going to fight it with everything we've got." When my mother was first diagnosed with cancer, our first encounter with an oncologist was, to my mind, shocking, but as my mother pointed out to me later, "pretty typical." This particular doctor spent the entire session with my mother looking down at a computer screen, mumbling under her breath about how we would—through radiation and chemotherapy—go in and "kill it." "It," of course, was the cancer: the enemy.

She barely acknowledged my mother's presence in the room (and ignored me completely), so intent was she on facing down the fascinating foe—cancer—that she had spent so many years studying. I remember the stacks and stacks of research documents and books that lined her office walls, amid the dead plants on the windowsill, and thinking that "healing" was not really her forte, but "fighting cancer" certainly was. It did not seem to occur to her that this "enemy" was *inside* my mother's body; it was literally a part of her. It is an unfortunate paradox that plagues our medical profession: The war we conduct against illness winds up being a battle against the very thing we need to survive—the body.

Now, I'm not advocating that we shouldn't try to vanquish cancer from our systems, or that illness is not painful and debilitating. But what I do want us to reflect upon is how our mechanical perspective on the physical very often leaves us with an adversarial relationship with the body in which we reside. It is somewhat akin to hating the apartment or house you live in but having no means to uproot or move.

We may never come to "love" our bodies, but we will gain immeasurably if we learn to tune in to the negative self-talk that would denigrate, judge, or distance ourselves from the very house in which we live. We need to come home.

Second, once we've reframed our relationship with the body, turning the enemy into, if not a friend, at least an acquaintance we can tolerate, we can begin to explore the language it uses to communicate its needs, fears, and desires. To do this, I find the teachings from hatha yoga, with its focus on the integration of body, mind, and spirit, to be very helpful. I also borrow from the wisdom of the aikido traditions, as shared by Richard Strozzi Heckler in his wonderful book *The Anatomy of Change.* In these body-focused wisdom traditions, the entry point for engaging in dialogue with the self is through the body. We look to explore—and directly experience—our relationship with the world by directly rooting our thoughts and feelings in the sensations, pulses, and echoes from the somatic world.

The starting point is the breath. By sitting quietly, closing our eyes, and tuning in to our breath, literally stopping all movement and focusing our attention on the slow and steady flow of air that passes across the threshold of the nose and mouth, we begin to disengage from the buzz of the outside world and become present in our bodies. This process, as we all know, is known as meditation, and its powerful healing and restorative effects on the body have been well documented. Meditating, even for just a couple of minutes, can help calm the mind and bring us back into the present moment. In part two, I will share with you my favorite meditation practice, which is drawn from the Vipassana tradition of Theravada Buddhism. It is a potent technique for shifting the energy of the mind away from your swirling thoughts and onto the sensations and subtle pulsing messages from the body.

For now, though, I want to introduce three key attributes we can explore in dialogue with our bodies, once we've downshifted our focus onto the vehicle in which we reside. These are center, ground, and alignment.

Center, Ground, and Alignment

At first the concept of *center* may strike you as abstract or enigmatic in the context of the physical body. The reason is that for most of us, most of the time, the center of our universe is the mind. Our thoughts take the central role of protagonist in the play of our daily lives, and our brains—centered in the head—are where our focus goes immediately when we fixate on center as a concept. But there is a world of difference between thinking about being centered and feeling the sensations of energy at the core of our physical system. In many Buddhist and yogic traditions, the center, or *hara,* as it is often called, is located about two inches below the navel. This is the center of gravity in the body, and the source point for the flow of life energy, or chi or ki, as it is called in many Eastern traditions.

In shifting our focus from the mental model of the mind as the locus of energy, to the experiential stance of the body, the center is better thought of as the "core" point from which the energy of vitality radiates through the body. It is the source point for our intuitive, felt sense of the world, and if you think about it, at times of great change or upheaval, it will often send messages to us that speak louder than our thinking mind. In Western parlance, we sometimes refer to this felt sense of foreboding or possibility, pain or joy, as "thinking from the gut."

Likewise, the idea of being "grounded" is an intellectual frame that we assign to others or perhaps to ourselves, when we think about feeling safe, centered, and in control of our thoughts. Yet, the integrity of true grounding always manifests first in the body. We all know what it is like to be in the presence of people who speak eloquently and confidently, appearing to be knowledgeable on a particular subject, yet we come away feeling vaguely uneasy about them because there is a disconnect between the way they speak and the way they hold their bodies. If we stop and pay attention to their physical stance, we may notice that their sitting or standing posture is a bit off-kilter. They lean perilously to one side as they speak, or they lean way back in their chair, move constantly in an agitated manner, or even sway on their feet as they speak. The speech may be impressive, but the body is not grounded— and we can feel it.

Being grounded, in the physical sense, is a corollary to the energy of being centered: The flow of energy in the body moves literally from the core down through the legs, into the feet, and into the earth. When someone is truly grounded, and not caught up in their thoughts and fears, there is a clearly noticeable alignment between their posture—centered, grounded, calm—and their spoken communication. From the felt connection with the earth, with feet planted firmly on the floor, all the way to the top of the body, where the eye contact is likely to be direct and focused, the grounded person exudes a sense of being, not just comfortable in their head, but at home in the body as well.

Harkening back to my example of how to "dance" in the throes of change, by engaging in a two-step process of attention and intention, we can now add the physical dimension with the ideas of center and ground. When operating in a posture of alignment, with our life energy unblocked and flowing, the body will literally reflect the state of our attention—and intention. What we are seeking here is the practice of mental, emotional, and physical alignment, such that the focus of our mental activity—the dance of attention/intention—is reflected in how we show up in our bodies, and in the world.

The energy of the body, as I said before, is a trustworthy barometer of the extent to which our thoughts are in sync with the reality of our physical situation. The goal, in shifting through the stages of change, and in releasing our fears along the way at each juncture along the road, is to check in with both our mental energies—to see where we are focusing our attention and intention—and our physical bodies—to take note of whether we are centered, grounded. Discovering and experiencing directly that sense of integrity between mind, body, and heart is key if we are to fully embrace and utilize all the energy and vitality that is truly available to us at any moment.

The body can be our best advocate for moving seamlessly through major change, for sending us the message that some aspect of our identity, our story of self, has outworn its usefulness. It can be the internal barometer that notifies us that it is time to gain a new perspective, to shift our stance on life. Our challenge is to get out of our heads and listen. My client George is not happy about the neck pain that has shown up just when he is seriously contemplating major changes in his career trajectory. Yet, it has caused him to pause, slow down, and, most important, recognize that no matter how carefully crafted his vision of the future may be, he is going to need to be centered, grounded, and aligned—in his body and in his life—to fulfill his dream and change his life.

Chapter Three

THE MYTH OF THE SYMPTOM

"The average, healthy, well-adjusted adult gets up at 7:30 in the morning feeling just plain terrible."

—JEAN KERR

In this chapter, I want to examine how the cultural and economic discourse that runs in the background of our society's view of illness focuses far too often on fixing the machinery, getting the car back on the road, so to speak, by simply alleviating the symptom. Unfortunately, this auto mechanic approach to health causes us to blatantly ignore or miss seeing entirely the deeper issue, *of fear,* that often confounds our well-being. Sadly, I submit that in today's factory-style health care system, where the insurance industry chides hospitals, and doctors, to get us in and out in a flash (my very, very good GP tells me his insurance providers allow him seven minutes per patient or else he doesn't get paid), the old adage often holds true: We miss the forest for the trees.

To begin to tease apart this theme, let me share with you a personal story. A few years ago when I was in the midst of the frenetic final study push for my PhD oral exams and I was feeling extremely anxious and stressed, my doctor was kind enough to prescribe Xanax for me, which as most of you will know is a common anti-anxiety drug. I'll always remember the little vignette that took place between us at the time, for although he was willing to prescribe the drug, he didn't do so without a bit of old-fashioned "counseling" thrown in for good measure.

I remember his exact words: "Now you know, doc"—he's very respectful of the fact that I too am a doctor, which is already very unusual!—"I'm happy to prescribe the meds for you, but bear in mind, these are only going to relieve your symptoms. You've got to do the heavy lifting and get at those underlying issues." We both laughed at this, given that he knows perfectly well that "getting at the underlying issues" is what I do for a living. I was grateful for his wise words of counsel. At the time, I did talk with a therapist about my anxiety, and I did meditate deeply on my own inner demons. Safe to say, my anxiety, as is quite often the case, was emblematic of a deeper, more insidious emotional foe than my occasional headaches and disrupted sleep patterns might have indicated: fear.

In this case, a deep, residual fear of failure had resurfaced, bubbling forth in the form of incessant worry that I would be "found out" by my colleagues and teachers as a "fraud." Twenty years later, it was all eerily reminiscent of long-buried memories of tearful test-taking traumas in my childhood. Ironically, as with many friends and clients who have had similar experiences, the truth of the matter tends toward the other end of the spectrum: I have historically done very well as a student. So why, in the context of a final exam, might I be insistently terrorized by an anxiety-producing inner drama that threatened to unmask my success as some sort of masquerade?

Well, as we will explore together in greater detail in part three, one of the most common symptoms that successful people of all stripes tend to suffer, especially upon reaching a pinnacle moment that signals a shift to a new level of accomplishment or achievement, is an irrational but very painful *fear of success*. On the cusp of earning my doctoral degree, I was in the final throes of a major shift of identity, not fundamentally different from making that inevitable leap from grade school to high school, or from high school to college. Becoming a doctor of psychology would alter my career trajectory in many positive ways, but it also represented an undeniable loss—of the comfortable and predictable life I had constructed in the corporate world.

I'm always amazed at how surprised my clients are to discover that they can be overwhelmed with anxiety—or even become depressed—when approaching a milestone in their career or family life that is emblematic, not of failure, but success. Even postpartum depression, which emerges with a complex set of emotional and physical symptoms that is difficult for the medical establishment to explain, might be understood more readily if we take note of the loss that accompanies the arrival of a child. For the mother who is supposed to be thrilled—and on some level usually is—about the blessing of giving birth, there is still a very real shift of identity, and a major loss, associated with becoming a mother: a loss of freedom, of flexibility and movement, of an identity as unencumbered by a dependent other. Giving birth can represent one of the highest forms of achievement in life, but it also changes everything. Success, in the form of PhDs and promotions and babies, may signal the culmination of a long, arduous period of hard work—a literal and metaphorical labor of love—but it also requires us to shift gears and let go of a story of self that we may consciously or unconsciously be reluctant to release.

Understanding how anxiety—and its root in fear—can emerge and undermine our progress in life even in periods of advancement and growth, is a key reason I wanted to write this book. Fear of success is just as common as fear of failure, and both can be show-stoppers in terms of the discomfort, anxiety, and worry—the symptoms—that they produce. But they are not the same; they arrive at different moments in a cycle of change, and they serve very different purposes. Fear of failure typically appears when we are practicing, studying, and focusing on achieving a personal or professional goal: It signals that the end of an era is approaching, that something new is on the horizon. It is a time for moving forward, not shrinking back or hiding out, but staying fully engaged, with discipline and effort, in the agency of the impending change.

Fear of success, which lies right on the other side of its sidekick, fear of failure, typically emerges in the wake of the change made manifest—the PhD conferred, the baby arriving—and signals the end of a full cycle of renewal, a time for celebration, gratitude, rest, and acknowledgment of a particular kind of loss: The loss of a story of self—in a particular role or specific job—that no longer fits.

Harkening back to my case of test-taking jitters, my mini-session with my family doctor made me realize that I was experiencing my own version of a perfectly normal, yet deeply etched pattern of fear of failure that accompanied the sequence of growth—and loss. This revelation did not automatically make the anxiety disappear, but it did give me a better understanding of what was happening; it raised my *fear awareness,* so to speak, which helped to quell the voice of self-criticism. When the next bout of worry descended, before I reached for the Xanax I was able to pause, breathe, reflect, and, most important, lighten up a bit, to accept my failings and fears, even chuckle. I still popped a couple of Xanax (I'm human!), but the bottle sits today on the shelf, half full, just in case.

The story above describes my particular version of how fear shows up to disturb and disrupt our lives even in times of positive change and in peak moments of happiness and success. But what it also points at is one of the major cultural myths we in the West have come to accept as part and parcel of our biochemical-mechanical medical model of illness: The symptom is the disease.

CURE THE SYMPTOM—MISS THE DISEASE

I saw a television advertisement for a new miracle drug recently on the market to treat, or should I say, as the marketing pitch claims, "cure" asthma. In the ad, the pharmaceutical company describes asthma as being caused by "a constriction and blockage in the linings of the air sacs in the lungs." The basic symptom of asthma, as most of you familiar with the ailment will know, is difficulty breathing. At first glance, it seems logical to say that this is *caused* by the constriction of air sacs in the lungs. But is it really this simple? What *causes* this constriction? Isn't that like saying a forest fire is caused by flames? When the firefighters arrive on the scene, like doctors looking to stanch the bleeding, they seek to douse the flames. They might say later that the fire caused a great deal of damage to the landscape, but they would look deeper for the cause of the fire itself. Yet, in the commercial world of health and healing, we simply accept that the flames caused the fire, and worse, that dousing them alleviates the illness at its source. But this is blatantly false.

The ad goes on to claim that by taking this new medication, the lung passages will be "opened up" and your asthma will be, well, "cured." Now, I'm all in favor of what would be more appropriately called "symptom relief," but that kind of phrasing, although useful with common cold remedies, doesn't have the heavy-duty selling power of "cured." Regardless of how exaggerated the claim of a cure may be, what incenses me most about these types of advertisements is the faulty logic they employ, implying that the symptom of the illness is the illness itself. This reductionist and surface-level perspective on illness gets perpetrated on us every day by the insurance and pharmaceutical industries.

The deeper truth about asthma is that we don't know what causes it, not really. It is not caused by its symptoms. Research by neurologists, lung specialists, and developmental psychologists has linked asthma to environmental conditions, emotional trauma, and even neglect. In one study, researchers found that in some households with children, a large percentage of which turned up having extreme cases of asthma, many had high levels of toxic mold in their basements. The mold was then thought to be the cause of the asthma. Fortunately, one of the researchers was a social psychologist who bothered to ask the question: Why are these kids being stuck in the basement for hours on end in the first place? Of course, that study would involve taking a very hard look at the parenting activity going on under those roofs, which is not only difficult to study—it is not something that most parents are particularly open to exploring.

Very quickly, if we are even willing to walk down the stairs and peer deeply into the basements of our causal theories, diseases like asthma become multidimensional conditions with varied and complex sources—emotional, environmental, and genetic. The problem is that as a culture we prefer to place a simple Band-Aid on symptoms and ignore the meatier exploration of the real cause. Of course, economics plays its part as well, for where profit is the motive, how does getting to the heart of the matter pay? If it turns out that a physical illness like asthma has psychological, environmental, or genetic roots, what kind of pill can we manufacture for that?

Likewise, we get caught up in similar circular logic for all kinds of other ailments: stress, anxiety, and in particular, depression. Whenever I read or hear that depression is sometimes caused by a biochemical imbalance in the brain, I can't help but ask: How do they know that this so-called imbalance caused the depression and not the other way around? Perhaps the emotional shutdown caused by the symptoms of depression actually depresses or disrupts the natural flow of serotonin, dopamine, and the other happiness hormones that control neuronal activity in the brain. Perhaps our psychological response to fear, loss, or even minor external disruptions in life could bring about alterations in brain functioning, causing the biochemical flow of hormones to shift out of balance.

The fact is that psychiatrists and neurologists whose specialty is understanding the brain and the complex interplay between consciousness and biology do not really know the ultimate cause of depression, nor do they know why the brain becomes out of balance biochemically; they just know that the symptoms of depression tend to appear in tandem with disturbances in our brain's biochemistry. In the past twenty years, pharmaceutical research has led to the discovery of a number of medications that appear to positively impact—and relieve—the symptoms of depression and anxiety. As I said before, I'm all in favor of symptom relief, and do not hesitate to refer clients with severe symptoms to doctors who can support them in feeling better. However, just as with my trek to the doctor for Xanax and his wise response to my request, medication for emotional and psychological breakdowns is just the beginning of the conversation. The idea that we are *curing* the disease by simply relieving the symptom is, to my mind, a dangerous cultural fantasy.

Pain itself, as expressed in symptoms, is fundamentally a language, a symbolic expression the body uses to send us a wake-up call, a message that we are out of balance; that we have lost our way. It seems that we have fallen into a deep trance in this culture when it comes to our approach to health and healing: We see the symptom as the disease. We blindly follow our doctors' orders to "cut IT out" or "cover IT over," but we rarely bother to dig very deeply into what this "it" really is. Instead, we lapse into a willingness to accept a blatantly illogical, if soothing, story: no symptom, no disease. Yet, at a deeper, more reflective level of awareness, we all know that this is blatantly false. The trouble is that taking this approach to illness at face value causes something else to occur that ultimately may be more damaging: We miss the messages from the body and fail to decode their meaning. Instead, when we ignore them, cauterize them, or just pop the pill for relief, they tend to get louder. Unfortunately, I've seen far too often the following sequence: What shows up as anxiety in an early stage becomes panic later, and soon thereafter, a heart attack. We would do well to heed the call.

I'm convinced that many of our physical symptoms, especially as they relate to mysterious ailments like autoimmune diseases, asthma, anxiety, and depression, are the body's way of bringing to consciousness the one thing we most want to avoid: the fear that accompanies change, perhaps even growth. Behind the constricted air sacs, the sweaty palms, the heart palpitations, the headaches, and sometimes the deepest lethargy lies the monster that would eat us alive: our own fear of life's inevitable shifts.

Of course, I run the risk of oversimplifying and applying a bland label—a Band-Aid—myself, if I just leave it at that. Recognizing that fear is the causal root of many of our ailments should not and does not provide a catch-all basket in which to toss off our pain. The opposite is true. Knowing that fear underlies much of the disease in our culture is the beginning of a conversation, not the end. For just as the theory that all will be well if we fix the symptom is a myth, so too is the idea that "knowing the cause" brings on a cure. What is possible, however, once we become aware that fear is running the show, is to engage in a different kind of dialogue with ourselves, not one focused on "fixing" or "curing" but rather listening and learning, for perhaps we are not even broken.

Gary's Story: How a Life-Shifting Illness Helped to Manifest a Dream

While we are on the subject of how we might understand the symptoms of pain and bodily breakdown as opportunities to learn, shift, and grow, I want to share the story of one man's journey into the darkness of illness, and how he has not only engaged in a life-affirming, creative dialogue with his symptoms, but become a role model for how to navigate sickness for countless others along the way.

Gary is the kind of person—healthy, vibrant, high-energy—who made it through the first six decades of his life with nary an illness beyond an occasional flu. So it was a terrible blow when two years ago, after experiencing severe lower back aches and pains in his ribs for many months, he was diagnosed with multiple myeloma—a debilitating form of cancer in which the diseased cells replicate, not into a localized tumor, but throughout all the bones in the body. It is a very serious malady with a low cure rate, but the good news is that there are many treatment options, all of which involve various forms of chemotherapy. For the past two years now, Gary has experimented with a rich array of chemotherapy "cocktails," with varying degrees of success.

His story of suffering for the sake of healing would not be particularly unique except that Gary, as a practicing psychotherapist, social worker, and spiritual-oriented individual, has come to view his cancer with a uniquely creative and potent lens: He doesn't see his cancer as the "enemy." He recognizes that this invader has come to him from the inside of his own body, that some part of him is wounded and hurting, and rather than take on his own body in a war-like stance of aggression, which would be the norm in our culture, he has engaged with the disease with respect, curiosity, even awe.

He has even begun to write about his relationship with the disease, in a blog he calls "Cancer: A Love Story," where he shares with readers the ups and downs of day-to-day life with cancer. In his regular updates, he treats his body, and his cancer, more as a difficult and enduring partner in life rather than an affliction.

What is remarkable about Gary's story is that he has come to write about the experience of having cancer so brilliantly, with humor, tenderness for self, respect for the doctors and nurses who care for him, and, most important, gratitude for each day that he sees the sun rise once again. But that is not even the punch line. This is: Ten years ago when I first met Gary, all he spoke about was his dream of being a writer. He was still working full time as a therapist at that time, but he had started a novel and written a few chapters of a memoir about his journey to Africa with shamanic healers. We shared many conversations about finding time to relax, dream, and write—and we commiserated on how life always seemed to get in the way.

Here we are ten years later, Gary has cancer, *and* he has become a writer, with a following. He writes beautiful prose, shares his story, using wise words filled with humor, humility, and grace, and with the gift of his writing, he is offering up a new kind of narrative about the ravages of disease. By writing about his illness in this manner, he is becoming a role model for many.

His life shifted in a way that he would not have chosen, and certainly in a way I would never wish upon him or anyone. Yet, shift it did. But instead of being taken down by the diagnosis, he turned the experience into an opportunity to live out his dream of becoming a writer. Cancer has provided him with the impetus to reframe his life, to reignite his creativity, and to even reinvent his career.

THE PARADOX OF STRESS

The timing of the universe is always impeccable. As I arrived at the point in this book where I planned to tackle the subject of stress—stress reduction, stress management, and the like—I found myself reflecting on what might be a rather controversial stance on the subject, and lo and behold, I started to feel stressed out! How perfect. It always helps to be intimate with one's subject matter. I'm no stranger to stress. I don't, in fact, know anyone who is not closely acquainted with the painful, intense feelings of discomfort that we associate with the symptoms: pressure, usually in the head and the neck; muscle constriction in the chest making our breathing tighter, shallow; heaviness, worry, confused thinking—a sense of being overwhelmed. We've all been there. There are a thousand variations of how stress shows up to disrupt our mental, emotional, and physical equilibrium.

What was stressing me out, as I thought about what I wanted to write about this ubiquitous form of suffering that seems to inordinately plague our culture, is what a paradox stress is. My current feelings of stress notwithstanding, I've got to say it: Stress is good. We need stress. Let me try to illustrate my point. Whenever I feel particularly stressed, stuck, or overwhelmed, I like to take a long bike ride or go for a run. Aerobic exercise, as we all know, is one of the best ways to reduce the symptoms of stress. Research has shown that physical exercise releases endorphins into the physical system that appear to counter the negative buildup of stress hormones like cortisol.

Near my home in the Hudson Valley, there is a long, winding country road that is perfect for biking. It is curvy and generally free of automobiles, with lots of steep inclines and long dips for catching my breath. At the outset of each ride, I always face an immediate fork in the road, literally, and a choice. On the left, the ride is mostly straight, flat, and downhill. On the right, the ride is more episodic, with steep hills, sharp curves, and long drops. You would think that if my goal is to reduce stress, get in the flow, and feel free, I'd go left. But I never do. The fact is that I like the hills. I need them. Frankly, the ride to the left is too easy, too flat; it is almost tediously static. In a word: boring.

The paradox of stress reduction is this: When I think about the most stress-relieving part of a bike ride, it is not those occasional downhill glides with the breeze flowing through my hair and no need to pedal or brake, but rather when I "hit the hill." In those moments when I feel the tension heat up in my leg muscles, when I gaze upward and feel a rush of adrenaline in the face of the incline ahead, when I downshift (to lighten the stress!) and become excruciatingly present to the oncoming climb, those are the moments when I feel the most focused, energized, and relaxed. In my case, the stress created by shifting the focus out of my head and onto my body, onto the present moment and its uphill exertions, releases the stress in my mind/body: the worry, anxiety, and, most of all, the fear that saps my energy and holds me stuck. Now I'm either a very odd duck, or it would appear that stress is not always the enemy that it is purported to be. In fact, it is this very stress—in this case, of physical exertion—that alleviates the real culprit: fear.

Unfortunately, stress has become one of those terms against which we carry a grudge. We are bombarded with ads for programs and workshops and CDs all purporting to help us reduce stress, yet this may be one more example of where the symptom is NOT the disease. The deeper truth is that we thrive on stress. Without it, we would wither away and die.

I'm reminded of two clients I saw back to back recently, who for a period of time made me feel a bit like a ping-pong ball on the table of stress. Each of them came to me complaining of being stressed out. On one side I had Sally, whose life appeared to be overflowing with stress, and on the other I had John, who complained about feeling stressed but whose life, it appeared to me, was sorely lacking in it. He, like me on those bike straightaways, seemed bored.

Viewed from the outside looking in, Sally's life appears to be overflowing with stress: She has a high-paying job as director of public relations for a major bank, which requires endless hours of work including nights and weekends. She has two strenuously active children ages seven and twelve, who have an endless litany of projects and programs and enough activities to make anyone's head spin.

On top of all this stress-inducing drama, she has an investment banker husband who works twenty-fours hours a day himself, and rarely participates in parenting or relating to Sally much beyond a shared video game and endless logistical e-mails. And so Sally comes to me each week complaining of being overwhelmed by stress—pressures at work, tension at home, endless to-do lists, and no time for herself. It is a common complaint for people who are trying to balance the continuous demands of career and family life circa 2009.

At the other end of the stress spectrum, we have John. A sixty-three-year-old retired architect, John lives simply and comfortably on a small pension that he built up over his thirty-year career. Having never married or had children, his life appears, again from the outside looking in, as a luscious landscape of freedom. John is able to do what he wants when he wants. He has close friends, and although he sometimes desires a closer companion in his life and misses the intimacy of a romantic relationship, he didn't come to me pining away for a girlfriend. His complaint, when he did arrive on my doorstep, was that he was stressed about his own lack of a to-do list, which was showing up as a general malaise, a lack of enthusiasm and passion for life.

At the outset, I couldn't help but think, as these two stressed-out clients passed each other in the hallway, that if they could just take each other's place for a few months, or maybe a few years, all would be well. Sally could sure use a little more freedom, and John could benefit from a bit more activity. They appear, at least initially, as opposites, to be sure. But that's the problem with stress: If you don't dive below the surface symptom, you can all too easily mistake the symptom for the disease. It turns out that John and Sally are not really opposites at all, but surprisingly similar, and that *stress* is not really the problem for either of them.

Sally, when pressed to explore her story of woe, turns out to thrive on being busy: She is passionate about her job, loves taking care of her kids, and doesn't, deep down, really mind running around supporting their high-energy lives. What she really feels is fear: fear that she is losing a connection with her husband; fear that he and she are becoming increasingly isolated from each other; fear that she might end up alone.

John, likewise, is actually quite content with many elements of his life. He thrives on his newfound sense of freedom in retirement, and he enjoys having the flexibility to putter about with multiple hobbies that he has put off for years. Stress is not his real complaint; loneliness is. He, like Sally, fears isolation, separation, and a lack of intimacy with a significant other. Funny, rather than switch places with each other, I might do them both more good if I were to introduce them (although don't worry, I won't). They are, like many of us, caught up in the story called "stressed," but at a deeper level, where the rubber of truth hits the road of the heart, their core issue is fear.

And so the crux of the problem with stress is that far too often it is not the problem. In some cases, a bit more stress may even be the solution. Both Sally and John, in facing their fears, actually need to turn up the stress quotient: They both need to move through their fear of isolation by "being more related," which will require that they each take on the added stress of engaging with potentially scary others—Sally's husband and John's potential girlfriends.

At the end of the day, stress is a necessary component in building a building, or a life. As any structural engineer who designs and builds suspension bridges will tell you: Stress is a key ingredient in the recipe for success. Without the right level of tension, achieved through a balance of weight, distance, and pressure bearing down on the different elements of the structure, the bridge will fall.

We humans, as delicate systems composed of interrelated emotional, physical, and mental elements, are in many ways no different. We too require stress to stay afloat. The difference is that unlike a suspension bridge, whose foundation, set in concrete, remains fixed (although in truth it too is always moving, in sync with the movement of the earth), the human system is fluid, movable, and in a constantly dynamic relationship with its environment. The loop of tension that holds up a bridge is closed; ours is open-ended. Our goal need not be to banish stress from the system, but to navigate that delicate sense of balance that keeps us upright and moving forward, flexible and adapting to the winds of change.

ANXIETY AND DEPRESSION: TWO SIDES OF THE SAME COIN

I recently sat through a heartrending ad for the latest antidepressant, which touts that some 80 percent of the American population will be taken down by the pain of depression at some point in their lives. Very soon thereafter, I happened upon my old dog-eared copy of M. Scott Peck's famous book *The Road Less Traveled,* opened it carelessly, and found myself reading the following passage: "Since mentally healthy human beings must grow, and since giving up or loss of the old self is an integral part of the process of mental and spiritual growth, depression is a normal and basically healthy phenomenon."

In that moment, the following question arose in me: Why isn't the statistic about depression more like 100 percent? I've certainly never met anyone who hasn't suffered with some combination of the symptoms of depression— lack of energy, trouble sleeping, feelings of despair, feelings of hopelessness— at some point in their lives, especially if they've managed to live through a few wars, recessions, divorces, physical ailments, and, most important, the loss of a loved one.

Life-Shifting Action Step:
De-stress the Distress

The chart below is divided up into three categories of stress: good stress, which is the kind of pressure and exertion we feel when things are perhaps difficult but motivating and energizing, even fun; bad stress, which is the stress that shows up as pressure to perform, achieve, or exert ourselves toward a desired goal but that can get out of control; distress, which is stress that shows up as anxiety, anger, or other symptoms of fear. Take out a piece of paper or journal, and fill out your own forms of stress—good, bad, and distress—for the categories listed below. Reflect on the distinctions between types of stress by journaling your answers to the questions below.

	Good stress	Bad stress	Distress
Family			
Work			
Money			
Relationships			
Community			

Questions for reflection

1. Do you notice any common patterns, trends, or themes in your list of good/bad stress?

2. Do your experiences of good or bad stress ever overlap? Why? How?

3. Are there ways you could change your life patterns to increase the good stress and lessen the bad?

4. When you are feeling distress, is there fear lurking in the background?

5. In moments of extreme distress, what might you be afraid of?

6. If actually increasing the level of stress—good stress—might be possible, how would you do it?

I have a similar curiosity about anxiety. When I think back on all the times I've felt the symptoms of anxiety myself—constricted breathing, incessant mind chatter, insomnia, headaches, irritability—I can't help but notice, in retrospect, that my anxiety attacks almost always accompanied some major change that was afoot in my life: a potential promotion at work, a pending move to a new home or a new city, a change in relationship, a rift in my family.

During the period when these changes were occurring, I was also confronting a shift—a life shift—in my way of viewing my life, my very identity, and part of me was holding on tight to the status quo. On the one hand, I didn't want to change, which created a great deal of tension—and fear—in the context of a deeper truth: I did want to grow. These anxious moments appeared when there was an obvious disconnect between my "old self" and the sense of safety and comfort I felt within that well-worn identity and a "new self" that was emergent, unknown, and, truth be told, rather terrifying in its awkward "newness." And so the symptoms of anxiety would surface, and sometimes linger, often far too long for my taste.

In addition, if I reflect on the times in my life when I've felt truly depressed, for a length of time that would constitute a diagnosis of clinical depression (i.e., more than a few days or weeks of symptoms), they too were times of great change.

The pangs of anxiety and downward pull of depression emerged just when I felt the yearning from somewhere deep inside my soul, my heart—you know: that unfathomable place where the seeds of growth are born—to leave my corporate career as a human resource executive and head out on my own. The entire transition from the seedling of an idea—becoming an entrepreneur—through those early halting baby steps into the insecure but amazingly free and exciting realm of the self-employed, I was by turns anxious *and* depressed, sometimes both at the same time. In retrospect, it all seems so—well, how does one phrase it? Normal. I feel quite sure that every client who has ever reached out to me for support has come into my office experiencing some combination of the symptoms of either anxiety or depression, and often enough, both.

The deeper truth about these symptoms, as most of us recognize if we stop and reflect on our own experience and the experiences of those we love, is that anxiety and depression arrive on the scene to try to protect us. They rev us up (anxiety) or shut us down (depression), to actually prop us up as we surf the wave of fear that inevitably rolls in on the ebb tide of change. But anxiety and depression don't try to protect us from just any old fear, such as fear of being mugged at four in the morning when you should know better than to be wandering the streets of New York City alone, not *that* kind of fear however real. No, they arrive to fend off the big ones: fear of major upheaval; fear of great loss; fear of losing who we know ourselves to be.

What makes the matter worse, and the tension even more unbearable, is the confounding truth: Some part of us *knows* what it is happening. Some part of us wants to change. Some part of us wants to grow. And, as desperate as we are to find the cure for the symptom and to make the pain disappear, there is a deeper, more grounded life force within us, what my Jungian colleagues and M. Scott Peck would call the unconscious that knows better. I call it soul.

I am not fundamentally against the pharmaceutical companies and their purple pills, or even their relentless advertising. There is a blessing to be gleaned in bringing the emotional and physical ravages of anxiety and depression out of the closet, to bringing them into the light of day, such that they become mainstream conversation. For it is just that conversation, with self and a loving other, in the form of a therapist, a coach, a trustworthy confidante, that more often than not breaks us through the knot of fear that is generating the symptom in the first place. It takes a great deal of courage to ask for help. And when the pain takes us down to a point where just getting out of bed in the morning is well nigh impossible—and yes, I've been there—then the pharmaceutical fix may be the right first step on the road to recovery.

What does upset me about the marketing of symptom relief through drugs are two potentially dangerous side effects that never get mentioned (unless maybe you can read lightning fast, as they scroll by on the bottom of the screen): first, the idea that we can reach for a pill, feel better, alleviate the symptom, and then not have to change (i.e., not have to grow); and two, that experiencing the symptoms of depression and/or anxiety somehow demonstrates that something is fundamentally wrong with us.

What we need to reflect on, rather than beating ourselves up about it, thereby making the symptoms worse, is why we get depressed and anxious in the first place. At the end of the day, these symptoms are simply reflections of two sides of the same coin: the coin of change. And change, although it requires us to, as M. Scott Peck puts it, "give up" ways of being that no longer serve us, is the key to emotional, physical, and spiritual growth. Change is a core requirement of becoming; it is the natural order in nature, and we humans are not immune to nature's ways.

Unfortunately, when something hurts in life, we rarely think that it might be a signal that something *good* is trying to be born in us. We habitually turn against ourselves, making the experience of anxiety or depression worse, by judging it—and ourselves—as bad. Fortunately, after many hours of therapy and years of suffering through multiple bouts of depression and anxiety, I have finally learned to accept the wisdom of the body. When I wake up in the morning, my mind racing with thoughts of imminent disaster, my body aching to roll over, go back to sleep, and fend off the day, I just breathe, relax, and welcome the arrival of the onslaught of change. I turn my attention to listening within for a deeper voice, one that lies beneath the mind's clattering chatter of end-of-the-world scenarios, and I ask: What is being called forth?

So when you find yourself under attack from "the blues" or feeling revved up in a frenzy, your thoughts spinning out of control, here is your challenge: Can you relax, slow down, and have compassion for the self that is morphing within you? Can you tune in to that inner voice, beneath the chatter of the mind, the one that speaks from within your own human heart? Better than any pill, that's where the answer is found.

ANGER: THE KING OF POP

My client Walter just wants to have, as he puts it, "a harmonious workplace." So when he blew up at his bookkeeper last week and called me feeling guilty, I had a sense that something was awry. Walter and his partner run a fairly smooth operation: a small, boutique computer software firm with a cozy downtown office that houses three or four administrative staff, an office manager, and a few part-time programmers. It is generally a congenial place, and whenever I've had occasion to visit, the staff are pleasant and friendly, if a bit harried. It turns out, however, that two of the women in the office don't get along. They come from very different ethnic, religious, and geographic backgrounds, and often have opposing viewpoints on everything from how to raise children to how to change the copy machine ink cartridge. They rarely speak unless forced to do so.

Walter is tired of their sullen, seemingly hostile interactions. He wants the office to be "upbeat" and "like a little community." He finally took one of the women aside and while trying to coax from her the reasons behind the poisoning silence of interoffice warfare, he got frustrated, and ultimately angry, pretty much demanding that she be more collegial. In the aftermath of the clash, he knew, before I even said anything, that his own behavior wasn't exactly role-modeling the very thing he desired most: harmony.

Of all the symptoms of disharmony (that very often presage disease), the one whose terrain we find the most challenging to navigate is anger. Of course, on the surface, anger is quite natural, quite normal, and quite common. We see it every day in a thousand forms, from violent protests in the streets of Iran, to caustic exchanges between late-night comedians and politicians, to cutting remarks between friends over politics, to sarcastic salvos between lovers over housework, money, even sex. Just about anything can ignite the fire of anger. None of us is immune.

Anger is most easily understood, I think, by most of us as a buildup and discharge of the energy of thwarted desire. We want something and we don't get it. Some goal, some hope, some dream—some picture of the way life is supposed to look—gets dashed, and very quickly, whoever did the dashing becomes the enemy. Subsequently, we feel an internal energy shift, it can turn on a dime, and the feelings of frustration, irritation, and anxiety build within us. Eventually, if the desire is strong and the blockage to its achievement becomes rigid and impenetrable, anger erupts.

We are often taken by surprise by our own anger. It appears to emerge out of the blue, like a volcanic eruption. One moment we are calm, relaxed, and enjoying the day, and next thing we know, the guy driving in the next lane cuts us off, and suddenly we pop, and this searing fireball of emotion gets flung, literally, out of our system and onto the world, onto this supposed enemy, who is more often than not a stranger in a hurry, or worse: an employee we genuinely like, a family member we cherish, a partner we love.

We think we understand anger. We have books on the shelf that supposedly teach us how to manage it. A friend of mine actually cowrote a wonderful little book about how to manage your anger. It is filled with lots of aerobic exercises for "dousing the flames" of anger, yogic breathing to calm the rising temperature of ire, empty pages for jotting down "what not to-do" lists when something sets us off. It is a useful book, and I'm sure helpful to many; I've tried a few of the exercises myself when in the throes, or aftermath, of an outburst. But in attempting to manage anger, I wonder if we don't miss the point. All our attempts to manage life—you know, that endless stream of management mantras: time management, stress management, change management, and anger management—are fueled by our need to control life, and the life energy that swirls within us. But can we really control life? Can we truly control time, or stress, or change, or anything, or anyone, least of all, when in the throes of anger, ourselves?

The truth, I think, is that we don't really understand what anger is, where it comes from, or why it grips us so often and so deeply, and with such disastrous results. If we stop and look beneath the label "anger," and listen to the feelings that get generated behind the behavior, what we will come upon most often is fear. We are afraid of each other. We are afraid that we won't get what we want. We are afraid of life.

And so we get angry. But why? Why do we choose, in what feels like a nanosecond, to get angry when rationally, intellectually—and in retrospect—we always *know* better? One reason is that anger is the great dissembler; it is the king of emotional "pop"—a masked marauder of displaced fear. Unable to be with the true feelings—the lack of control, the disappointment, the residual despair of past hurts—we will do just about anything to avoid touching the pain of our very real vulnerability. More often than not, I find that the expression of anger—over office politics, harried drivers, unemptied cat litter—is not really about what is currently happening but is instead the residual trigger of a deep and painful memory from long before, from a time when as children we really were afraid, we really were unable to control our environment, when we really were dependent, as it were, upon the kindness of strangers (and yes, for most of us, our own parents were strangers, unfathomable in their power over us, derelict in their duty to meet our every need and want, and unconsciously, we still hold a grudge).

Take Walter, for instance. Where does his outsized angry response to his office dynamic really come from? He knows that his angry eruption was out of proportion to the situation. So why erupt, why lose control? Why make things worse? From a calm place of reflecting, with a little probing from me, a new awareness emerges: He grew up in a chaotic family environment where there was constant bickering and little sense of calm or safety. He remembers it vividly, for it is alive in him still, in the cells of memory. This phantom of the past has a positive valence as well: It drives his desire to create an office "home" that is the opposite of what he experienced as a child—an environment of safety, serenity, and collegiality. Hence, when this desire for harmony gets blocked by employees who unwittingly fail to carry out his unconscious plan, Walter's fear—truly his childhood terror of chaos—returns full on. Unable to understand or engage with the pain that this long-distant fear retriggers, he erupts in anger. It is a defense against pain, pure and simple: a reflex.

We've all been there. Ultimately, if we truly hope to learn to manage anger, we need to understand what it really is and see where it really comes from. It is most often a symptom of past hurt, past pain—past fear—that is alive in us and, sometimes literally, dying to get out, to get released. We all "act out" at times. Unfortunately, whole families, offices, even countries, expel their anger onto each other with little awareness of the underlying fear, the underlying pain that is seeking to be healed.

I recommended that Walter apologize to his employee for his outburst and calmly make a request: that she share her story, whatever she is willing or able to express. His job is simply to listen deeply, to recognize her pain and her fear as his own. The anger of her sullen silence and the anger of his outburst are both symptoms of the same disease: the discomfort of fear. The starting point for unmasking and healing the symptom of anger is to become aware of the fear beneath, to see how it drives us in those unavoidable moments of vulnerability, when the hurt child bursts through and throws a tantrum.

❂   ❂   ❂

The next step is developing greater compassion for ourselves, not to become harsh parents of our own inner kids. Beating ourselves up over the inevitable outburst just makes things worse. We may be an angry lot, but we can also take solace in the fact that we are all in the mysterious school yard of life—together.

Life-Shifting Action Step: Tracking Your Triggers

In this exercise, think about a time when you have felt angry or experienced conflict with your partner, children, friends, or perhaps a boss or subordinate. Take a few minutes to reflect on what triggered your anger. Then reflect on the following questions:

1. What happens in your body when you feel triggered by anger?

2. If you reframe the encounter and think of it as being about fear, what might you be afraid of?

3. What do you most fear about your own anger?

4. How might you act or speak differently if you were to be aware that your true feeling was one of fear, not anger?

Chapter Four

THE TROUBLE WITH HAPPINESS

"You cannot make yourself happy, but you can find joy in sadness. If you desire happiness, you will be disappointed, just so as if you desire contentment. If you desire nothing, you will find both."
— AUTHOR UNKNOWN

Perhaps one day, a few hundred years from now, we humans will look back on this time of historical upheaval, political and economic strife, and see clearly, with the advantage of wisdom and hindsight, that with the commingling of cultural stories from the East and West, a rupture was inevitable.

The Eastern approach to life most associated with Buddhist and Hindu philosophies would have us believe a quintessential noble truth: Life is suffering. The goal of enlightenment, from an Eastern perspective, requires that we recognize that everything in life is impermanent, that change is inevitable. In this context, any form of striving for achievement, success, or material wealth is a fool's game, one we must inevitably lose.

The Western story, the narrative most of you reading this book have been steeped in since birth, tells a different tale, invoking life's highest value as the "pursuit of happiness." The great conundrum that emanates from these seemingly contradictory views of life is something I have experienced firsthand. Upon visiting what we might consider poor countries, at least materially, in the East, I found myself immersed in the cacophony and chaotic rhythm of what appear to be, at least on the surface, lots of happy folks. On the other hand, if a visitor happened across what is usually considered the most prosperous country in the world, the United States of America, he or she would likely find a great many people caught up in the throes of depression.

Clearly, we live in a time not only of great cultural rifts, but of consummate paradox. How can it be that in lands where the core belief is that *life is suffering* people are often quite content, while those who would salute the flag of *happiness* often experience a great deal of suffering? Very likely, if we follow my lead from the last chapter and dive below the surface symptom, whether happiness or suffering, we'd find a great deal of anxiety and depression, as well as joy and pain, on both sides of the Pacific.

Ultimately, we are all trying to find our way through the mystery of life, and even though we may approach it with what appear to be divergent core beliefs, the underlying reality remains true: We are all seeking peace in the face of change; we are all fearful of the unknown. I raise this specter of cultural collision not to judge the inherent value of either an Eastern or Western perspective, but rather to point us in the direction of exploring, in the context of life's cycles of change, how the cultural stories we hold dear can land us in dangerous territory: a territory marked by disappointment, and fear.

Here in the West, one of the immediate problems we run into with anything and everything related to happiness is just how elusive the concept really is. Consider an analogy. Substantial research has shown that as our culture becomes more and more obsessed with physical appearance and vaults "thin" (downright skinny if you're a woman) and "fit" into iconic territory, incidences of poor self-esteem, low self-worth, even depression, associated with physical appearance in young people in particular, have exploded. As the bookshelves, magazine racks, and now Internet sites clog with pictures of sculpted muscular, six-pack-toting fellows and elegant stick-figure females, the importance we ascribe to beauty and a slim physique actually seems to foment suffering, for one very obvious reason: Most of us never measure up.

I submit that the same dynamic holds sway in the kingdom of happiness. In a world where the real process of living is more cyclical and replete with constant shifts and upheaval, anchoring ourselves in "happy-land" may be a laudable goal, but its achievement, at least for any serious length of time, contradicts nature's ways. Just as the beauty of any rose is doomed to fade, so too the bloom of happiness is transient, and any attachment to its arrival's being permanent is bound to set up a clinging, anxious longing. In a word: unhappiness. Buddhists are clearly onto something. Attachment to and idealization of all things "happy" may actually bring on the very thing we most try to avoid: suffering.

For this reason, my road map for getting your life in gear will not point you in an upward, straight-line trajectory toward happiness. Rather, I believe life is a cyclical journey replete with numerous highs and lows, where although we may arrive at a plateau of fulfillment—a stage I call realization, which may be accompanied by the experience of contentment, peace, even ecstasy—we rarely hang here for long. Inevitably, we round the bend, and just like the seasons, head directly into the next period of loss, transition, and change.

Eckhart Tolle's work, which attempts to synthesize the Eastern approach to life within a Western framework, focuses on how to step out of our conscious habits of mind, our story, and remember that we exist in an unfathomable ocean of consciousness—an empty place where there is no happiness or unhappiness, but only "now." Tolle notes that "striving to be happy" is a conceit of the ego-mind, a reflection of our fear-based attachment to the future in which we lose touch with the present moment. His approach to happiness brings together, it seems to me, the best of Eastern and Western narratives, asking us to relinquish our egoic—and egotistical—need to control and manipulate life.

I'm not against happiness per se; it's just that, at the end of the day, I'm not convinced that all this commercial focus on happiness is healthy. Hanging our hopes on happiness is like capturing a monarch butterfly in your hands: You might get lucky and get one if you try really hard, but then what? You can't really enjoy its beauty once it is crushed in your fist. Hold on to it longer than a few seconds and it will surely die, and you will be anything but happy. You will feel sad, sorry, and most likely quite guilty. For me, helping people to "shift their lives into high gear" is about helping us all to be more present in our lives, less fearful and attached to transient highs and lows. My intention is that we (and me too!) become more awake and adept at moving through the inevitable cycles of life's journey; that we become less attached to the cultural elixir of happiness and more focused on relishing the experience of each stage in an endless life cycle of change.

THE ASYMPTOTE OF JOY

An asymptote is a mathematical term for a line that curves toward a fixed point, usually described as zero. An asymptotic line curves in such a way that it flows infinitely toward its goal, the crossing point, but never gets there. Joy, satisfaction, contentment, and all those pleasant dictionary terms that deign to evoke happiness are basically asymptotic: They move in the right direction, toward the laudable goal of "being happy," but they never quite arrive, or if they do, they don't stick around for long.

Life just doesn't seem designed for endless contentment (as people who, when on holiday, decide to up and move to the Caribbean often discover): Most of us rarely settle into happiness for long periods of time. We get a glimpse of joy, perhaps have a peak experience (and mind you, I'm a big fan of joyful moments!) or a few blissful sunny days, yet, in due course, clouds, storms—rainy days and Mondays—inevitably arrive to break up the monotony. Is it possible that our denial of the unattainable nature of happiness winds up creating and reinforcing its opposite?

I recently discussed this very subject with my dear friend and former therapist, Judy, who shared with me that although she is generally quite content with her life, she sometimes finds her mind wandering into unpleasant territory, asking, "Is this all there is?" On the face of it, Judy has every reason to be happy; she has a profession as a psychotherapist that she loves and where she is able to give back by helping others to heal, a husband of thirty years, and a healthy and successful daughter, who is happily married with three wonderful children. Judy loves being a grandmother and although her long marriage has not been without its upheavals and necessary cycles of reinvention, she and her husband have settled into a generally peaceful and compassionate partnership.

Judy, as I will gently remind her, is nearing the end of a cycle in her life, a full realization stage, where the identity she has created for herself—professionally and personally—has provided a great deal of happiness and just rewards. The bad news—if you want to see it this way, and Judy sometimes does—is that there is "rupture" in the air surrounding Judy's pleasant and comfortable life. She can feel it. She confesses to me that she has been having trouble sleeping; she feels restless, anxious, sometimes even bored. Like many in our happiness-obsessed culture, she wonders if there is something wrong with her, thinking that she should be able to just relax—and be happy.

For Judy, the end of a cycle may be in the works; she may be moving into a period of upheaval, hopefully one that will arrive gently and, with the support of a loving family and close friends—like me—will lead not to harsh self-criticism (which could pull her into depression), but will instead shift her out of her fear of not being happy enough and on into a period of inquiry, with the energy of possibility. In the best of all possible worlds, Judy will allow herself to relinquish the plateau of complacency with lots of self-compassion, welcoming the rupture as a call from her soul—signaling that something new in her is still yet to be born.

As Carl Jung noted in the theory of individuation, which I talked about in chapter one, the core challenge we face in our happiness-obsessed culture is to accept a counterintuitive truth: The boxes we build around our identity are destined to be broken open. Our egos may cling to a fantasy of ultimate fulfillment—retirement on the golf course in Florida—but the soul has other plans: to constantly push us forward, to break apart our comfort zones and fling us up against our growth edge.

Much like those spiritual seekers who head to the East to grasp at enlightenment and seek to transcend their earthly status, only to find themselves back at home one day and in need of a job, we all ultimately must reconcile a more banal truth about life on earth: We are never "done." We don't settle into a heavenly landscape of happiness upon retirement, and we don't dissolve or leave our earthbound bodies just because we meditate for twenty years in a cave. We are earthly creatures, subject to the up-down cycles of nature, required to forge our way on the hardscrabble path of life. The fact that we never settle down into a land called "happiness" or "enlightenment," however, is great news, for it means that some part of our nature—what Jung calls the soul—is constantly calling us forth to grow: to plant and till new seeds of possibility that expand our boundless human potential.

THE TYRANNY OF "SHOULD"

If you could delete any word, any single word from the English language, because you thought it would make life ever so much more enjoyable, what would it be? There are the obvious choices: hate, rage, anger, violence. Perhaps you might think, given the theme of this chapter, "I know, he's going to want us to banish 'happiness' from our vocabulary." Perhaps I would consider this, but that's not the word I would ultimately choose. My choice for the term that life would be ever so much better without is "should"!

Happiness, as we've started to understand, is a particularly elusive goal. Our cultural addiction to it and our lifelong dance with it may be a toxic combination. Yet, what really gets us in trouble is the double whammy of suffering that ensues when, driving along the bumpy and far from linear road to happiness, we pick up the mantra of an extra passenger whose voice rings loudly in our heads, shouting, "I *should* be happy." "Should" is a particularly egregious and dangerous term, because so often when it appears, it is a signal, a flash point, for resistance—and resistance, playing its role in this toxic game, is almost always a tip-off for fear. Now, perhaps "fear" is the word I'd most want to get rid of, but as we are learning, fear is actually a very important, and helpful, companion on the journey of life. Not so with "should."

Let's walk through an example so you can see how happiness, difficult to experience even in the best of times, gets totally derailed in the wake of "should." My client Peter and his partner have been together for fourteen years. They have had their ups and downs—as all couples do—but recently their relationship appears to be on the skids. It seems that Roger (the partner) tends to be harshly critical of Peter, putting him down with complaints about his procrastination, his lack of focus, his inability to meet financial goals, and his lack of sharing in the housework. According to Peter, whenever Roger is feeling particularly anxious—or I might surmise, insecure—his rants can accelerate to vitriolic levels, edging toward verbal abuse. On top of this, Peter doesn't feel supported by Roger in his desire to grow personally and professionally as a financial planner. Roger, a social worker, seems content to have reached a plateau in his own career and may even resent Peter for wanting to grow, change, and evolve. Recently, Roger's irritability and recalcitrance have led to Peter seriously considering ending the relationship.

Of course, as with all intimate partner dynamics, the situation is complex; there is no right or wrong player. I'm sure if I were to have Roger as my client, there would be an even-steven reverse narrative of legitimate complaints about Peter. Everyone in the dance of relationships plays his or her role, for good or ill. What is particularly striking in the example is the stark evidence of something I see every day in my practice with clients: Peter carries around very strong assumptions about his life and the relationship, and where he *should* be at this juncture of his life (he just turned fifty). He recently stated to me, "Perhaps I should have left the relationship a long time ago." And further, "Don't you think I should be happy? That I should get unconditional love and support from my partner? I should be treated better."

Here's the issue I want to raise around the insidious moniker of "should": We are so attached to the concept of being happy in this culture that we beat ourselves up whenever life appears other than aligned with this lofty—and quite often unattainable—goal. In all three examples above, "should" is a euphemism, a stand-in, for "something is wrong with my life." I don't accept life as it is. Either IT (life) or I (me) needs to change.

What's so poisonous about the word "should" is that it gets us coming and going. Equally capable of projecting our dissatisfaction with the status quo on the outside world, the tyrannical "should" makes the world—our career, our partners, our finances, the weather—all wrong, then tirelessly confounds our mental world, turning our thoughts to daggers aimed at making me/us wrong. Either way, "should" is a killjoy.

In the case of Peter and Roger, Peter's "should" is all about Roger: Roger should be different, and then and only then Peter might be happy. In other cases, the derailing troublemaker on the road to happiness is ourselves. We play out something along these lines: "If only"—"if only" is a sly variant in the "should" narrative—"I were different, better, more motivated—something other than how/who I am—then all would be well." Really? Do you recognize this pattern in any of your own thought processes?

What is the antidote to the debacle of "should"? When I think about supporting my clients or myself, I attempt to look beneath the surface chatter of the mind, to nonjudgmentally observe the emotional content that underpins "should." In its many internal and external guises, "should" is often a sign of resistance to *what is*, and resistance, at its core, is almost always fear.

So we can now return to my point about happiness: Our attachment to its ongoing realization may generate fear. Can you see the connection? Take a moment and think about what the deeper voice—the one bubbling up from the heart—might be saying (when in the throes of "should"): "I am afraid to let go of my partner. I am afraid to change. I am afraid that he doesn't love me. I am afraid that my life will be a failure. I am afraid that my life *is* a failure." YIKES! Do you see how the monster of fear lies in wait under the surface mantra of "life *should* be different"? Now let's return for a moment to my fantasy word-banishment quiz. At this juncture, I want to change the rules. I recommend that we keep both words—"happiness" and "should"—but banish them from ever being used in the same sentence. That *should* do it.

Byron Katie, in her powerful book *Loving What Is*, has the right idea: The source of our unhappiness—and our fear—can be found in our attachment to having things look other than the way they really look. We need to learn to step back, breathe, and accept life—as Katie says, to "love life"—just as it is. Life is not a straight line upward toward a mountaintop called "happy." Life is at best an endless (although in this form it does end!) series of cycles that, like the seasons, promise us nothing more than the inevitability of change.

Happiness, in the context of "should" is a paradox, because only by letting go of the "should" component—which is based on fear and our need to control—can true happiness ultimately emerge in our lives. I believe we could be happy, but only if we learn to stop resisting life, embrace change, and resonate, relish, and revel, deep down, head to toe, in the mud of what is, which is what becoming a "life-shifter" is ultimately about.

MONEY, MEANING, AND THE MADNESS OF MORE

When I reflect on what's happening with the economy on a psychological/cultural level, somehow I always end up harping once again on our addiction to material, consumable, instant, microwave-safe happiness . . . and all the trouble it gets us into. It just seems to me that the deeper issue we face, as a

Life-Shifting Action Step:
Exorcising Your "Shoulds"

This exercise can be performed as a powerful ritual for *exorcising* the negative effects of *"should"* on your life. Take a piece of paper and make a list of the top five "shoulds" that show up in your day-to-day narrative. The list may include ways that your life, your job, your career, your relationships should be different.

Now create a sacred space in your home where you can be alone, quiet, and not interrupted for a few minutes. Light a candle and sit quietly before it. Take a few deep breaths and read your "should" list to yourself. When you are ready to let go of your "shoulds," place the list in the flame, and slowly and intently watch the paper burn (be careful to do this ritual in a safe space). Take long, deep breaths and relax into the experience of burning your list. This ritual may seem silly or overly contrived, but if you do it regularly, whenever you find yourself repeatedly saying to others, or to yourself, that "things/you should be different," it can be a powerful reminder to let go and be present and more accepting of "what is."

nation and a culture, is a crisis of *identity*. We've lost sight of who we are, and what *really* matters.

Now, I don't want to run off at the mouth about "truth, justice, and the American way," yet somewhere along the way we have reframed and dumbed down the narrative of the "American Dream" to consist solely of home ownership, the acquisition of an endless parade of instantly obsolete gadgets, and two cars in every garage. Perhaps the trouble we have with happiness isn't so much with our desire to be happy but with the path we've chosen to get there: We've just drunk way too deeply on the Kool-Aid of consumption, becoming inebriated on the false belief that we'll all be blissful if we just have *more*—more houses, more cars, more wide-screen TVs, more highways, more beachfront resorts, ad infinitum. Clamoring always for the almighty "more" strikes me as a form of madness—a pathological disease that is more symptomatic of a deep depression than of the so-called happiness it is designed to create. Why do we feel so empty that we are in constant need of a fill-up, a pick-me-up, a buildup?

Somewhere along the trajectory of material wealth and prosperity, we seem to have caught a consumption virus—a happiness disease—for which we pay dearly by living in constant financial anxiety, our sense of identity tenuously attached to real estate, the stock market, and more than anything else, our résumé, all of which are subject to only one constant: change.

So where do we go from here? Wiser, if disheartened, we move forward, as individuals, as a culture, as a species. As Jung might say, the "shadow" side of our addiction to happiness—at least in material form—has reared its ugly head, but breakdown also, always, precedes breakthrough. Rupture is an inevitable and ultimately positive stage in the cycle of life; it emerges when a peak period of satisfaction, achievement, or happiness shifts inexorably toward complacency and self-indulgence.

The other thing we would do well to remember is that there is a major difference between *having* and *being*. I was recently struck by just how muddy these "having and being" waters can get if we fail to pay close attention. In their new self-help book *The Passion Test*, Janet and Chris Attwood lay out their prescription for what can only be described as happiness, as they say: "having it all." The core theme of the book resonated with me: that it is crucial to get in touch with your passions—to reflect and remember and reconnect with what you most care about—if you hope to manifest a life of meaning, value, and ultimately success. The premise of the book is sound.

My only concern is that I wish they had been a bit more circumspect in defining exactly what they mean by *passion*. It seems that, from their perspective, finding your passion, or as they say it, "discovering what you love," can include what you want to do, what you want to have, and what you want to be, any or all of the above. My trouble with this is that it may lead us down a treacherous path where discovering one's passion includes a list of items such as "being a multimillionaire" or "having a mansion on the beach."

Self-help authors, it seems to me, should know better than to lump *doing*, *being*, and *having* into the same category and then line them up as passions of equal status. They just are not the same. When so-called experts suggest to readers that the path to happiness is a catch-all highway on which every form of passion is of equal value, I fear that this approach may promote its opposite: It may foster distress.

There has to be a better way to reconnect to your passions than by listing all the stuff you love and want to have, do, or be. Of course, the challenge is that to really do the work of reconnecting to passion, meaning, and value in life—to rediscover what really matters—you have to get tough on yourself and ask some difficult questions: Who am I? What is most important in my life? Where am I going? No easy answers here. No quick fix.

The trouble is that the acquiring part of life, however effortless it may seem in the act of pulling out that credit card, far too often takes us off track, away from the deeper calling of our soul for growth and expansion and change, and down an exhaustive path of having and getting—more, more, more. On that path there is never, ever enough.

Life-Shifting Action Step:
A True Passion Test

In order to discover your deepest passions, to access your soul's visions, dreams and fantasies of what is truly possible in life, you have to move beyond self and culturally imposed stories of how money and material wealth are theoretically the supposed keys to success. As "unrealistic" as the questions below might sound, it is a powerful practice to give yourself the gift of fantasy and reflection about *what really matters*. Take a page in your journal and just write whatever thoughts come up in response to the following questions. Be careful not to censor or judge yourself. Don't try to be practical. Just ruminate, fantasize and dream. You may look back on your notes a few years from now, and be very surprised by what has happened along the way!

1. If money was *not* a factor in how you designed your life, what would your soul be called to create?

2. If you were stranded on a desert island and could only have five items/things with you beyond life-sustaining food and water, what would they be?

3. If you were writing your own obituary, what would you want it to say?

4. If five years from now you woke up from a long slumber and found yourself unencumbered by responsibilities or a need to pay the bills, free to embark on the ideal day, what would it look like?

Chapter Five

THE ROAD MAP OF CHANGE

"When one door of happiness closes, another opens; but often we look so long at the closed door that we do not see the one which has been opened for us."

—HELEN KELLER

Over the past fifteen years of counseling people from all walks of life—corporate executives, housewives, doctors, lawyers, even students—I have found that the vast majority of the time clients arrive at my doorstep with some variation of the same complaint: They feel lost. With the backdrop of a culture that proclaims on every billboard—television, radio, and newspaper—that the road to happiness is found in accumulating material wealth, and typically with parents who, perhaps lovingly but forcefully, pushed us onto the practical path of finding a well-paying job, acquiring a spouse, and having a family, it is jarring to find that even when we achieve these goals, we may still end up miserable.

As I have been discussing throughout part one of this book, our sense of self is a story we craft while driving along a road filled with twists and turns, and the more we become attached to the outcome called "happiness" as defined by external forces—our families, our partners, our culture—the more likely we are to career off course. At some point along the journey of life, the voice that is uniquely ours—the voice that emerges from a deep, mysterious place in our psyche that I call the soul—will demand to be heard.

The breakdown, when it occurs, may appear in the guise of a variety of symptoms such as body aches, anxiety, and depression, for the message of change, of energy that is pushing or pulling us in a new direction, will most often show up first in the vehicle itself: the body. Attending to the symptom may take us on a detour to the doctor's office, and in some cases the medication or advice we receive helps us recover our bearings and get back on track, at least temporarily. Yet, somewhere along the way, the call to change—the need to release our attachment to one fully formed story or an externally driven identity, to dive deep and explore the depths of our very being—may get loud enough that in spite of the "fix" from the medical regime, we still experience a deep sense of dread, a feeling that despite all of our hard work and discipline, we just "don't know who we are anymore." This sense of being lost on the road to happiness will very often bring on a "crisis of meaning." We discover that the roles, responsibilities, and life path that we have chosen, or that has been chosen for us, just doesn't result in a meaningful sense of joy; there is no peace, no calm, but rather a sense of upheaval, of having taken a wrong turn somewhere along the way.

What has been most noticeable to me over the many years I've been researching the phenomenon of clients being called to "shift gears" is how normal the cycle of self-renewal really is, how beneath the story of unhappiness—burn-out in a job, misery in a marriage, overwhelming debt in the accumulation of a "lifestyle"—the call for change simply signals that our soul is calling forth, through symptom, malaise, or loss, something new to be born.

The core myth of our Western culture—that we live our lives in a linear, straight path, traveling inexorably toward happiness, joy, and supposedly retirement is just that: a myth. Life does not have a singular destination—other than our real death—but instead comprises a series of cycles in which we grow, develop, peak, and need to be reborn, all along the way. Fundamentally, what causes us to feel lost in those moments when the destination we've reached no longer bolsters our sense of self, but undermines it, is that we lack a *road map* for the way life really works.

In this chapter I want to introduce you to the map I've designed to help my clients, and myself, move with less effort and less fear, down the harrowing highway of change. As you will see, it comprises six stages, each of which represents a distinct moment along the road to complete transformation and renewal. I use the word "moment" specifically, because it has become clear to me, having witnessed hundreds of people go through this cycle, that the amount of time we may spend at each stage will vary greatly. The moment of shift, when we release a particular set of fears and move on to the next stage, can happen in an hour, in a day, or it may take months. In fact, through the experience of yoga, I have discovered that the body, mind, and heart may completely reinvent itself in a matter of hours, even minutes. In addition, the length of time we spend in one particular stage may be very short and the next very long. Like the journey itself, the trajectory of time along the path is not linear or predictable; the only thing that is for sure is that you will go through each stage, sequentially, in making a full shift toward rediscovering, reinventing, and refinding your sense of self.

LOST IN TRANSLATION

Before we jump into the road map, I have one more point of clarification to share with you and that is what I mean by *shift*. To be sure, I believe that when we travel through an entire cycle of the life-shifting road map that I describe later in the chapter, a complete transformation will occur: You will wake up one day, fully embrace the experience of the final stage (realization), and notice that you have dramatically shifted how you see yourself, how you feel in your body, how your story of self has been completely redrawn. You may not even recognize this new you, you just know that something about how you describe yourself, how you engage with your life, is very different.

"Transformation" is a word that, unfortunately, has become overused in the self-help world, representing a change of just about any kind—a new job, a new relationship, even just moving to a new city can be misconstrued as the mark of a transformation. Not true. There are different degrees of shifting, and to utilize the tool set in part two and to journey successfully through a full cycle of self-renewal, it is important to recognize the extent to which you are really "shifting gears" or simply moving back and forth within one stage where the surface story may look different, but the underlying dynamic hasn't changed. Equally likely, in the midst of moving through the stages, a shift may feel transformative, and it may well be in some aspects, but it does not denote a full life shift of renewal, but rather points to your being in transition. Hence, before we can embark on the journey to truly reinvent the self, we have to understand the distinction between the requisite modes of shifting. There is a clear difference between the three modes: transition, translation, and true transformation.

Transitions are what we might describe as the "mini-shifts" along the path. They represent the transitional moments in which we shift from one stage to the next. Each stopping point along the road of change has a particular quality of thinking, feeling, and being, and as you move through the cycle and pass through different stages, you will likely encounter a different set of thoughts, and even very different fears along the way. For many people, the transitions through the first three stages feel a bit like downshifting: The quality of the experience is likely to have a downward "pull" to it—from feelings, thoughts, and sensations of resistance, through an experience of release or letting go, on into a phase of rest, even immobility.

The transitions that occur in the first three stages all signify a movement toward an ending—and the retreat stage is likely to feel like a culmination or even a completion. But it is really a halfway point, a rest stop, because at some point perhaps days or weeks after settling into what may feel like a "bottoming out" zone, the energy will shift again—and the second half of the cycle—the upshift—begins. The last three stages are energetically reconstructive, where thoughts, feelings, and sensations of rejuvenation and renewed motivation will emerge as you shift into the direction of something new and exciting. A full cycle of self-renewal will include six transitions, each of which feels like a powerful shift—and it is—whereby your emotional, physical, and mental energies will change significantly as you move through distinctly different types of fear.

My clients are often surprised to learn that fear—and its attendant surfeit of symptoms—will continue to be your companion even as you move through the "upshifting" stages of the cycle. We all resonate with the idea that letting go of some aspect of ourselves is scary, but we are less cognizant that developing a new way of being in the world—a new career, a new relationship, a new identity—can be equally unnerving, and frightening, even when it feels exciting.

What is most surprising to people, however, is not just that fear joins us for the entire road trip, in various guises, but that we can fool ourselves all too easily into thinking we are making a shift when in actuality we are stuck in what I call "translation." Translation occurs when even though we may tell ourselves that change is occurring, the quality of fear involved remains the same. The symptoms may shift; we may move from anxiety to irritability, from headaches to stomach pain, from sullen silence to a sudden burst of anger—but the thing we fear (which will be different depending upon the stage) doesn't budge. Translation is sometimes hard to spot, but it is most recognizable at times when we find ourselves seemingly moving in circles, repeating old patterns, taking two steps forward and two steps back. We all know what it feels like to think we've made a shift, yet suddenly wake up to find ourselves right back where we started—in the same old job, in the identical relationship dynamic from the past, in the same quagmire around money, or family, or our career.

Translation can be a formidable obstacle along the path of transformation, for it often shows up as changes we make to our external situation—what we might call "window dressing"—but the internal context, the psychological landscape of our thoughts and feelings, remains stuck. The biggest hurdle to overcome in discovering that we have not really transitioned from one stage to the next, but that we are "spinning our wheels" in one stage over and over, is to finally begin to acknowledge, accept, even welcome the fears that are keeping us in a holding pattern—and to utilize the tool set in part two to move us through them. But, most important, we need to try not to be overly harsh and self-critical at this juncture. We all get stuck. Translation, although not a true shift in the sense that we are hoping to make, is part and parcel of the way our ego has been conditioned: to protect us by avoiding change. Translation will often show up in the form of rationalizations, denials, and the king of self-protection: procrastination. That's OK.

My point in setting out the three distinct flavors of shifts that typically occur along the road to self-renewal is not to set up a hierarchy of judgment, whereby transformation is best, transition is good, and translation is bad. Rather, since each of these three are normal occurrences along the road—and each denotes a distinct relationship with fear—it is important to become conscious of the differences: to take stock of where we are at any given moment so we can simply recognize when we go astray, and get back on the path of real transformation.

THE SIX STAGES OF CHANGE

Working with people who are stuck somewhere along their journey and in need of roadside assistance, I have come to see that the map of life's journey seems to have very specific stopping points along the way (as outlined below). As we will see when we encounter true stories of individuals who have traversed the full cycle of self-renewal in the third part of this book, a key step toward becoming more comfortable in the driver's seat of your life is to be able to recognize *where you are* on the journey. Then, and only then, can you stop by the side of the road, take a bit of a breather, get out your tool set, and get to work—letting go of fear and getting your life in gear. We start by reading the road signs:

1. The Rupture
("check engine" light comes on or you see "accident ahead")

The moment on life's road trip when you realize that something is amiss, you have a flat tire, need a tune-up. After about five thousand miles of safe cruising in my Volvo, I recently turned the key on a very cold day and the engine refused to turn over. Instead, an "engine performance reduced" warning light came on—a sure sign of a vehicle entering a rupture stage! Some ways you may recognize this stage: feelings of fatigue, stress, anxiety, general discomfort with the status quo of your job, your relationship, or your living situation. The bottom line: Something just doesn't feel right.

2. The Release
(sign for "yield"; slow down)

By slowing down and reflecting on where you are in your journey, you come to realize that some aspect of your identity—how you know yourself to be—in relationship with your career, significant others, perhaps your family, is no longer working. It is time to let go or release some element of your personal narrative in order to make room for something new. This may be particularly painful, especially if you have been holding tight to a specific self-image or self-perception, but it can be done—and the tool set in the next section will show you how.

3. The Retreat
(sign for "rest stop")

Time to stop and rest, to take a break from the normal routine and allow the transformative processes of the release stage to become integrated—mentally, emotionally, and physically. After a period of release, which may involve letting go of a job, a loved one, or a self-imposed sense of identity that no longer serves you, it is perfectly normal to feel naked, even exhausted and emotionally drained. Depending upon the nature of the release you have experienced, there may be a period of uncertainty and feelings of emptiness, even boredom. Retreat is a time for patience and waiting, a time for reflection and contemplation. Something new will be germinating within you but you may not yet know what it is.

4. The Revival
(sign for "on-ramp")

A time of new beginnings, in which you may feel a sudden burst of energy and vitality. In the cycle of self-renewal, this stage represents the period of the birth, the infant, and the toddler all wrapped into one. You may feel exuberant and refreshed, yet vulnerable and insecure. It is a time for daydreaming and crafting a vision for a new relationship, career, or sense of self. It is a time for experimenting, playing, and feeling free to explore new ways of being in the world. Just like when you have excitedly purchased a new car and you want to show it off to the world, but you are at the same time cautious and sensitive, afraid of being judged or criticized, it is a time for moving back into the mainstream, but slowly, with a light step. The key to the revival stage is to stay in "play" mode; there will be plenty of time for work later on.

5. The Rehearsal
(sign for "caution: new construction")

Exiting the revival stage will be evident with a strong signal called "commitment." At some point along the path of exploration and play, you may find yourself focusing on a new mode of operating, a new career path, or a new relationship. At this juncture, the new work of constructing your next identity has begun. The rehearsal stage is all about getting in shape for the next road trip, becoming purposeful again.

Life-Shifting Action Step:
Mapping Your Journey

Take a blank sheet of paper and starting on the left side (aka at "birth"), draw a line of your life across the page that marks both the ups and the downs.

Questions for reflection:
Is your life line a straight line heading upward?
Is it curved or jagged?
What are the high points and low points along the trajectory?
Did you use up the whole page or is your life line scrunched up on one side?
How does it make you feel to see your life scratched out in a single line?

Have someone you love do this exercise and share your life lines with each other. What do you learn about your relationship to life?

6. The Realization
(sign for "freeway: all clear ahead")

After you rehearse and practice and work hard to hone your skills in the new venture of your choice, there will very likely be a period of time, hopefully a long time, when the stars all line up on your side of the street. The road is clear ahead and you get to cruise along smoothly, just taking in the view. It is time to celebrate and be grateful for all of your hard work, to shift into fifth gear and relax. It is time for honoring yourself and your accomplishments as well as for giving back. Mastery marks the realization phase and wisdom emerges from all your hard work. This is the payoff stage: Enjoy the ride!

THE CYCLE OF DREAD

If you are like most people, the line of your life that you drew in the sidebar exercise from the last section was *not* a straight horizontal line across the page. As much as we might like to hold to the fantasy that life is a pleasure cruise from one wonderful exotic locale to the next, we all know that this is not really how things work. The road map of life is more like a series of hills and valleys, with occasional detours down rocky and uncharted terrain. That's not to say that there are never periods of relative calm, when the road flattens out and we can put on the cruise control and take in the view. Yet these don't—or rather, *shouldn't*—last.

After knowing the vehicle is in good shape, and mapping the terrain of your trip, staying safe along the way—avoiding accidents, breakdowns, and detours—is clearly the most important factor in determining the speed and success with which you will fare on your journey. Unfortunately, fear is the decelerator even as we hit the accelerator. Think of it as defensive driving, because the reality is that no matter what stage we are in along the path of change and renewal, fear will be there right beside us as our constant companion. It appears to be a combination of hard-wiring deep in the ego-structure that is formed in childhood and also a key factor in our individualistic Western culture: We generally distrust the unknown "other" and get easily frightened by anything or anyone new that comes into what we consider our home territory, or "safe space."

What's key is that we do not avoid our fear responses; rather, in order to stay on course and grounded, anticipating change with enthusiasm and perhaps even excitement, we have to tackle our fear head-on. We can do this by learning to recognize and understand the type of fear—which may appear with a variety of symptoms like depression, anxiety, and stress—that accompanies each stage, each stopping point along the way.

In fact, just naming our fear, becoming awake to its presence and impact on us as we travel, will go a long way toward defusing its power and supporting our shift—the smooth transition—from one stage to the next. I call this raising our "fear awareness." Once we are able to map the fear, what I call the "cycle of dread," along the terrain of the six stages of self-renewal, we can utilize specific tools to help us accelerate the shift, not only from one stage to the next, but from dread to delight—joy, excitement, and vitality. Fear is a sneaky backseat companion, however, for although it follows us all throughout the journey, it tends to change its stripes, hide out, and get camouflaged in a variety of symptoms, transmuting its quality, nature, and content as we transition from stage to stage. Imagine driving cross-country picking up strange hitchhikers along the way.

Our job, as we will see in the next section and in part two is to learn to unmask our dread, to bring the fear devil right up into the front seat with us, to utilize specific tools and practices to diminish its grip on us, transforming our backseat driver into a front-seat partner. Then, and only then, can we feel safe and exhilarated by the ride and enjoy the journey.

Below is a synopsis of the cycle of dread. See if you can recognize any of these frightful passengers who have joined you through the ups and downs of your journey thus far.

THE CYCLE OF DREAD

1. **Rupture Stage**
   Dread Factor: Resistance to Change
   The most common symptoms of fear associated with the rupture stage are usually anxiety (our system revs up and won't idle) or depression (our system shuts down and won't move). Both of these symptoms, along with irritability, boredom, stress, and exhaustion, are usually signals that our ego is in fear mode—digging in its heels to keep with what is comfortable and familiar, no matter that we think we might desire something new and different.

2. **Release Stage**
   Dread Factor: Fear of Endings

In spite of the ego's protestations, or sometimes *because* of them, the end comes. Nature runs its course, with or without the blessing of our egos. A decision point is about to be reached and the end of some aspect of our identity—a relationship, a job, a home situation, a friendship, an addictive behavior—is on the horizon.

As a result, some aspect of our sense of self, some story we have told ourselves, is dying. We all dread—and are culturally conditioned to avoid—this existential truth.

In those challenging hours, days, or weeks before the definitive end occurs, we may be gripped with a new fear—in the form of terror, anxiety, nightmarish fantasies—as our ego, in its final attempts to avoid letting go, may pull us off the road and drive us into a ditch, sometimes metaphorically, sometimes literally, ending us up in a sick bed, even the hospital. What we most need to allow, during this difficult transition, is grieving—the normal expression of feelings, thoughts, and sensations that accompany loss.

But since our culture is focused so heavily on productivity and maintaining a strong ethic of work, action, and all matter of "doing," we may not get a great deal of support for grieving. Grieving takes time. We need to be gentle with ourselves, practicing self-acceptance and compassion for the process of change. This is the most common point along the road of transformation where we may slip into the rut of translation, spinning our wheels, and avoiding the transition to full release. The key to making this transition, as we will learn in the next section by putting the tools to work, is to allow ourselves to grieve—to breathe, relax, and accept the inevitable. By raising our awareness that experiencing a fear of endings is perfectly normal at this juncture, we become able to allow, accept, and honor the process.

3. **Retreat Stage**
    Dread Factor: Fear of Paralysis
    In the emotionally draining aftermath of an ending, it is absolutely necessary to stop and rest. Feelings of inertia, emptiness, and loneliness may emerge and they need to be honored before you can move on. The retreat stage may last just a few days or may drag on for months, and in the middle of it we may fear that it will never end.

We may become overwrought with feelings of boredom, frustrated with our lack of clarity or direction, or anxious about the future—similar to what was experienced in the rupture stage. But since these sensations arrive in the wake of a release, the associated feelings of dread are likely to be quite different, with qualities of paralysis and lack of energy for any kind of movement.

The retreat stage is a delicate moment in the cycle of renewal, for we may have the desire to skip this stage and "get back in the game," which we may recognize as the "rebound" reflex. We may feel confused and lost such that our fearful ego wants to "go back" and reclaim that old sense of stability. This mini-cycle is a clear sign of translation—where our fear may pull us back toward the known—and if we aren't vigilant and accepting of the nature of how the cycle of change works, we may end up back in the old job that we hated or back in a relationship that we know, deep inside, is over.

4. Revival Stage

Dread Factor: Fear of Inadequacy

Gradually, the stuck feelings will give way and we will begin to sense that something new may be on the horizon. The energy of vitality begins to return. But in this stage of being a beginner, as we try out new ways of being—dating again, considering a new career, learning a new skill, or practicing a new craft—we may be fearful of looking stupid, feeling foolish, and become overly self-critical.

Being a beginner requires the fortitude to make mistakes and keep playing, to be open and willing to try. If the fear of feeling/being inadequate becomes strong enough, we may find ourselves detoured back into the rupture stage, another form of translation instead of transition. This marks another key danger zone along the path: In this child-like energy of renewal, we need to be watchful and supportive of our newly emergent vision of the future, as residual fears from childhood may come to the surface and sabotage us.

5. Rehearsal Stage

Dread Factor: Fear of Failure

As we continue to build the skills and capabilities that will move us toward a new identity—a new relationship (or reinventing our current one), a new job, or simply a new way of living—self-criticism can morph into stage fright, which in turn results in harsh self-criticism and second-guessing. Once we have made a commitment to something or someone and we have entered into "practice mode," fear of being judged a failure, of not being good enough, is likely to rear its ugly head.

By raising our fear awareness of how natural this type of fear is—fueled by our ego's desire to protect us from harm—we may learn to put the fear to use as our guide. The voice of judgment becomes a barometer by which we measure our progress: As its volume decreases our competence increases. Eventually, it remains only a whisper in the background and we shift gears, owning the new identity and moving into the next stage. But we need to learn to watch for its presence, listen with compassion and understanding to its needs, so as to not be derailed by its ferocity.

6. Realization Stage

Dread Factor: Fear of Success

At some point we experience a sense of completion. We relax into the relationship, the career, the new "home" of who we know ourselves to be. The fears of inadequacy and judgment recede and a newly forged sense of harmony and alignment emerges. Yet even in the midst of celebration and achievement, we often feel fear. Who hasn't experienced pangs of self-doubt, questioning the validity of an accomplishment or the sustainability of a new or reconstituted relationship? We may feel compelled to work harder, drive faster, fearful that our success may be a fluke. Fear of success is an odd duck. It appears at unlikely moments, just before the wedding ceremony: "Do I really love this person?" Or at a pinnacle moment of career achievement: "Do I really deserve this award?" It may also show up as fear in the guise of guilt: the retread of childhood conditioning that we know as "who do you think you are?"

Now that you have an overview of the six stages of a full cycle of renewal and the accompanying fears that are likely to trip you up along the road, you may feel a bit overwhelmed by all the different steps you will go through—and intimidated by all the various types of fear that show up for the ride. Before we go any further in this primer, then, let's take a time-out and read a real-life story of how one man, caught in the throes of a major life change, found his

way through each of the stages and remade his world, his life, and his iden
anew.

Stuart's Story

A forty-five-year-old general counsel for a major media and entertainment firm when we first met, Stuart was, by all reckoning of the outside world, exceedingly successful and highly competent in his life and work. But when he first appeared in my office, he was already into his second year of taking antidepressant medication. The good news is that the medications had worked, to some extent, and the dark emotional pit of depression into which he had fallen had lifted.

Yet, the deeper truth still held: Stuart felt unfulfilled as a lawyer, unhappy in New York City, and trapped in a lavish lifestyle for which he was paying a stiff price: his health. Despite the antidepressants, Stuart had severe migraine headaches and lower back pain, and to make matters worse, was constantly riddled with unexplainable skin infections. As he would sometimes say, he was "uncomfortable in his own skin."

Born of middle-class Jewish parents—Holocaust survivors—in Brooklyn, Stuart had grown up regaled with endless stories of the importance of getting a good job, being a doctor or a lawyer, always having a "profession" to fall back on. A loving and devoted son, Stuart studied diligently, became a corporate lawyer, and followed the path laid out for him. Yet, in his deepest memories of childhood, the moments of great joy for him were those carefree summers when he was away at camp—off in the mountains of northern New York state, camping, swimming, and playing in the fields and meadows. Ironically, performing the tough work of country life—mowing lawns, pruning trees, weeding gardens—was the time Stuart remembered as being happiest.

Thirty years later, life became unbearable for Stuart. After a long client engagement had him working fifteen-hour days for months at a time, Stuart's emotional and physical systems just gave out. Overworked, overweight, and exhausted, he dropped out of work for two months, slept for days on end, unable to get out of bed, and even had fantasies of suicide. The antidepressants helped, enabling him to return to work and at least go through the motions. But the rupture was real, and Stuart's general unhappiness refused to go away.

When we first met, he was distraught that the antidepressants weren't "stronger." "I can't give up my job. It's true that I hate it, but I have bills to pay, a wife to support. Besides, what else would I do? I am a lawyer." Stuart's identity as a successful lawyer was a tough nut to crack: He believed that this was *who he was.* In the rupture stage, resistance to change can be strong.

Let's jump ahead four years and see where we find Stuart today. He lives in Tuscany, the proud owner of an olive farm in the countryside outside of Rome. He writes to me occasionally to regale me with stories of olive harvests and winemaking, and his wife has become a local chef! Step by step, Stuart moved through his fear of change and slowly shifted gears to reconnect with his inner passion. Key to the process of Stuart's amazing self-renewal was his becoming aware of his fears along the way. First, there was the fear of change— and his resistance to it—that landed him in a rupture in the first place. His ego-self, having spent many years building up a successful corporate persona, ultimately ran afoul of a deeper core truth: that he is much more than just a lawyer. He is a nature lover, a craftsman, a lover of culture, a dreamer.

Moving through the rupture stage only took a few months once he weaned himself from the antidepressants and got fully in gear. Working with the tools I will share with you in part two, Stuart was able to shift gears and begin to release his attachment to the identity of corporate lawyer. This letting-go process, of course, brought with it a whole new set of fears. Allowing a long, successful career to *die* was an agonizing yet necessary process, one through which he by turn grieved and dreaded, as he literally mourned the end of an era. Following this came what Stuart likes to call his "fallow" period: a retreat time, when he took a leave of absence from his job and traveled for a couple of months on a solo sojourn to, as we might put it, find himself.

What he found along the way was not always pleasant. New fears emerged as he traveled alone on this part of his journey—fears that he would be lost forever, never find his way back to the so-called real world, that his family, friends, and colleagues would forsake him, leaving him alone, broke, and isolated (fortunately, Stuart's wife was very supportive; she just wanted him to finally be happy). Pangs of guilt—last-gasp attempts by his sundered ego-self to beat himself up—would suddenly emerge and even at the ripe old age of forty-five, he would wonder if he had let down his parents. Of course, the highways and byways of his retreat stage also had high points, moments where he would gasp in delight as he spontaneously arrived at a panoramic view of the countryside, or taking an afternoon siesta in a summer meadow he would find himself giddy with the excitement of his newfound freedom— enveloped in the energy of possibility.

Along that seemingly aimless road for two months, he also discovered Italy—a country and culture he had always remembered loving as a child, when he studied art, history, and music, especially the Renaissance. How perfect that Stuart would shift gears from the retreat stage to the revival, entering his own personal renaissance, while traversing a landscape where the entire Western civilization broke free from its multicentury rut—the Dark Ages. Stuart's passion for culture, his love of nature, and a long-lasting love of great food—and olives!—all seemed to coalesce in this Tuscan cradle of Western culture.

Two years later, after exploring many possible variations of job, work, and country life—first still tethered to New York City (and part-time legal work) and finally cutting bait and committing to purchase the farm in Italy (the rehearsal)—Stuart moved through additional fears (of people thinking him crazy, of feeling out of control, of failure) before he was reborn an olive farmer. At the first olive harvest, I suggested that he create a ritual celebration to mark his entry into the realization stage. He invited his parents—who as you might expect had been at the very least wary and, at times, downright scornful of his choice to leave the legal profession—to fly to Tuscany, join the community harvest gathering, and crush the first olives. A little while later I received a little bottle of pressed extra-virgin olive oil in the mail: literally, and figuratively, the fruits of his labor. In Stuart, we have proof in the pudding (or in the oil, I should say) that you can renew your life and live your dreams—but you have to be willing to work through your own cycle of dread.

Now, at this point some of you may be thinking, "OK, wait a minute. This is all well and good for corporate lawyers with supportive spouses and a wad of reserve cash like Stuart, but what about the rest of the world? I can't just take two months off to drive around Italy, and I sure as hell can't leave my job! Does this transformation stuff really have to take four years?" Stuart's story is dramatic. But whether you transform yourself from lawyer to olive farmer or shift from full-time to part-time work or make the leap from full-time mom to empty-nester, the stages of the process will all show up—and the associated fears will come along for the ride. I guarantee it.

My client Trudy loves to hear about Stuart's story of full-blown life change. She uses his story to inspire her as she works through what appears to be a simple shift—going back to school and starting a new career after raising four kids. She has no plans to move to Italy (as glamorous as that might sound) but the fear, angst, and vulnerability she experiences—of letting go of her identity as mother, homemaker, and chief chef and studying with classmates younger than her own children—are just as real as Stuart's. No matter how simple the shift, or how dramatic the reinvention, the process of change is invariably the same.

We all wish we could go from rupture to realization with a snap of the fingers or take a pill as a quick fix—that's what the meds are for, right?—and miss the pain of confronting and moving through our fears. Unfortunately, this fantasy is just that: unrealistic. The reality is that no matter how straightforward the process of reinvention—of our work, our relationships, even our health— somewhere along the road you will hit speed bumps, internal (and maybe external) traffic cops, and all manner of scary obstacles. But there is good news: Each moment of fear we experience throughout the "cycle of dread" can be shifted from dread to delight. All it takes is a set of practices to support us in making the transition from one stage to the next, releasing one set of fears and tackling the next, to move through an entire cycle—and remake our sense of self fully anew.

Chapter Six

FEAR FACTORS

"Nothing in life is to be feared, it is only to be understood. Now is the time to understand more, so that we may fear less."

—MARIE CURIE

The first step in facing our fears is looking at how the emotion (usually expressed as anxiety, stress, anger, overwhelm, sadness, or even illness) plays itself out in our particular situation. Most of our fear-based responses to what occurs during each of the six stages of a major life shift can be traced back to our early life conditioning. We took our cues on what was frightening, what was supposedly dangerous, from our parents and other authority figures in our lives. Through a developmental process called mirroring—a literal absorption of the powerful affective energy of authority figures—the brain becomes wired to respond to the fear that we witness in those we love; it becomes our fear as well.

For example, if your mother was fearful of not having enough money and exhibited anxiety or agitation when money was the subject of conversation, it is highly likely that you will repeat this pattern. Chances are that if your father was afraid of the neighbors and suspicious of people who were not like him, you may be, too. We are all conditioned in our response to life by what was modeled for us as children. Even in our adult vehicle with all the fancy gadgets and safety belts, we still get scared, for there is a little kid in all of us that is still sitting in the backseat, or glued to the TV in the dark bedroom, terrified of the same monsters—insurance companies, doctors, lawyers, and ex-spouses—that plagued our parents.

WHEN PAST IS PRESENT

Even seemingly insignificant tales of childhood terrors may strongly influence what is fearful for our adult selves. For example, I remember being left alone in the backseat of my parents' car for a few terrifying hours one night when I was about nine years old. My sister, a rebellious teen at the time, had come down with a stomach virus of some sort and had to be rushed to the hospital. My parents were overwrought and panicked. They couldn't leave me home alone in the middle of the night, so they scooped me out of bed and dragged me with them. I remember with harrowing detail the excruciating sense of fear that I felt as I sat in the dark in the backseat of that car, for what was likely about two hours but felt like an eternity. Ever since then, I have often noticed that when I'm out shopping or sightseeing with friends and they wander away from me for even a short time, I will begin to feel tense, and even have mildly anxious thoughts of foreboding. These feelings are irrational, of course, triggered by the residue of a long-buried memory of trauma, but no less palpable and distressing.

This conditioned fear may show up as a story line underlying fearful situations in all the domains of our lives—anxiety about work, worry about the kids, stress about our partner's behavior. This is why it is essential to reflect on our childhood experiences—to bring the past up to date and out of the dark recesses of our lost memory, for what remains active in the unconscious is still alive in the present until we release it. The past is present and the goal of "shifting" through fears from the past is to become aware of how they control us.

As you will discover in part two of the book, a key to shifting your relationship with fear is to practice stepping back from the immediate reactivity it causes in you, to nurture a reflective posture in which you can begin to connect the dots between your present response to a painful situation and the early conditioning that may be erupting on the scene but no longer is either required or serves the adult you. In working through the first two tools for transforming fear, recognition and responsibility, you will notice how fear-based reactions to all types of life circumstances—issues with money, concerns over personal relationships, or work and career choices—may be trigger points for repetitive patterns that were set in place many years ago. Let's take a look at an example of how this dynamic, where the past is unfortunately still very much present, showed up in the shifting career challenges of one of my clients.

Margaret has a high-powered job as a marketing executive with a large pharmaceutical firm. Her reputation for delivering strong results to her clients comes from working long hours and being demanding both of herself and of her team. She has a "take no prisoners" leadership style and is known for being direct and sometimes even abrupt in her communications. In her personal life, she is married to a rather quiet, unassuming computer programmer, who clearly lets her "wear the pants" in the family. The same goes for her social life. When I ask her about friends, she notes that her friends are very loyal to her but will look to her to coordinate all their gatherings and maintain the social circle. Clearly, Margaret is a doer who takes pride in being a strong performer.

The trouble starts when we learn that Margaret rarely takes a day off, resents her boss (who, ironically, is quite similar to her in style), and tends to be overly critical of herself when things don't go as planned. And although her staff are quite loyal to her—as she is to them—she gets hurt when in feedback sessions she learns that she has a reputation for being aggressive, overly controlling, and even abusive at times.

When asked what irks her most at work, in her friends, or about her husband, she is quick to reply, "When people don't follow through. I don't have any patience for ineptitude. I can't stand slackers!" Margaret's angry response is a projection, a way for her to expel painful feelings onto others rather than have to face them herself. She has deep feelings of insecurity, which, despite her outward success, are fueled by a residual childhood fear: that she might not measure up. Deep down, she fears that she might not "look good" or always be strong enough or maintain her power. She is afraid of being seen as weak or vulnerable. Yet, of course, the truth is that she is vulnerable, that she is sometimes weak—as are we all.

By taking a step back and reflecting on what her anger is really about, Margaret was able to raise her awareness of her deepest fear: that she might not always be successful. But where had this drive to excel come from? Clearly a strong positive quality—and a necessary one for a leader—in some circumstances, this tendency to push herself and others beyond what is required to get the best out of them (and her) emerges from deeply held beliefs about success, work, and how to operate in the world. Being a high-level performer and needing to achieve success at all costs is the driving influence of Margaret's work ethic, her emotional response to others, her daily rhythm: It is her identity story.

When asked about her relationship with her parents in this regard, Margaret was at first challenged to find the connection. Her simple reaction to my question about her childhood stated the obvious, "I'm not sure how my parents influenced my way of being at work now. I've always been this way, kind of driven to succeed and get ahead. My dad always wanted us kids to do well, to do better than him, in fact. I guess I always thought that his pushing us to excel was a good thing. He was certainly driven. Hah . . . driven to yell and scream at us if we brought home even a B. Well, now that I think about it, I suppose it was a bit harsh. . . ."

Slowly, painfully, the memories emerged. Margaret's dad clearly loved his kids; she has the smiling photos and slide shows to prove it. But there was always an underlying energy of disapproval as well; sort of a below-ground stream of criticism and fear that was part of her father's make-up (clearly a response to his own upbringing during the Depression) that would bubble to the surface and erupt in anger if he witnessed what, in his self-story, appeared to be his kids being "slackers." Margaret ultimately came to see that she had developed her need to achieve in response to her father's high expectations, that as a child she believed that she would be loved by her dad only if she pleased him consistently. Her fear was that she might lose his love if she failed to perform; in response, she was determined to be strong, to always outperform, and to be worthy of his love.

The first step toward raising your fear awareness is to identify your own fearful driving forces from childhood. This is not a Freudian rant on blaming your parents. It is a story that we have taken on, an identity that formed over many years as a result of being a witness and a participant in a dynamic and complex family and community system. Our fearful response to certain external cues may not look rational or productive in an adult world where we should (there's that word again) know better or have more control over our behavior, but we need to be gentle with ourselves: We learned our responses to the world at an earlier, more vulnerable and sensitive time. We were molded by our surroundings, our environment, and the emotional responses that we witnessed being played out before us. They may be etched deeply, but they are not etched in stone; they are not who we are. Rather, they point to the starting point for change.

On the other hand, the goal of the cycle of self-renewal is not to vanquish our fears altogether. We don't want to become fearless, as some New Age teachers would have us believe. "Fearless living" is, of course, an oxymoron of the highest order, for life itself is not always safe or benign—and our fear is a natural response to real or perceived threats. Anyone who tells you they are fearless is exhibiting the full-on expression of another hardened story of identity—a defensive posture designed to keep the monsters of vulnerability, weakness, even death, at bay.

We may never fully vanquish our fears, but we can learn to shift through them with greater mastery, calm, and ease, as we drive across the rocky landscape of life and come out stronger at the end.

THE FIGHT OR FLIGHT FEAR RESPONSE

Studies have shown that just like animals humans have one of two basic responses to fearful situations, whether real or imagined: Either they move toward the perceived danger and prepare to fight or they retreat and try to get away from the situation. This is called the fight or flight response and it is well documented. However, the reality of how we tend to deal with fear is more complex than any either/or situation. The majority of us tend to use *both* fight and flight responses depending upon the circumstances. We may, in fact, use both responses in the same situation, moving toward the perceived danger in an attack mode and then quickly switching into a retreat stance. Or we may react the other way around—we may initially remain passive, or go numb, but later, at a certain moment (sometimes unconsciously in a passive-aggressive mode), we may attack. Think of how two boxers duke it out: They jab, parry, attack, retreat.

These modes of self-protection have evolved and developed over thousands of years. They are instinctive and unconscious in most cases, harkening back to a time when the environment for humans, an acutely vulnerable species throughout most of its evolution, was a truly dangerous place. Unfortunately, even in situations where the imminent threat is less real than perceived, we can still fall back into conditioned ways of operating passed to us from our distant ancestors.

For instance, a person who senses that his job may be in jeopardy—as he witnesses others around him being laid off—may react initially to his fear of job loss by working extra hard even when the additional effort has no significant impact on the business context. Leaning into his fear, this surge of energy and activity may just add to his stress, make him behave erratically, and even have a negative impact on the quality of his work. On the other side of the coin, for some the threat of job loss brings on a fear response so debilitating that they are overcome with dread and find themselves retreating from activity and from others just when they need most to be engaged.

At times of grave danger, this instinctive response may well still be useful, though for the most part, our lives are rarely threatened; yet, depending upon our level of stress, anxiety, and vulnerability at the time, an emergency response may be just what shows up. Hence, it is extremely helpful to raise your fear awareness in the domain of extreme stress, real or perceived danger zones, and acute conflict. Fear is always at play here, even if we don't recognize it.

Here's an experience I went through not too long ago that gives a good example of this situation. I was driving down a country road about one hundred miles north of New York City, enjoying the view of snow-capped mountains and forests in wintry hibernation. Thinking that I was basically alone on this particular side road, I admit that I was cruising along a tad over the speed limit. I was driving within reason, mind you, but being perhaps a bit cavalier. Well, alone I was not. Just as I rounded a corner, a huge male deer, with a full head of antlers, leaped out of a snow bank and landed right in front of my car. In that moment of panic, I had two choices: slam on the brakes and pray, or push on the gas and swerve around him . . . and pray! It was a split-second response: I chose the latter. Hitting the gas and swerving (and still praying), I somehow managed to miss him by an inch and drive past him before he could even freeze or leap. Another driver might have slammed on the brakes and they may very well have stopped in time—or (more likely since the road was icy) they may have slid right into the stag.

OK, what did I learn from this moment (besides that I shouldn't speed)? That my "emergency response" tends to be "fight mode." Under most difficult and scary situations, I have a tendency to lean into the conflict, to take people on (not always the best choice, needless to say), and move into avoidance mode only when the first attack response fails. If you are more of a "flight" type than a fighter—at least initially—then very likely the emotional experience of fear will feel like shutting down, cowering, or paralysis—becoming frozen. If you are an avoider, you may have been asked what's wrong by someone during a difficult moment and all you can muster is "nothing" or "I'm fine," which everyone knows is not true. On the other hand, if you are an aggressor type in a crisis or confrontational scenario, you may mistake fear for aggression, anger, or rage.

My client Julie has a particular dynamic with her boyfriend that illustrates how our individual fight-flight response can get entangled, not only with deer in our headlights, but with those we love, who sometimes trigger us the most. Fondly, even in moments of great difficulty, Julie and Mark use nicknames— "Octopus" and "Turtle"— to quickly call a time-out whenever a breakdown occurs in their relationship. No matter how small or huge the flare-up, when the conflict heats up and boils over in anger, Julie, like an attacking octopus, becomes a fighter, moving in toward Mark, engulfing him with questions and diatribes, almost suffocating him with her voice-raising anxiety. Mark—aka Turtle—under the same circumstances, moves under cover and retreats, becoming silent, sullen, and insufferably obstinate. No progress gets made toward resolution, reconciliation, or reconnection until one of them breaks the stalemate.

What does help, however, is raising, in both cases, their awareness of how each is having his own individual fear response to the emergency moment: the dread of conflict and fear of being torn apart. One fights, the other flees, but they are both responding to the situation like frightened animals. This awareness, of course, does not prevent the inevitable breakdowns from occurring. But the length of time that they stay encased in their conditioned roles has shortened dramatically as they have learned to have more awareness, compassion, and even a bit of humor regarding their unique zoological follies.

So, as you can see in the dynamic between Julie and Mark, anger is very often a projection—an outward extension—of fear. Shutting down and becoming frozen can also show up as a response to fear. For many of us, recognizing that feeling numb (avoider) or feeling rage (aggressor) is actually an emotional symptom that overlays fear is something we find startling. Yet fear is most often the underlying experience in most negative and unpleasant situations. To transform dread of change into delight in change you need to recognize what your core beliefs are in regards to fear; it is also useful to raise your awareness of how you deal with so-called emergency moments. There is no pass or fail way to answer this because *there is no right or wrong way to handle crisis.*

We all succeed and fail according to the circumstances—context, participants, relationships—and, probably most important, how much time is available and what tools we have at our disposal. But knowing how you instinctually respond in times of crisis helps raise your fear awareness, and that awareness, as we will learn in depth in part two of this book, is the key to shifting gears—in the best of times, and even more important, in the worst of times.

THE GIFT OF BELONGING

In an age of HMOs and shrinking health care options, it never fails to amaze me to hear that one more insurance company has joined up with a university or medical school to "try to prove once and for all" the efficacy of psychotherapy. Of course, very often their hidden—or blatant—agenda is to prove that therapy either does not work or that patients only need a few focused sessions to get back to work on the treadmill of productivity. Yet, instinctively, we all know the benefit of the "talking cure."

Innumerable studies have shown that social support is crucial to enhanced survival rates in people with severe illnesses. One study showed that women with breast cancer who attended group therapy lived twice as long as their more isolated counterparts. Another showed that leukemia patients with strong supports of family, friends, and therapy had much longer survival rates than those without them. We all know how much value we get from sharing our deepest fears, in a context of safety, with a dear friend or a loving, supportive companion.

We all need to share our stories of childhood fears: How else will the grip they have on us be released? The pharmaceutical industry would dearly love us to believe that taking just the right pill at just the right time will dissolve our fear, calm our anxieties, and shift us out of our depression. Studies continuously validate that the right drug can be helpful, although in reality the placebo effect seems to be involved at a much higher rate than most drug companies would like to admit (as much as 50 percent of the success rate for some antidepressants). But the truth is far more obvious and hardly needs to be proven: We need one another.

The sad truth is that we live in an isolating age. Our family and community structures, once the backbone of society, are increasingly fragmented and broken. We live in "apart"-ments, often alone or with an increasingly smaller and smaller number of close companions. Our day-to-day lives are filled to the max with work and our interaction with coworkers is often truncated, text-driven, and intermediated by computers, BlackBerries, and iPhones. No one I know of has ever felt moved, touched, or healed by a PowerPoint presentation.

We do a great deal of communicating, but very little actual sharing of our deeply held stories of fear, pain, and insecurity. In fact, the very thing that we seek out a coach or a therapist to provide—a place where we can relax, let down our hair, be seen and heard—is considered taboo in the workplace. We are prompted to be strong and fearless in our work lives, such that the "entrepreneurial spirit" has become a billboard along the highway prodding us to be competitive, driven, focused, and assertive. We strive to win. Perhaps we do succeed, yet at what price? We may garner material wealth and the trappings of success, yet far too often we end up feeling lost, alienated, and disconnected.

What's missing from the picture of modern productivity and material success is the very thing we most crave: a safety zone, a place where we can reach out, ask for, and give support—a place of belonging. I'm struck over and over again, in my leadership coaching work with corporate clients, at how the quantity of our time together is rarely a crucial element in whether the engagement is successful. What matters is the quality of the interaction, the depth of the conversation, and most important, the level of safety the client comes to feel, no matter how short or truncated the interaction. The gift of therapy, of coaching, of support groups, of church suppers and bridge clubs doesn't really need to be proven, for we all know intuitively the power of belonging. Safety heals.

We all want and need to feel supported, to not feel judged, criticized, or evaluated. But the experience of feeling safe is not time dependent; it is not a quantifiable thing that can be released into the body with a pill. Safety emerges in the dynamic container of empathy, listening, and mirroring that can occur spontaneously and even instantaneously when two or more people are actively, consciously being present with each other. It can be activated in a split second and deeply felt in just minutes, because it is, at bottom, fueled by the always available energy of compassion, and love. The human being is a natural force for healing; we long for connection and community because we know, or our souls know unconsciously, that inside a safe container of belonging we can release our stories of fear.

YOUR INNER COMMUNITY

I can't begin to recall how many times I've bought self-help books that promise to help shift me out of my blocks and wounds and all manner of tribulations, and as much as I read them and enjoy them, I have one bad habit: I rarely do the exercises at the end of the chapters. I read them, reflect deeply, and organize them neatly on my mental to-do list. I might even try out an exercise that seems particularly appealing on a client or in a workshop. Yet, rarely do I actually engage with the material myself beyond reflecting, meditating, and note-taking. This avoidance of action doesn't stop me from learning a great deal and garnering innumerable benefits from the wise teachers and authors who have found their way to me. But it does point toward a place where I sometimes falter, and my resolve breaks down: getting engaged on my own.

I imagine that I am not alone with this failing. If you're a self-help book reader like me and you are coming up to the end of this "primer" section, you're now about to reach the "point of no return" with this book. It is a natural paradox: Book lovers are less likely to be action-oriented. We are cerebral, reflective, and contemplative by nature—or at least according to our story.

Life-Shifting Action Step:
Finding Your Flight Crew

This practice is designed to help you clarify how supported you feel by others in your close social sphere. Find a quiet moment to reflect and with a notepad or journal, complete the following sentences:

1. When I feel fearful, I go to _____ to feel safe.

2. When I share my fear with _____, I feel _____.

3. When I feel _____, the fear dissipates or dissolves.

The key to this exercise is to pay attention to the energetic and emotional response you have to the experience of being vulnerable with others. If you share your fear and come away feeling *more* fearful or drained of energy, then this is *not* the right person for you to share with. The goal is for you to identify one or two people with whom you feel completely safe, able to share your story and be supported by the healing, comforting energy of feeling heard.

Yet, if you are like me, and about to move into the Life-Shifting Program section of this book, it is time to pony up to the bar, pay the tab, and leave that story with the bartender.

Those of you who are thinking types may be drawn to self-help books because they feel safe. Curled up on the sofa with a self-help book, or a good novel, you can cast off the armor of any of the myriad identities that you need—or think you need—to wear during your regular life: wife, mother, executive, parent, athlete, and so on. In a certain sense, your relationship with a good book is a safety zone, a place of comfort, nurturing, and connectedness with another—the author—where you allow your ego to become a bit more permeable, open and receptive to new ideas, new possibilities, even new neural pathways; it is, as I described above, a place of belonging.

Yet, it is also a place where you may find yourself hiding out, avoiding deep emotional or physical engagement with the world, or within yourself. The truth is that the healing powers of a book are limited, and to a certain extent paradoxical: You need to get up off your chair, get out in the world, and find support, safety, and connection with others if you are to truly shift out of fear and move through change. Books can help. Road maps like this one can surely foster a sense of direction, and provide a foundation from which to spring into action. But just as reading a guide book on India—or even perusing an interactive travel Web site—is not going to look, feel, smell like India, or shift you into the experience of the Far East; a book can take you only so far. You must take that next step, buy the ticket, and board the plane.

But you don't have to go it alone. There is another place of safety and belonging available at all times and in all places: an in-between zone where a whole community of guides, coaches, and therapists are ready to join you for the ride, but you have to look for them in a place many of us avoid, deny, or think is crazy: *inside*. It is an unfortunate writing of the narrative that would have Jung's most startling discoveries regarding the unconscious and the process of individuation—theories that in popular translation have become the core principles of countless New Age philosophies—as having been born of his "psychotic breakdown" at midlife. Surely he did come apart or dissociate from his workaday personality as a psychiatrist when he began tuning into the inner voices and images that appeared in his dreams. But was this insanity? If so, may we all become insane at some point: Might it be where the genius lies waiting?

Mary Watkins, a professor of depth psychology at Pacifica Graduate Institute in Santa Barbara, California, writes and teaches about what she calls the "imaginal dialogues" that we all conduct with our "inner community." She uses the word "imaginal" as coined by Lionel Corbett from his book *The Religious Function of the Psyche* for a specific purpose: to shift the cultural narrative that we hold with regard to what is "real" and what is "imaginary"— to open up a space in between the two cultural norms that allows for an inner realm of images, voices, and characters to come alive.

We all consider it *normal* for a small child to have imaginary playmates or for adolescents to write to themselves in a diary. These are considered developmental activities in which the structure and capacities of the burgeoning ego-identity become stronger by engaging in practices that bolster one's sense of self. Yet, once the ego is fully formed, or as some might say, hardened, into a story called "adult," we are supposed to ignore or dismiss the inner voices, the dream images, and self-talk as dangerous, even neurotic.

The sad irony regarding this loss, of what was a rich and inviting inner world when we were children, is that these same voices in our head, the images in our dreams, and the intuitive "hits" that flood our emotional and mental systems at certain pivotal moments in our lives are always available to support us; we just fail to listen. When we do listen in, or tune into the frequency of our inner, subjective voice, what we most often hear is the *rat-tat-tat* voice of self-criticism, self-recrimination, and judgment. These are the troublesome "inner parents," with whom we are all too familiar. They tend to be the loudest voices we hear, often drowning out the rest of the inner family: supportive sisters and energy-boosting brothers, who like real, loving siblings are available to give us a leg up, to open our eyes and ears to what's possible—even when we are feeling fearful or down.

It may feel like a stretch of the imagination for you to think of yourself as having an "internal community," but before you pooh-pooh the idea as unreal or decide that I am talking about figments of your imagination, stop and think about it for a moment. Do you ever wonder why the images and stories and felt experiences you have in dreams, whether of the daytime or nighttime variety, have such a powerful pull on us? Did you ever find yourself lost in thought—caught up in a story of your own making—even when in the presence of a group of other people, some of whom may be speaking directly to you? Do you ever go to a movie or read a novel and find yourself not only totally absorbed but directly impacted emotionally and physically (by the appearance of tears or laughter, for example) by the "fake" situation? Did you ever wake up in the morning feeling fearful or anxious, with a strong voice of negativity pounding in your head, and then find yourself singing in the shower, all at once thinking differently about the day—seeing sunshine, blue skies, and positive things happening?

If you recognized yourself in any of these scenarios, then you have had the direct experience of hearing from, and listening to, internal characters, who speak with real voices, evoke real pictures, and impact you emotionally, physically, and, of course, mentally. These characters are, in truth, very much like a cacophonous and chaotic family—with sometimes loving, sometimes harsh parents, sometimes supportive and sometimes combative siblings. In a strict, adult frame of reference, this community of characters is imaginary—not "real"—but they are so powerful and impactful on our emotional systems that they deserve not to be dismissed but to be honored. This is why Watkins and others, who study the psychological effects of internally generated images and symbols, label them as "imaginal." They are located, perhaps, at a distance from the hard, dusty road of "fact," but still are quite vivid, evocative, and visible on the horizon of our psyche.

Let's look at an example of where our inner guides may arrive to rescue us from the devastating impact of our worst fears, just when we need them most. My client Adam recently retired after a thirty-year career teaching learning-disabled children ages six through twelve. Despite his long, stable career and stellar reputation as a teacher, he came to me carrying a story of isolation, social phobia, and negativity that has made his shift to retirement difficult and lonely. Adam tends to speak of himself in broad, judgmental strokes, using harsh indictments: "I have no friends" and "don't know how to talk to people," "I live under a cloud of bad karma."

Clearly his troupe of inner voices is less than supportive and his story of self appears filled with an overarching narrative of self-doubt and self-criticism. Yet, when I ask him to describe his strengths and positive characteristics, he goes on to note that he "stays in shape and regularly runs marathons," and that some of his colleagues at his former work "reach out and invite me to social things, but I usually say no and stay home. That's my way."

I don't want to minimize the story of fear that undermines Adam's shift into retirement. His sense of self-worth as a teacher, honed over many decades, has clearly been ruptured—as the identity marker of "teacher" now fully realized has ended its useful life and needs to be shed. In the wake of this shift to a new stage, a new cycle of self-renewal, the harsh voice of self-criticism that reverberates in his head is a symptom of fear—a symbolic holding tight to a fictional story of failure and self-defeat that his ego uses to keep him stuck.

So what gives? How does someone who is so "bad" get up in the morning, regularly run five, ten, even fifteen miles, and ultimately enter and complete a marathon? When I asked him to recount his most satisfying experience in recent years, he regaled me with a story of going to Paris, running a marathon, and having his sister waiting at the finish line to congratulate him. What a loser!

So what prompted him to become a runner? Well, to hear Adam tell the story, he recoiled at the death of his mother from lung cancer, jolted by the view in the mirror, as he put it, of him lying in a coffin like her—as a result of his habit of smoking three packs a day. It was a fearful voice that spoke to him—he even went on to say that "perhaps it was my mom, speaking from the grave"—but nevertheless it moved him, prodded him, and broke him out of the pattern of self-destructive habits and onto the running track. Fear-driven perhaps, but loving as well, this voice inside helped to shift his grief at losing his mother toward motivation to live, to be healthy, and to move forward. He listened to this voice—one that emanated ultimately from that same inner circle that was now prompting him to cower in retreat.

Surely, Adam has a deeply held narrative of separation, self-criticism, and fear of others, and his shift process from the rupture stage into release and retreat—in preparation for a new beginning—will not be easy. Yet, one of the keys to the castle of change lies right inside of him: the voice of the athlete that gets him out of bed at 6:00 a.m. for a run needs to be reawakened and heard. He needs to feel safe again with the members of his inner community who are currently holding him hostage—not allowing the voice of support and the energy of possibility to enter his conscious sense of self. It will be my job to help him reconnect to this voice; it is in there. In fact, there is a whole family of supportive, loving characters who are always available to help us shift from dread to delight. We only have to listen.

REVERENCE

Think for a minute: How did your parents handle your childhood fears? Were you admonished for being "silly," forced or shamed into swallowing your anxiety and putting on a "stiff upper lip"? Unfortunately, far too often, parents and older siblings denigrate the child-like terrors that traumatize little hearts and minds. When I was very small, the hum of the furnace in our family basement would terrify me—as my four- or five-year-old imagination would conjure up tigers and bears and monsters growling at me from somewhere beneath my bed. My mother took my tiny terrors in stride, even going so far as to take my hand one night and walk down to the basement with me, arm in arm, to vanquish the monsters lurking beneath the stairs.

Why are simple parenting techniques so crucial for a healthy development of self? Because, unfortunately, if as young children our fears are trounced upon as "childish" or we are shamed into thinking there is something wrong with us for feeling fearful, the resulting sense of inadequacy lingers for years. As tiny tots, in infancy and early childhood, we are extremely vulnerable creatures, with little of the adult armor of identity that will ultimately protect us from the painful realities of a harsh and sometimes unloving world.

If we are traumatized at a young age, and our fear is denigrated or dismissed, the wound remains. In this context, I don't think it is simply a coincidence that the single most common symptom I see in my clients—and my friends at times—is a lack of self-compassion. Far too often, somewhere along the rocky road to adulthood, we picked up an extra bag marked "should," as I described earlier in chapter four. It shows up in the voice that calls out to you, even now as an adult, saying, "You shouldn't be afraid. You shouldn't feel anxious. Your fear is childish. Your fear is holding you back. You are *bad* for being afraid."

Even the healthiest among us recognize this voice. This searing, strident inner scream that can shake us from a slumber in the form of a bad dream or nightmare, and can reverberate through our inner community, no matter how loving, is the infamous VOJ (voice of judgment). This is why I approach all my clients, my friends, my family, and myself—when I can remember to do so—with a different voice: the VOR (the voice of reverence).

What is reverence? We usually reserve the word "reverence" to evoke feelings of esteem and veneration for a great and powerful political or religious leader, such as the pope or president. For our purposes, I want to shift the focus only slightly, away from lofty external power figures, and back on to the only center of power that really matters when the topic is fear: you. No matter how old you are, it is never too late to learn the skills of compassionate parenting of self and it is never too late to quell the VOJ and turn up the volume on the VOR.

If you hope to get real benefit from learning how to transform your fears and shift through major changes when they occur, you must start with having reverence for yourself as you move through the highs and lows of endless self-renewal. There are three components to reverence, in this context:

1. Self-acceptance: the ability to look in the mirror each day and see yourself as both imperfect and perfect.

2. Self-compassion: the ability to express love and caring and be supportive of yourself even when you fail, make mistakes, or appear to be lost along the path of happiness.

3. Self-acknowledgment: the ability to celebrate your achievements and make time for experiencing the joys and pleasures of your own gifts through rituals, affirmations, and sharing yourself with others.

The VOR can appear in any of the above guises. It is the king of your inner community and though it sometimes can be overwhelmed by the cacophony of various internal family members who would rather shout at you through the megaphone of the VOJ, the energy of reverence is always available to you.

So as we bring this primer to the life-shifting process to a close and shift gears and head into action with the transformational tools for working through fear, I want to remind you to be gentle with yourself. Listen in to your inner community of voices as you approach each tool in the pages ahead. Watch and witness, as a gentle observer, how you respond to the practices I suggest for each step along the route to reinventing your identity.

Do you hear the VOJ calling for you to cease and desist as you get out of your chair and head to the meditation cushion? Remember, you have an infinite amount of life energy available to you at any given moment, but the flow can be all too easily stanched by the shutting down that occurs when we get caught up in the VOJ—a story of shame and self-criticism that leaves you feeling bereft and alone. Whereas a shift in the story, to a place of compassion and self-acceptance by bringing out the VOR, will bring your head, heart, and body into the present beauty and bounty of your loving, soulful connection to an ever-evolving sense of self.

The VOR is about listening for a deeper voice, one that resonates from the center of your being, a voice that calls to you, sometimes from far away when the energy of fear is afoot, but that you can still hear, even if only in a whisper, saying, "I love you. You are a good person. You are going to be OK." With the VOR singing in your ears, you will always have the ability to shift, to transform . . . to break out of the box that binds you: to live.

PART II:
LIFE-SHIFTING 102

The Program: Six Transformational Tools for Releasing Fear

INTRODUCTION

"Fear is the shadow of our own separate self trying to find a secure place in its world of false imaginings. Costumed in separateness, fear is our shadow."

—ROB RABBIN

My friends love to hear my bear story. And I love to tell it. No matter how many times I retell the story, the same thing happens: People perk up and move in closer, those on the periphery turn toward me and tilt their heads to hear, everyone's eyes get wide and focused, and the energy—like a pleasant sense of anxiety—becomes palpable. Here's the story: About two years ago, late in the evening on a cool but pleasant March night in upstate New York, I took my first foray out onto my deck for what is a favorite spring and summer ritual: a nightcap under the stars. Sitting quietly, gazing at the burgeoning beauty of the rising moon and twinkling stars, I suddenly realized that I was not alone (and I was alone at the house at the time). A black shadow—like right out of a Grimm's fairy tale—flashed on my right at the bottom of the deck stairs, about ten feet away. At first I thought nothing of it, assuming that my neighbor's dog was out wandering the neighborhood and making a typical visit. Moments later, however, when the black shadow appeared again, and a gleaming golden Labrador retriever coat failed to shimmer in the moonlight, I found myself peering closer, stiffening in fear, my adrenaline rising.

Turns out, there was no dog; instead there was a full-grown, very hungry (I know this because the next day I discovered a fifty-pound bag of bird seed completely emptied out!) black bear. In the split second that I realized this was not a benign four-legged visitor from across the lane, I panicked—at least on the inside. I felt a rush of anxiety unlike anything I'd felt except when sitting through the film *Halloween* (or maybe the one with Glenn Close and the rabbit).

My black visitor proceeded to saunter up the stairs and head directly toward where I sat frozen in my chair. He (or she) came right up and plopped himself down inches away from me, and, no exaggeration, stuck his long snout right into my lap, all the while rolling his head back and forth the way bears do (I recognized the head gesture—having watched *National Geographic* specials as a kid). But this was not on television: I was alone sitting nose to crotch with a wild black bear! Later I learned that bears hate loud noises and that I should have just shouted or stomped my feet and my not-so-little friend would have quickly dispersed. But, unaware of how to politely remove a live bear from my deck, I simply sat there, stark still, trying not to breathe.

Eventually, surely not more than a few minutes later (it felt like an hour), he stood up, took one last snout wave in my direction, and sauntered on down to the far side of the deck and down the other flight of stairs. At that point, as if coming out of a trance, I jolted back to my senses and made a mad dash into the house. I was shaking, literally, with fear—but strangely I also felt wide awake, agitated with excitement, maybe even joyful. I was acutely aware, in that moment, of how close together the experiences can be—of dread, and delight.

Have you ever noticed that our friends love to hear about our "fear stories"—our run-ins with hurricanes, lightning strikes, airplane turbulence, wild animals, and the like? We all love to share and hear about our close calls with life. Likewise, from the safety of a dark, warm, and cozy theater, surrounded by close friends, we enjoy watching movies that are chock-full of fear-driven drama, murder, monsters, and mayhem. Rarely do we ever stop to ask ourselves: Why are we drawn to watch, tell, and hear stories of fear?

The true answer may be unreachable, hidden in the depths of our collective unconscious—reflecting a time long ago when life for humans was anything but safe, when lions, tigers, and bears roamed, literally, in our backyards, and danger lurked around every corner. I think that as we've lost touch with the plethora of real dangers that plagued us in earlier times, some part of our psychological makeup remembers the potency, power, and motivation to create, learn, and shift that these fears generated in us. We actually love fear.

Yet, since our day-to-day lives are relatively calm by historical standards (at least in some parts of the world), we are drawn to stories that stir us up, awaken the physical (adrenaline rush), emotional (stress and anxiety), and mental (fantasies) energies that actually empower and motivate us *to change*. Think about it: We all know that speeding along the highway at ninety miles an hour is dangerous, at least twice as risky as driving at fifty. We also know that most of the time, with all the traffic that flows into our path on any major city artery, in the United States at least, that our short spurts of high-speed travel are unlikely to impact our arrival time in any measurable way. Yet, we still get caught for speeding. The truth is we love the feeling of high-speed movement; we love the energy of risk-taking, surviving the roller coaster, getting that speedometer to break the hundred mark.

Fear, as we discussed in the last chapter of part one, is a normal, present part of our life experience. Sadly, as a species we've lost touch with the power of fear to help us shift and grow as human beings; we've developed a bifurcated relationship with fear such that any positive attunement we have toward it has been relegated to the province of entertainment; something we witness from a distance on the six-o'clock news. The real experience of fear, as it shows up regularly in our lives, is considered bad—something to be denied, ignored, and pushed away at all cost. Yet, this form of dissociation or splitting off from the actual experience of fear represents a great loss, for it is ultimately our fears—awakened, acknowledged, embraced—that spur us to shift actively through the stages of change.

When the Buddhists share a cosmic tale that divides the world into two competing stories, one of love, the other of fear, they do not mean for us to rid ourselves of the latter and solely embrace the former. This "get rid of fear" approach to human nature is a Western conceit that is, in fact, born of fear itself. The Eastern wisdom around the nature of fear is to recognize the inherent duality—of fear and love, suffering and joy, happiness and pain— that comprises human life.

My Buddhist teacher Goenka does not suggest to us, during our meditation retreats, that we should seek to banish or push through our fear, for this approach to life just reinforces the power of the dictatorial stance of the ego. Rather, we are encouraged to step back from our need to control our experience, to simply and compassionately witness our own discomfort, to observe without judgment the swirling thoughts and worries that confound the mind. The goal is to recognize how the story of fear is just that, a story, and that if we welcome it as just one more aspect of life, we quickly pass through it to the other side where an equally powerful story—of love, compassion, and joy—awaits. We need both.

The nature of fear is a story just like the self that gets created moment by moment in the inner and outer dialogues that occur between the story I call "me" and the world. That is why we left off the primer in part one talking about reverence, for our goal in working through the cycle of dread is not to judge or criticize our fears but to embrace and accept them as part of the story of self. Our goal is not to control them or push them away but to dialogue with them and listen in for their meaning.

All the tools in this section's toolbox work to transform fear by recognizing first and foremost that fear—and its attendant symptoms—*is perfectly normal*. The paradox of fear is that when we seek to dictate how our experience of fear should unfold—and hold tight to a fantasy that we should not have fear and that we should be happy instead, we actually reinforce the negative energy that holds us stuck. On the other hand, if we acknowledge the existence of fear as a normal response to the dynamic force of change that is always afoot— even if it isn't directly visible through the windowless box of our comfortable lifestyle—the fear loosens its grip on us; our egos become more permeable, receptive, and willing to go with the flow of life. Fear is not the enemy; it is a signpost, a guide that once recognized can actually steer us through the vicissitudes of any major change cycle, keeping us from getting stuck.

The six chapters that follow outline in detail the transformational tools for moving through fear. They are designed to be utilized in a sequence, starting with recognition and moving through response-ability, refocusing, reframing, realignment, and finally reconciliation. As you read the text and the accompanying practices, you will notice that there are places where the ideas naturally connect and even overlap. The tools tend to work well in pairs: recognition/ response-ability, refocusing/reframing, and realignment/reconciliation.

In some sense, each pair represents two sides of a coin, bringing together the dual energy centers of attention and intention—in an ongoing dance to support your move through your fears and shift from one stage of change to another. In part three, we will delve more deeply into the six stages of change and see how the tools can be applied to transform specific fears that show up at each juncture in a full cycle of self-renewal. For this next section, however, the idea is for you to become more comfortable with seeing, experiencing, and working with fear, no matter what stage of change you are in.

As you read through the series of tools, you will also notice that I have designed the practices to take advantage of each of our energy centers: mental, emotional, or physical. Although energy always flows through the human system in all three domains, each of us has a natural and conditioned tendency—an affinity—to approach the world emphasizing one or two of them and ignoring or dismissing the others. As I have noted before, there is a reason why self-help books tend to emphasize specific healing modalities such as positive affirmations (mental domain), intuitive or feeling-oriented activities (emotional domain), or practices like yoga, aerobics, and the like (physical domain). All of these can be useful for transforming fear and helping you shift your energy as you move through change, but most of us have a strong pull toward one and tend to ignore or dismiss the others.

The chart on page 113 provides you with a simple way to determine your natural tendency to being a thinker, feeler, or doer in life. You may already have a fairly strong sense of how you approach your fears, but it can be enlightening to assess just how comfortable you are in each of the three domains. Armed with a higher level of awareness regarding your natural tendency, you can consciously choose practices that may bring you to a new growth edge, pushing you through the self-imposed box of your identity. As I discussed in chapter two, the goal of life-shifting is ultimately to "learn to dance" with change—and fear—and to do this successfully, we need to develop flexibility and strength in all three domains.

One additional note for those of you who may be familiar with Carl Jung's notion of types or have been exposed to personality assessment tools like the Myers-Briggs instrument, which originally was based on Jung's work. Jung believed there were four fundamental energy domains that comprise the human psyche and show up as personality traits: thinking, feeling, sensing, and intuition. Since Jung himself had a strong affinity for his intuitive as well as his rational side, and for him the number four represented wholeness, he crafted his approach to personality with these four distinct sections. I'm a big fan of the Myers-Briggs personality instrument and others that have been developed along these lines, but I also have found, working with hundreds of clients over the years, that intuition can be a challenging element to pin down.

I've witnessed people gain access to their intuitive side through deeply felt heart-based affect (emotional), through strong gut reactions (physical sensations in the core), and mind-blowing visions and fantasies (mental). My personal perspective on the intuitive tends to reflect the way Jung often spoke about the mysterious echoes through the psychic system—emotional, physical (sensate), and mental—that signal the emergence of the soul over the ego. Hence, I am not leaving off the intuitive side of our energy system, just folding it into the other three domains, for I believe that the soul speaks to us in a wide variety of voices, symbols, and somatic stirrings—all of which can be "intuited" just by tuning in, listening deeply, and being open to the call.

As you read through the series of tools described in this part of the book, and jump into the practices and exercises, I encourage you to watch yourself closely—to use the reading about the tools to explore your own particular relationship with fear, and to raise your awareness of how fear is just another story woven into the tapestry of self. Ask yourself these questions as you read through this section: Which of the six tools are you drawn to? Which ideas excite you? Which of the action steps do you feel an affinity for, and find yourself willing to set aside the book and practice? Do you notice an urge to stick with one domain of practice? If you are a "thinker" type in your natural orientation, what happens when you contemplate getting into action or working more directly with your intuitive/feeling sense of self? What do you find confusing or difficult to understand? Do some of the exercises—perhaps a meditation or visualization or movement—strike you as unrealistic or silly? What would you *never do?* Is this your fear speaking? If so, welcome it. Jump in and play.

PART II:
LIFE-SHIFTING SELF-RENEWAL
DIAGNOSTIC #1

INSTRUCTIONS FOR TAKING
THE DIAGNOSTIC EXAM

Go through the items below on all three lists one by one. Reflect on how you normally think, feel, and operate in the world. Mark "T" for the items on each list that resonate for you. Mark "F" for the items that do not typically apply to you. There is no right or wrong way to score this diagnostic. When you have completed the list and marked every item, add up the total number of "T" or true answers for you and determine the percentage that apply to you by dividing the total number by the total for each list (30).

Cerebral type: Thinker

1. Enjoys analyzing and dissecting subjects ❏ T ❏ F
2. Enjoys rhetorical conversation ❏ T ❏ F
3. Thinks in hypotheses, frameworks, and models ❏ T ❏ F
4. Decides using logic and analysis ❏ T ❏ F
5. Tends to respect the rational argument ❏ T ❏ F
6. Expresses feelings as thoughts ❏ T ❏ F
7. Likes facts and data ❏ T ❏ F
8. Enjoys studying and research ❏ T ❏ F
9. Enjoys reading non-fiction ❏ T ❏ F
10. Respects intellectual rigor and debate ❏ T ❏ F
11. Expresses compassion with logic ❏ T ❏ F
12. Head-centered in approach to life ❏ T ❏ F
13. Experiences concrete visions and fantasies ❏ T ❏ F
14. Enjoys brainstorming ❏ T ❏ F
15. Enjoys solving problems ❏ T ❏ F
16. Likes to dissect ideas ❏ T ❏ F
17. Always wants to have more information ❏ T ❏ F
18. Tends to enjoy technology, computers, gadgets ❏ T ❏ F
19. Writes in an organized, thoughtful fashion ❏ T ❏ F

20. Enjoys political discourse   ❏ T ❏ F
21. Tends to ruminate, philosophize   ❏ T ❏ F
22. May procrastinate by getting caught up in planning   ❏ T ❏ F
23. Fear expresses in depression, boredom   ❏ T ❏ F
24. Thinks before acting   ❏ T ❏ F
25. Motto: Let me think about it   ❏ T ❏ F
26. Can be overwhelmed with data   ❏ T ❏ F
27. Fear mode: frozen then fight/flight   ❏ T ❏ F
28. Tends to day dream rather than night dream   ❏ T ❏ F
29. Insights and intuitions come in words, thoughts, ideas   ❏ T ❏ F
30. Meditation challenge: quieting the mind   ❏ T ❏ F

Total Number of "T" or True Answers _____
Percentage of True Answers x/30=_____

Empathic type: Feeler

1. Expresses feelings directly   ❏ T ❏ F
2. Decides with the heart   ❏ T ❏ F
3. Drawn to images more than words   ❏ T ❏ F
4. Appreciates subjective reality more than scientific fact   ❏ T ❏ F
5. Expresses feelings with compassion/empathy   ❏ T ❏ F
6. Values relationships more than ideas   ❏ T ❏ F
7. Wants to feel passionate and engaged with people not things   ❏ T ❏ F
8. Can be mercurial, melodramatic   ❏ T ❏ F
9. Debates with passion rather than logic   ❏ T ❏ F
10. Focuses on the pain of others   ❏ T ❏ F
11. May have bouts with guilt or self-doubt   ❏ T ❏ F
12. May have difficulties maintaining personal boundaries   ❏ T ❏ F
13. Tends to have vivid, colorful night dreams   ❏ T ❏ F
14. Enjoys reading fiction and/or poetry   ❏ T ❏ F
15. Loves music over silence   ❏ T ❏ F
16. Can be overwhelmed by emotions   ❏ T ❏ F
17. Procrastination tends to become drama   ❏ T ❏ F

18. Tends to love the arts over sports ❏ T ❏ F
19. Writes in metaphor; uses analogies ❏ T ❏ F
20. Loves stories and narrative ❏ T ❏ F
21. Can be dismissive of logic ❏ T ❏ F
22. Heart-centered in approach to life ❏ T ❏ F
23. Fear expresses in anger/sadness ❏ T ❏ F
24. Can feel overwhelmed at times ❏ T ❏ F
25. Loves just being in nature ❏ T ❏ F
26. Fear mode: flight not fight ❏ T ❏ F
27. Needs a great deal of rest/sleep ❏ T ❏ F
28. Insights show up in pictures/images ❏ T ❏ F
29. Can appear indecisive or wishy-washy ❏ T ❏ F
30. Meditation challenge: can be swept away
    by emotions ❏ T ❏ F

Total Number of "T" or True Answers _____
Percentage of True Answers x/30=_____

Somatic type: Doer

1. Prefers practicing over theorizing ❏ T ❏ F
2. Enjoys conversation while moving ❏ T ❏ F
3. May avoid reading or writing ❏ T ❏ F
4. Results-oriented, may be impatient with
    procrastinators ❏ T ❏ F
5. Practical and pragmatic ❏ T ❏ F
6. Needs to have concrete goals ❏ T ❏ F
7. Appreciates multi-tasking ❏ T ❏ F
8. Prefers physical exercise over contemplation ❏ T ❏ F
9. Likes to build things or take things apart ❏ T ❏ F
10. Can become overwhelmed with activity ❏ T ❏ F
11. Enjoys physical activities, athletics, and sports ❏ T ❏ F
12. Tends to be group oriented, avoiding solitude ❏ T ❏ F
13. Enjoys nature for hiking, movement, exploration ❏ T ❏ F
14. Respects physical prowess, strength ❏ T ❏ F
15. Communicates in short bursts ❏ T ❏ F
16. Tends to focus on logistics, action items ❏ T ❏ F
17. Prefers making music more than listening ❏ T ❏ F
18. Loves to watch sports, contests ❏ T ❏ F

19. Loves active creative hobbies: cooking,
    pottery, knitting   ❑ T ❑ F
20. Loves competition   ❑ T ❑ F
21. Fear mode: fight not flight   ❑ T ❑ F
22. Tends to ignore or dismiss physical ailments   ❑ T ❑ F
23. Prefers to work with hands   ❑ T ❑ F
24. Can be reactive, aggressive   ❑ T ❑ F
25. Tends to be in constant motion   ❑ T ❑ F
26. Fear expresses through over-functioning, anxiety   ❑ T ❑ F
27. Tends to be dismissive of depression   ❑ T ❑ F
28. May not sleep enough   ❑ T ❑ F
29. Intuits through the core: respects gut reaction   ❑ T ❑ F
30. Meditation challenge: difficulty sitting still   ❑ T ❑ F

Total Number of "T" or True Answers _____

Percentage of True Answers x/30=_____

FINAL THOUGHTS ON THE DIAGNOSTIC

You will likely score higher in one domain than the others on this exam. The higher the percentage on one list, the more likely that this is your natural mode, or way of being in the world. If you scored fairly evenly on all three lists, you may have a balanced approach to life that includes mental, emotional, and physical responses to the world depending upon the context.

Be honest with yourself and watch how you respond to the life-shifting action steps in the following chapters of part two. You may find yourself dismissive or avoidant of some suggested practices or drawn to a series that follows along thinker, feeler, or doer lines. This is OK and normal. You may want to come back to this diagnostic and repeat the exercise after you have read part three and explored how you operate in the throes of different stages of change, transition, and fear.

Chapter One

THE TOOL OF RECOGNITION: KNOW THY ENEMY

"Fear is a question: What are you afraid of, and why? Just as the seed of health is in illness, because illness contains information, your fears are a treasure house of self-knowledge if you choose to explore them."
—MARILYN FERGUSON

Unless you are truly in a dangerous situation—where you are threatened with physical harm—fear will most likely emerge disguised, as I explained in chapter three of the primer, as symptoms. Irrational and out-of-control thoughts, unexplainable (at least initially) emotions, such as anxiety, anger, or depression, and unpleasant body sensations (sweaty palms, heart palpitations, nausea, or body aches) may show up on your doorstep as a very unwelcome coterie of strangers. Recognition, by way of an enlivening conversation with the internal emergency call systems, whose flashing lights and whirring alarms are screaming "call-to-arms," is your tool for *tuning in.* Using recognition, we stop, shift our perspective to one of witness, and ask ourselves these questions: What am I really afraid of here? What is triggering these feelings, thoughts, and sensations of fear?

When you can name your fear—giving it a concrete label and identity—even if it turns out to be inaccurate or only partially accurate—you will go a long way toward dissolving its power over you. Armed with greater self-awareness about what is *really* happening—some part of you is feeling afraid—you may be able to regain control, slow down the momentum of the experience, and diminish your feelings of confusion or overwhelm. Once you are able to shift your energy and attention to the present moment, observe without judgment your physical sensations and the flow of your feelings, and even converse with your own internal community, you become less driven by fear and more part of the dance.

TUNING IN TO THE VOICE OF FEAR

Sometimes it's hard to recognize our fears—or the messages they carry—in our normal waking state. Hence, Jung believed that dreams could be a powerful access route to the unconscious, a way to listen in to the deeper messages of soul—or what he called the archetypal or true self—that are kept at bay by the workaday, defended ego. I like to use his practice of Active Imagination in working with dreams, but also in shifting our stance with regard to our daily internal visitors when we are awake—our inner community. As I discussed in chapter six of the primer, our interior world, which more noticeably comes alive when we are asleep and our defenses are relaxed, is always running in the background of our lives. It is made up of a cacophony of voices—a community of internal characters—that we can either reject, criticize, and judge (and one of those voices conducts that exercise: the voice of judgment) or we can recognize, accept, and even learn from them.

Most of my clients come to me with a dark cloud hanging over their inner community: They view their inner world as a war zone, replete with competing voices, incessant, meaningless chatter, and endless turmoil. It is often a jarring moment—of recognition—to see that this "stance" against the internal world is just that: a judgmental perspective on the self. Not dissimilarly from the medical establishment's tendency to treat illness in the body as an "enemy," we too easily fall into a trap of despising our own inner community—forgetting that it is *ours;* it is inside us. It is part of us.

Helping a "Thinker" Access His Fear

My client Peter arrived at my office in the midst of the rehearsal stage of a major change cycle—he was starting his third year of medical school after a restful summer period in which he had worked as an intern at a medical clinic. Having survived, even thrived during the first two years of medical studies, he was surprised to find himself experiencing difficulty sleeping and extreme attacks of anxiety as he began the hands-on phase of his medical education—working directly with a team of surgeons, making early-morning rounds, attending the surgery procedures, even having to, as he put it, "sew up the patient" under the glaring, watchful eye of the attending physicians and nurses.

Peter, like many of us, is a "thinker-type" individual. Drawn from an early age to books about science, history, and literature, Peter loves to analyze situations and people, thinking about what makes things work. His interest and desire to explore the world intellectually makes him well-suited for the medical profession, as he loves to work through problems and look for the underlying causes of symptoms and illness. His training, however, reinforces this tendency to seek logical, rational conclusions, so that when it comes to his own inner turmoil, Peter quickly becomes frustrated when he cannot figure out what is wrong. When we first met, Peter was totally absorbed in the "should" game I wrote about in chapter four, believing that he *should* be confident and more relaxed in med school. After all, he had been a straight-A student up to this point, so why, he wanted to know, shouldn't he be able to slough off his anxiety and "get down to business"?

Of course, Peter, being a very thoughtful and self-aware young man, was not dismissive of his emotions, and on some level he understood that his anxiety and stress might have emotional roots. He tended to want to think his way through the feelings, though, and like many in the medical profession, sought to understand feelings by reducing them to biochemical processes in the brain. When it came to his own fears—and the emotional response they elicited in him—he became distraught and frustrated with his inability to "peel back the onion," as he would say, and "root out the chemical cause." He was seriously considering going on a regiment of antidepressants but felt like "a failure" for not being able to "surgically remove" his own anxiety.

I found it interesting that Peter was open to the idea that his anxieties and symptoms might be a conditioned response to earlier childhood experiences, but unable to pinpoint a specific trauma or breakdown during his upbringing (although he did speak of feeling a great deal of pressure from his parents to succeed), he would immediately focus on the possibility of his anxiety being genetic in nature. Where we found common ground, and an access route to the deeper emotional pain that ultimately was connected to fear was when we discussed how the limbic system in the brain, the seat of emotion, developed through a process of mirroring—through symbol and affect—the signals of safety, love, and belonging transmitted from mother to child. It was, in fact, when I asked him about his earliest memories of being with his mother as a young boy, that he brought up, seemingly out of the blue, what to him was a strange phenomenon: He had been having an intense, recurring dream—of himself as a young child.

Trained to dismiss dreams as the detritus of an overworked mind, Peter was initially dismissive of the dream. When I asked him to reflect on the dream, to bring the images and narrative as he remembered them into his current awareness, and most important, to think about how he *felt* during the dream sequence, his facial expression shifted.

From the typical, taut analytic scowl of self-recrimination that I was used to seeing, there was suddenly a softening, his cheeks reddened, his eyes watered, and his shoulders slumped in an unmistakable gesture of sadness. I asked Peter to take a deep breath and share the dream with me:

> *I am very young, maybe about four or five years old. I'm alone in a long hallway, seemingly lost. I walk and walk and walk down this endless corridor, unsure of where I am or where I'm going. I feel very frightened. Suddenly, I find myself in a large, dark, and cavernous room. There is a long rectangular table in the center of the room with a number of medieval-looking, high-backed chairs arranged along each side. Seated in the chairs are my parents, my brother, my teachers, and a number of strangers who appear to know me, but whom I don't recognize. There is an empty chair at the end of the table and as I walk into the room, someone, I don't remember who, motions for me to come and sit down. I sit. As I look around the table, a powerful feeling of dread rises in me. I notice that the people are all holding a stack of papers in their hands. They seem to be reading something on the paper and then turning to me as if looking for an explanation. A big man, perhaps my father but it is not clear—could be a teacher—hands me the papers he is holding and gives me a blank, judgmental look. I have done something wrong. I can feel it. I am terrified of these people. I want to run. But I don't. Instead I receive the papers from this dark, looming figure and look at them. They are all blank. That's the last image I have, as at that moment when I stare at the blank pages before me, I wake up.*

Peter is fortunate. Dreams can be powerful messengers that bring to consciousness an awareness of feelings—and fears—that we have either been avoiding or repressing, but most of the time they are not so easy to interpret. Peter's dream was very direct. When I suggested to him that he might be experiencing fear in the dream that was connected to his fear of being judged by the medical team he was working with, he was surprised but open to the possibility. It was, of course, perfectly normal for him to feel anxious—and fearful—as he was at the "apprentice stage" of his education and truly was being judged by the so-called experts. But since he couldn't allow himself to feel the fear in the daylight hours, while under the microscope of his teachers, the fear had broken through the hardened walls of his waking ego by emerging in the safety of his sleep world.

I suggested to him that next time the dream recurred, when he was lying awake filled with sensations of dread and thoughts of failure, that he breathe deeply and welcome the feelings. I even went so far as to suggest that he actively attempt to reconjure the final dream image—of him staring down at the blank sheet of paper—and to reconstruct the ending to the dream from a waking state, to create a different outcome. I gently suggested that, as he reconnected with the terrifying image of the judgmental people and the blank page, he try to play with it, examine it, even converse with it. At one point in our session, I had an intuitive hit about the dream myself and suggested that he conjure the image of a gold star right at the moment he was staring at the blank paper and gently stick it at the top.

He was initially reluctant—given that he wanted to dismiss the dream as of no consequence to his waking life, and most important, he wanted the dream to disappear. What was key for Peter, however, was recognizing that the dream, however insignificant his logically trained mind might want it to be, elicited strong feelings in him—exactly of the type he was experiencing in school at the time. The images in the dream were showing up in a fragmented, seemingly nonsensical frame of reference for someone like Peter, but what he was willing to consider was that the dream was providing him with a powerful narrative—an access route to his core issue: his fear of being judged and not measuring up.

When I pointed out to him that his strong commitment to his medical studies placed him squarely in the rehearsal stage of a major life change process, and that fear of failure was the *normal* fear response during this phase of growth, it was like a lightbulb went off in his brain: He relaxed, brightened up, and simply said, "I see." For Peter, the dream world became his way through the walled-off landscape of emotion that his highly trained ego-mind—remember: the dictator—had dismissed. He didn't need to be on medication, nor did he need to analyze or surgically hunt down and remove the source of his suffering. He only needed to reconnect with his emotional self, and to listen in more deeply to the language of his soul.

His fear was perfectly natural, coming up from the depths of his split-off unconscious, and poking through the defended walls of his logical mind during sleep. The gift of the breakthrough, for Peter, came in recognizing that to become a good doctor, he would need more than just rational insights and highly skilled hands; he would need empathy and sympathy, and most of all, compassion for his patients and their pain. The dream was pointing him toward reconnecting with his own feelings—and fears—so he would have access to his own emotional body when he most needed it: in helping others.

He recounted to me the following at our next session: One night he found himself actually thinking of me as he lay awake after the dream occurred, and his feelings of terror diminished somewhat. In the freeing space of seeing a safe image—me—juxtaposed with the scary image from the dream, he was able to reimagine the dreamscape, to visualize, without judgment or fear, the image of the blank page and place a gold star at the top. He shared with me that not only did the image become vividly alive—and he felt enlivened and awake but calm during the experience—but the faces of the dream characters re-emerged as well, but this time they were softer, kinder, even friendly. The last time he had this dream, he actually laughed out loud, feeling, as he put it, "a rush of joy and excitement," followed by a sense of calm.

The dream never recurred and Peter is doing well in school. Of course, not all of our fears are so easily quelled. But the example is telling, for it points the way toward the power of inner and outer dialogue with self that can shift the energy of fear once we recognize it for what it is: normal. The practice I suggested for Peter in working with his dream—to reconnect, dialogue with, and reimagine the dream images and their meaning—has long been a hallmark of many psychodynamic techniques in therapy. It harkens back to the process I mentioned earlier called Active Imagination, originally developed by Carl Jung.

Recognition of your fear starts with a shift in perspective, away from judging your symptoms, dreams, inner voices, and bodily pains as "bad," and over toward seeing that these may all represent ways that a deeply repressed desire for change, for a shift in energy, is calling out to you. My client Peter was fortunate to have a dream—and a dialogue with it—that woke him up to the reality, awareness, and acceptance of his fear. He was willing to consider a different way of "seeing through"—to a new sense of self. Ultimately, his fear was a harbinger of his shift from the rehearsal stage to the full realization of his next step on the ladder of self: being a doctor. By becoming aware that his experience of stress was really a perfectly normal fear of failure, part of the transformation process, he was able to relax and take the feelings—and dreams—in stride.

Helping a "Doer" Access Fear through the Body

Let's look at another example, this time with an individual who is less intellectually focused and more somatically inclined: a doer. As you reflect on these stories, think about how you relate to your own fears: Do you tend to want to think things through and find a logical source for your symptoms? Do you pay attention to your dreams or dismiss them out of hand? Do you tend to focus on your to-do list and avoid feelings by staying in action mode? If you fall in the latter category, you may relate to my client Yvette.

A tall, slim, polished, and seasoned corporate executive, Yvette is the last person you would think of as fearful. Having achieved her lofty goal of becoming a vice president of sales for a Fortune 100 manufacturing firm by age thirty-five, Yvette is no wallflower; she is a type-A, action figure. Extroverted, confident, and assertive, Yvette moves in the world with the bearing of a leader and elicits a loyal following from her subordinates. She is one of those people we all consider fearless and might even hold out as a role model for pushing through fear. Ever the planner, mover, and shaker, Yvette came to me at the point when she had decided, after a few years of success as a VP, it was time to leave the corporate world and live out her next dream: traveling the world and participating in nonprofit work to support the poor. The trouble, however, was simple: It just wasn't happening.

She had always known that once she achieved a certain level of financial and professional success, she would want to step off the corporate ladder and give something back. Yet, after carrying around this dream for a couple of years, she found herself unable to take the step—into her boss's office to resign—that would make her dream a reality. For a year or more, Yvette had been fantasizing about her departure, planning her exit strategy with her husband and family, getting all the ducks in a row. Yet, each time she approached her boss with the intent of stating her desire to resign, she froze.

Overwhelmed by anxiety and symptoms of panic—shortness of breath, heart palpitations, stomach pains, cold sweat—she would experience irrational thoughts of being fired, attacked by her boss, or worse. She found that in those final few steps toward her dream, she couldn't move. She would literally walk down the hall to her boss's office, become overwrought, turn around, and head back to her desk and bury herself in work. Later on those painful days, when she would hit the treadmill or run five miles as she did pretty much daily when the weather was nice, the only emotions she would allow herself to feel were self-recrimination, humiliation, and the real killer—

shame. Her head would fill with destructive thoughts like: "What is wrong with me? Why can't I just do what I want? I am a mess!"

When I first met Yvette, I was somewhat perplexed myself by her anxiety attacks, for they so completely contradicted the way she moved through the world. It was obvious from her strong presence, her fit physique, and confident bearing that she was used to being in control, and used to accomplishing whatever she set out to do. People who are somatic in their approach to life, who take care of their bodies, exercise, and exude high amounts of energy, can easily fool the world—and themselves—into believing they are invulnerable. But just as the "box" of self-identity Peter had constructed was hardened and seemingly impervious to emotions due to his strong intellect, the frame of good health, even vitality, as I discussed in chapter two, can become a self-imposed prison. Yvette may have been strong and fit physically, but underneath the composed exterior was a frightened little girl, and in the face of a major life decision and what she perceived as a powerful authority figure—her boss—she cowered.

When I first brought up the possibility that fear might be the underlying emotion she was experiencing in those fateful moments when she would approach her boss's office, Yvette dismissed the notion. "I'm not afraid of my boss," she exclaimed. "I've given him bad news before and stood my ground. I remember just last week I had to convince him to hire someone that he had initially disliked. We had quite a little row about the whole thing, but I held my own . . . and I won the battle. I got to hire the person I wanted. So it can't be fear . . . that's just not me." And so Yvette, like Peter, was initially unwilling to see fear as her problem.

It became clear to me, very early on in our work together, that the access route to Yvette's emotional self would be through the body. Unlike Peter, who, although dismissive, was intrigued by his dreams, Yvette totally denied herself any imaginal adventures into things like dreams or inner dialogue (only finding there the loud voice of her voice of judgment; she had no room for or access to the voice of reverence), and didn't have much patience for self-help books or reading in general. Hence, at one point, I suggested that she add yoga to her exercise routine, offering that it would give her a way of increasing her physical stamina and flexibility but also give her an opportunity to slow down and get more in touch with the emotional component of her symptoms. Never one to pooh-pooh exercise, she took the bait. After her first few forays into Vinyasa, or flow-style yoga, the tone of our conversations began to shift. She became calmer, softer, and more able to be gentle with herself as she described the persistent symptoms that plagued her plans to depart the corporate world.

Yvette quickly came to love yoga, for it gave her a way to be in movement, in touch with her body, and at the same time to slow down and reflect on her anxiety and explore the physical sensations of anxiety for what they were: fear. She learned to pay attention to her breathing patterns and notice how her breath would always give her a signal that she was getting anxious by becoming short and rapid. Soon enough, after practicing yoga for a few weeks, Yvette began to transform and shift the energy of her anxiety—and to speak, however reluctantly, of fear. Whenever the anxiety arose—as it still would when she thought about going to see her boss about her own situation—she learned to stop, breathe, and observe herself.

Soon, when she and I would get together, her self-talk began to take on a different, more vulnerable, and less strident, less self-critical tone. Not long thereafter, the moment came when she was ready to practice with the tool of recognition. She was able to lighten up on herself when the anxiety would hit and state the following: "As I think about going to see my boss, I become nervous, my heart beats loudly, I feel flushed. My thoughts race with fantasies of disaster. The prominent thought is this: I am afraid that my boss will hate me because I am being disloyal." All of a sudden the irrational thoughts and the physical symptoms of panic had a name: "fear of being disloyal."

From that moment forward, the entire experience of panic and anxiety took on a different slant; she recognized that what really scared her most was the potential perception by her boss of her supposed disloyalty. Recognition of what was really happening, and naming it, gave Yvette a newfound freedom to explore her feelings, thoughts, and reactions to the situation. She began to relax a bit and not beat herself up quite so much, beginning to understand that this particular demon—an irrational fear of being disloyal—was generating a powerful resistance in her.

By employing a practice like yoga, somatically oriented type-A individuals can slow down their reactivity and learn to tend to their physical sensations with more compassion and openness—to dialogue rather than argue with themselves. The simple act of breathing in tune with the body's rhythm is a key factor in connecting the dots between the physical frame where the symptoms of fear show up and the Pandora's box of buried emotion that is their source. Yoga gave Yvette the entry ticket to the tool of recognition, for the practice helped her to become less judgmental of her body's reaction to fear, and more in tune with the natural flow of energy between the emotional and physical systems. Once aware that although she couldn't control her anxiety with her mind or push it away by getting manic in her exercise routine, but rather could slow down and be present and gentle with her body and the emotions that flowed through, she was able to step off the disheartening treadmill of overwhelm, confusion, and indecision and accept her fear as normal, however anxiety-provoking and irrational.

The next step for Yvette was to become less reactive to her difficulty and, using her formidable strength as an accomplished adult, to take responsibility for the situation. By stepping back and accepting that she in fact does have an irrational fear of being disloyal, she was able to begin the excavation process into her past to discover where this fear was born. It turned out that when she was a little girl, her father, a military officer, always expressed his love for her in the context of her being well-behaved and—you guessed it—*loyal*. Always obedient to his wishes, she learned early on that her father's love was directly linked to her being a good girl, never disrespectful, never disappointing. This pattern of childhood bonding with a parent is perhaps not particularly uncommon nor abusive or even traumatic, but it did impact her in ways that only began to emerge many years later.

The job of recognition as a tool for responding to life rather than reacting to it—especially without self-judgment—is to help us see how our irrational fears connect to an earlier time, a developmental time in our lives when misbehaving or acting on our own impulses might have had grievous consequences.

As an adult, Yvette recognized that her boss, although similar in bearing and demeanor to her father at times, was *not* her dad. The abrupt rush of fear—the resistance to change—that emerged in the path to her boss's office, had nothing to do directly with her boss. Once Yvette was able to understand what was really going on within her on physical, emotional, and mental levels as she moved toward manifesting her dream, she was able to put the tool of recognition (naming the fear in the moment it was occurring) to work in real time. She was finally able to make that fateful journey to speak to her boss and gracefully resigned her post. The punch line, of course, is that her boss was actually very excited for her, perhaps a bit envious of her courage to take such a big step, but ultimately very supportive and happy for her.

If, like Yvette, you become aware of a reactive tendency or an irrational fear that appears connected to an experience of pain or trauma from childhood, you may want to choose a symbol from that period of your life to carry

with you. In moving through her fear of authority, I suggested th
carry a photograph of herself as a small girl—a smiling, happy pl
she could pull out in moments of anxiety: a reminder that she was no longe.
a little girl *and* of her need to be compassionate with the little girl's fear that
still lived in her. With this photo in hand, she found herself shifting out of a
state of self-criticism and into a state of compassion, a place from which her
natural and evolved strength could emerge.

Life-Shifting Action Step: Automatic Writing

This simple writing exercise is designed to help you break through
the mind chatter and connect you to a deeper awareness of your
core beliefs around fear. Take a page in your journal or a blank piece
of paper and write at the top of the page the following question:
What am I afraid of? Then just start writing. Write for 10-15 minutes
without stopping. Do not worry about writing complete sentences or
stop to think about what you are writing. Just write whatever comes
to mind. It may be phrases or just words or fragments. Just let it
come. If you find yourself stuck or over-thinking about the question,
just keep writing whatever comes into your mind. There is no right
or wrong answer and everything you write may be useful—but it
might not be obvious to you at first. Just keep writing. Practice this
exercise regularly starting with a question related to your fear—or
to the symptom you are feeling in the moment. For example: "Why
am I anxious?" or "What is my story about fear?" are great variations. The key to automatic writing is to unlock the mind from its
"box" called "knowing" and to step into your imagination, listening
for wisdom from a deeper place: your soul. The answer will find you.

Life-Shifting Action Step: Imaginal Dialogue

This exercise is similar to automatic or free writing, but it allows you to connect to your imagination through a simple visualization technique called Active Imagination. Find a comfortable place to sit, where you can be quiet for ten to fifteen minutes. Have your journal and a pen with you, or a blank piece of paper and a colored marker.

Close your eyes. Sit quietly for a few moments and take a few deep breaths. Notice your thoughts. Don't judge them. Just allow yourself to breathe deeply, relax, and allow the thoughts to flow through your mind. Notice any tension in your body and breathe into that spot that feels tight or anxious. After you begin to settle and feel quieter and more grounded, ask yourself a question about your fear, such as "What am I afraid of?" or "Why am I feeling depressed?" Whatever question comes to you, as it relates to your feelings of fear, is the right question. Allow the answers to flow through your mind. Don't try to get the *right* answer or be worried if nothing important or meaningful seems to come. After sitting for a few moments, still breathing and reflecting, allow yourself to ask these questions: "Who is feeling the fear?" "Who is thinking these thoughts?" and finally, "Who are you?" Allow yourself to breathe into the question and notice if an image appears—of any kind. It may be a person or a thing or a symbol—the content of the image *doesn't matter*; whatever arises in you is perfect.

After being with the image, whatever it may be, for a few moments, still breathing, and remaining calm and quiet, gently open your eyes and begin to draw a picture of the image. Don't try to draw a "pretty picture" or an exact replica of the image. Whatever you draw—a line, a face, a symbol—is always the right image. After you have drawn out the image, allow yourself to feel the emotional response—from within your body—that the image evokes. Take a few minutes to dialogue with the image. Ask it questions directly and just allow yourself to experience the flow of energy that comes from the image. Ask: What are you trying to tell me? What do you mean me to know? What do you have to tell me about my fear? Allow yourself to feel whatever comes up as you gaze at the image before you. Feel the feelings that it evokes. Breathe deeply and allow the image to work its magic on you. Surrender your need to *know* what it means. Just feel, in your body, the message it evokes in you.

If you practice this exercise regularly and begin to have an ongoing dialogue with the images and symbols that your unconscious mind brings forth in you, you will soon connect with a deeper knowing—about your fear, about your self, about your soul's desire.

{ Chapter Two }

THE TOOL OF RESPONSE-ABILITY: MIND THE GAP

"Fear is static that prevents me from hearing myself."
—SAMUEL BUTLER

Fear is not always hidden. I had a client just yesterday who is preparing to take the bar exam in a few months; she's overwhelmed with anxiety, scared to death of failing, and knows it. Ellen is in her late twenties, very bright, and exuberant about finally finishing school and kicking off her sought-after career as an attorney. Being a "thinker-type" individual, and psychologically oriented, she is well aware that fear is dragging her down and preventing her from focusing on her studies.

She even knows where her fear comes from: a childhood environment in which she was always pushed to achieve academically, where anything less than straight A's would bring obvious displeasure from well-intentioned, if extremely controlling parents. In an ironic twist, Ellen is, as she puts it, "not really afraid of my fear, I've seen this movie before," but she *is* stuck in what feels like a perpetual doom-loop of negative self-talk—and she's tired of it.

Knee-deep in the rehearsal stage of this change cycle of her life, Ellen may be fully aware of her fear, but it still has her in its grip, despite her understanding from whence it comes. "Tired" is her euphemistic way of putting what I see more dramatically etched in her furrowed brow, pale complexion, and slumped posture: She is exhausted with worry. For Ellen, as with many of you who may be quite readily aware of your fears, we need to move quickly and get to work with the next tool in the sequence: the tool of responsibility.

After reading about the tool of recognition, you may be thinking that *recognizing* your fear is a fairly straightforward exercise, and although helpful, not likely to extinguish the pain of it. Many of us, myself included, who are intellectually oriented and tend to think deeply about our problems, will be quite capable of making the connection between our symptoms—of anxiety, depression, irritability, and stress—and the fears that drive them. This is why the second tool, of responsibility, or "response-ability," as I like to describe it, is paired with recognition in the tool kit. The fact is that no matter how *aware* you are of your fear and its likely source, just naming it, although essential, is only the first in a series of steps we need to take to transform the energy of fear from dread to delight.

LEARNING TO RESPOND—INSTEAD OF REACT—TO FEAR

I describe the tool of responsibility as "response-ability" because there are two distinct meanings that can be applied in the use of this tool: (1) learning to be *responsible* for the energy of our reactions, and (2) learning to respond effectively to fear once it has been identified. Overall, this tool provides us with a perspective and practices designed to help us look at how we *meet and greet* change, and how we face off with fear: Do we become reactive and defensive? Or do we step back and reflect? The key to developing our ability to respond to the energy of fear when we become aware of its presence in our physical, emotional, and mental energy systems is *to create space* for it. The practices below provide an access route that will support you in shifting from a reactive to a responsive stance in the face of fear. They are designed to help you "stop, look, and listen" to create a much-needed gap between the energy of fear and the energy of compassion and acceptance that defuses its sting.

"Mind the gap" is a wonderful British slogan, utilized by the London Underground management to get passengers to pay close attention to the space between the train and the platform, because in the archaic London subway system there is almost always a chasm to cross as you step onto the train. Depending upon what station you're at, the gap can be six inches wide or more—enough to swallow a foot, an ankle, perhaps a leg. For our purposes, the expression points toward the need to tend to the space between the oncoming train of fear and the ground—that energetic "platform" of our life—on which we stand, either centered, aligned, or off-kilter. The tool of responsibility provides a set of practices that we can use to widen the gap, to create more space/time in which to reflect, to reconnect to our center and ground, to breathe, attend, and dance *with* the energy of fear, not against it.

If you think back to my bear story for a moment, you may notice that my decision, in the moment, to sit still and breathe—even though I was terrified and part of me wanted to bolt, which might have proved deadly—was a fortunate response to the arrival, literally on my doorstep, of very real danger. Lucky for me, I had the presence of mind to counter my own instinctual tendency to either "fight or fly"—to attack or run. The lesson was not lost on me—and I try to keep it alive in my life when the foes that appear in the shadows are a bit more sanguine but no less anxiety-provoking: It sometimes really helps to just breathe, feel the fear, sit still, and wait. Like bears, fear eventually gets bored—and moves on.

Let's get back to Ellen, who already has a heightened awareness of her fear, and see how she worked with the tool of responsibility, in ways that supported her to make the shift from being exhausted by fear to being supported by it. When I introduced Ellen to the idea of meditation, she was initially reluctant to try it. With the deadline for her exam looming on the horizon, her controlling ego responded to the possibility of just "sitting and thinking," as she put it, with a potent rational stance: "I don't have time for that!" But when I compassionately proposed that meditating, even for just a few minutes, especially when she was in the throes of anxiety, might help her to *stop* thinking, relax, and reconnect with her emotional and physical energies in a way that was supportive instead of draining, she was willing to give it a try.

There are many techniques for meditating that come from a wide variety of sources both scientific and spiritual, but they all have two things in common: creating an intentional time-out to sit quietly for a few moments or longer with no interruptions—no e-mails, no TV, no distractions—and focusing the mind's attention on the breath. Breathing is something we do all the time reflexively, so it is easy to forget that it can also be a tool for relaxation, tuning in to the self, and "creating space" for the energy of fear to move. Buddhists have known and practiced the art of mindfulness, or conscious breathing, for centuries. Our scientific community is just beginning to catch on to the power of meditation, and of the breath as a tool for relaxation, and healing.

Recent studies by neuroscientists of hundreds of Buddhist monks, who meditate for hours at a time, have shown that the brain waves of these individuals are substantially different from a typical Westerner's active mind. Scans of the monks' brains show much higher amounts of the alpha wave activity that typifies a relaxed, creative, content mind. These studies are beginning to understand the direct connection between the breath, the posture, and the release and movement throughout the brain system of hormones that produce feelings of serenity and peace. Energetically, meditation has also been shown to increase the flow of oxygenated blood throughout all parts of the brain, increasing the connectivity between the prefrontal cortex and the limbic systems—the cognitive, rational, and emotional centers. This is a literal, biochemical explanation for what we can experience ourselves directly:

Meditation can help us to break down the ego's walled-off sense of isolation and fragmentation and expand our sense of creativity and possibility.

For Ellen, once she realized that the key to success was not the quantity of her studying but the quality of the energy she brought to it, meditating was a godsend. By just taking a few minutes out of her busy schedule each morning and each night to sit quietly, to tend to her breath, and to be present to the physical sensations in her body, she was able to disconnect from the sense of overwhelm her overactive mind was producing. Meditation had an immediate effect on her day-to-day life in that it simply brought her back, if at first only momentarily, to the experience of feeling calm—and relaxed. But more important, at least for Ellen, is that by creating a space—a gap—in the constant stream of her fearful thinking, she was able to remember something even more significant: that she was a good student! In those calm moments when she shifted out of her head and into her body—through the magical mechanism of the breath and the energy of attention—Ellen was able to access memories that her fearful ego had long buried, memories of her history of success at taking exams in the past.

During the few weeks in which she committed to adding a meditation practice to her study routine, Ellen discovered the deeper meaning of her fear. It was actively pushing her to stop, think, and remember what she had forgotten about herself: that she always did well, that the source of her success was not the amount of studying she did (very likely an idea instilled in her by her parents), but in the energy of creativity and insight that was always available to her, and that had emerged every time she needed it most. Her magical ability to work through problems, to "think out of the box," was never connected to the quantity of information she consumed; it was an energy of creativity that came from a different place, a special place she had lost contact with in the midst of a frenetic attempt to "learn everything." It was her soul.

Her fear, of course, was an unwelcome visitor, and the voice of self-criticism that wanted it vanquished was trying to be helpful on some level. But the real gift was found when she recognized that she was overly focused on her fear. Fear was calling to her to pay attention, to listen in for a lost memory of whom she knew herself to be. Once she took the time to actually focus on her energetic state—physically, emotionally, and mentally—by meditating (which had been prompted by her fear—and her asking for help), she was able to access a different level of knowing and feeling about herself—a level of knowing that cut through the ego and flooded her system with that mysterious energy of intuitive wisdom.

Ellen liked to call this energy her "inner genius," but the label does not matter. What counts is that her fear prompted her to take a time-out, to reconnect with the deeper energy that was the source of her ability to ace any exam that one might place before her. Fear was the trigger. Meditation was the access route, through stopping, breathing, and shifting of attention away from the chattering mind and into the felt experience of her body sensations. As we might expect, Ellen did extremely well on the exam. She is on to the next stage of her career and recently got caught up in the daunting process of trying to make partner at her law firm. As she moves into the next stage of her cycle of development and change, she now has the ability to step back and listen to the message from that part of her that knows she will succeed.

By now, some of you may be thinking something along these lines: "OK, this meditation stuff sounds great, but I just don't have time for it. My life is so full with activities and to-do lists, the very thought of sitting still makes me anxious." Well, you're not alone. I have had my ups and downs over the years with meditation and although I know it is a powerful way to calm the fearful mind, it sometimes gets pushed to the bottom of my to-do list as well. If you are a highly mobile, active person, which is what our culture wants everyone to be most of the time, it may be daunting to consider making time for just sitting quietly. That's why I included a practice for the "doers" among us called "moving energy" that I learned from my wonderful spiritual teachers, Tom and Flame Lutes, which is described at the end of this chapter. It is an active, energetic tool, adapted from Native American medicine practices, that combines movement with specific breathing, sound, and meditation techniques, helping to calm our fears and create space between our thoughts.

But if you are still skeptical or resistant to the idea of "creating space" for the energy of your inner voice to be heard, I recommend a fun, light exercise to get you started on the path of response-ability. I call it the "egg carry" and many of my high-energy—some might say hyper—clients swear by it. The next time you feel yourself getting stressed out or in "high energy" mode of doing, doing, doing, go to the refrigerator and find a fresh, uncooked egg. Take it out and for the next ten to fifteen minutes carry it with you wherever you go. Never let it out of your sight. Even if you are sitting in front of a computer, typing away at e-mails or chatting on the phone, have the egg fixed somewhere on your body. You may laugh, but I put it in my lap while I do e-mails. Don't try to put a raw egg on the table or in your pocket: You'll be sorry. No, just simply carry the egg with you for about fifteen minutes. Notice what happens to your energy, to your attention, and to your thoughts and feelings when you are forced, even if rather artificially, to focus on something small, fragile, and breakable. You have to slow down. You have to pay attention, and your energy will shift.

After safely returning the egg to its container, reflect on these questions: How did you keep the egg from breaking? How did you shift your attention and your actions to accommodate the egg? In this exercise, you will get a visceral experience of what it means to slow down and be responsive to the world around you. If you move too quickly, or react too strongly, the egg will break. There is a meditative quality to the simple act of holding an egg, even for a few moments. Think about how this egg forces you to center, to ground into your experience and be more present.

To take this exercise into a real-world application, find something that can symbolize the delicacy of a fresh egg—a gemstone or a crystal, or a delicate piece of cut glass or similar token—and carry it with you as a reminder to stop, breathe, and be gentle in your response to life. For many of my type-A clients, the egg carry is the first step toward recognizing that you *can* slow down and not lose any productivity by taking a few moments to breathe, to focus your attention on your body, to be still.

So how do we create the space of "response" instead of "reactivity"? The following practices can help, and once you've identified the mode in which you will tend to react to the energy of fear—whether with anxious thinking, heightened emotions, or physical symptoms—you may want to craft specific practices of your own design. The key to responding effectively to fear once you are aware of it is to shift from either a thinking, feeling, or doing state to one of *being*—to accept your fear and make room for it, to be. Then and only then will it begin to loosen its grip on you, such that the gift it offers—as we will see with the next two tools—may become known.

Life-Shifting Action Step:
Vipassana Meditation

This simple meditation technique is designed to support those of us who, like Ellen, are actively in "mental mode" much of the time. I suggest you start by practicing this meditation a minimum of five minutes a day, preferably first thing in the morning or just before you go to bed at night. The goal of meditation is simple: to experience the space of awareness that exists between your thoughts. By meditating, even for a few moments, you can learn to step out of the mind chatter and become an observer of your own mind—and story.

Sit quietly in an upright position. If you have any pain in your back or legs, find cushions and supports to enable you to be as comfortable as possible, but to be able to sit still, without moving, for at least five minutes. Close your eyes and begin to deepen your breath. Allow your attention to shift away from the outside world and on to your breath. Feel the flow of air moving through your nostrils and down into your body. Listen to the sound of your own breath. Practice sitting with your attention on the breath for a few moments and then begin to notice if thoughts come up and pull you away from the focus on the breath. Just notice. Don't judge the thoughts but instead just bring yourself gently back to the breath.

Once you have settled into a deep, circular breathing pattern, begin to shift your attention to the rest of your body. Begin with your toes. Notice your attention shift to your toes. Wiggle your toes, feel the sensations in them, and breathe into them. Allow them to relax and slowly move your attention up your ankles, your calves, into your thighs and torso. If you find your mind wandering, gently come back to the breath. Notice any tightness, or sensations of discomfort in your body. Scan your entire body very slowly, moving your attention up through your abdomen, stomach, and chest, on into your shoulders, elbows, wrists, hands, and fingers. Focus on those parts of your body that feel particularly tight or where there may be pain. Breathe into those parts. Allow the sensations to move and just notice the shifting, pulsing energy as it moves through your body. Finally, come back to the breath and just notice how your thoughts move through your mind, coming and going, allowing yourself to simply observe, without judgment, the thinking mind.

Life-Shifting Action Step:
Shake and Bake: Move Your Energy

This practice is ideal for those of you who may have a resistance to or difficulty with sitting meditation practices. It can be a perfect prelude to sitting meditation, for it is designed to actively move the energy in your body until you are able to become still enough to focus on the breath, or to relax in a warm bath. This practice can be done in as little as five minutes, but it is best to carve out at least fifteen minutes where you can be free to move uninterrupted and without distractions. If you have a particular high-energy music that you enjoy—like African drumming, or Latin salsa—these can be wonderful supports to get you into the flow of moving with the body. However, it is important to remember: This practice is *not* dancing. The four steps outlined below can be practiced with music—fast, pulsing music with a strong beat is best—in the background, but the idea is not to find yourself dancing with the music, because the goal of "moving energy" is to do just that: to *move* the energy of feelings, sensations, and thoughts through the body. A crucial factor in shifting energy—and thus shifting your fears from reactivity to spatial response—is to break the customary and habituated patterns in which we typically move. That is why this activity is not a dance. It is an opportunity for you to breathe, move, and explore how the sensations of fear *move* through you as energy.

Step 1. *Pranayama breathing*: This breathing practice, which is sometimes called "fire breath," is a powerful entry point for moving your energy. It is not meditative breathing in the sense of the practices described above, but is designed to *use* the breath to build and expand your energy. Start by standing up in the center of a room, flex your knees, and shake your body lightly until you feel centered and grounded. Feel your feet (barefoot is best) on the floor and begin to rock back and forth between each foot. If you are using a dance rhythm–style music, just move gently back and forth—no dancing—and allow your feet to connect strongly to the floor on each beat. Feel settled in one spot. Do not move around a lot but stand upright, centered, and relaxed, breathing only through your nose and taking short, rapid breaths. Begin to breathe more quickly and deeply. You will know you are building energy awareness if you can hear your breath, even over the din of loud music. Breathe like this—in and out of your nose rapidly—for a few minutes until you begin to feel a warm sensation, even a stinging sensation, in your nose that spreads out through your body. Try covering up one nostril and breathing even more deeply and rapidly through the other. Move back and forth by putting your forefinger on one nostril and then the other. If you do this practice, even for just a few minutes, you will already very likely begin to feel focused, energized, and more alive—the energy of a renewed vitality moving through you.

Step 2. *Shaking (not dancing):* Now relax your breathing back to a normal, circular pace. With your feet planted hip-width apart and arms relaxed by your side, begin to shake your hands/wrists vigorously. Lift your arms above your head and just shake your hands, wrists, and arms—without falling into any kind of dance-like pattern. Slowly accelerate the shaking by including your upper arms, shoulders, and torso. Try to notice how you may fall into specific patterns of movement. Don't judge this—it is perfectly normal—but try to break the patterns. Don't worry about what this looks like (you will want privacy when you do this practice so you won't feel self-conscious and can just let yourself shake wildly, with abandon). Eventually, keeping your feet planted on the ground, bring your whole body into the shaking activity. Shake your hips, your buttocks, your neck, and your head. Allow your jaw to relax and shake. Be careful not to strain or over-exert the motion with any part of the body. Pace yourself, but try to shake out the entire body for at least ten minutes. About halfway through the shaking practice, add sound as described in the next step.

Step 3. *Making sound:* While you are shaking and moving your entire body, trying not to move in any particular pattern, slowly add a low humming or grunting sound. Keep breathing deeply as you shake, and just let sound—growling, moaning—emerge effortlessly. If you are in a place where you can make a lot of noise without disturbing anyone, let yourself scream or shout—whatever sound wants to come. This is a powerful addition to the shaking practice, for it will release pent-up feelings and emotions, and get you in touch with the energy of fear that may be bottled up inside. Shake and move and breathe for as long as you can, at least ten minutes.

Step 4. *Sitting:* Slowly allow yourself to let go of the sound, bringing the body's motion down to a slow pace, and ultimately bring your hands down to your side and finish with a light shaking of your hands/wrists—just as you began. Take one last full-body shake and a few deep breaths with a deep, loud sighing sound. Just release any last energy that feels bottled up inside. Then slowly settle down on the floor (you may want back support) and either sit quietly or lie down completely flat. Turn down the loud music (if you have it playing in the background) and just relax. Allow your breathing to become normal again, and settle into the delicious sense of peace and calm. Feel your entire body relax. Notice any residual tightness and breathe into it. Take at least five minutes to lie or sit comfortably and just observe your body, your mind, and your feelings. You may want to journal about what comes up for you in the space created after moving your energy. Often we will receive wisdom or meaningful messages from deep within the body after having shifted the habituated patterns of energy and unblocked the flow.

Chapter Three

THE TOOL OF REFOCUSING: THE MYTH OF FOCUS

"It is not the strongest of the species that survive, nor the most intelligent, but the one most responsive to change."

—AUTHOR UNKNOWN,
COMMONLY MISATTRIBUTED TO CHARLES DARWIN

It was a beautiful, moonlit night. Late summer in south Florida, it was still close to eighty degrees—a perfect night for a stroll on the beach. My friend Barbara and I had not seen each other for a few months, so it was a treat when our schedules aligned to allow us to wend our weary way southward, escaping the confines of New York City for a long weekend in the sun. After walking along a picture-perfect stretch of white sand for what felt like just a few minutes but must have been hours—given that the sun receded on one side and the moon rose on the other—we slumped down together on a park bench to rest. Silently we watched as the moon, almost but not quite full, rose over the ocean. It was a spectacular sight: Puffy, ethereal clouds formed, floated, and disappeared across the horizon, at times covering the soft, orange glow of the moon, at times breaking apart and receding, allowing the growing, glowing visage of the lunar surface to beam down directly. It was one of those moments when we, and I mean here the universal "we," all feel the interconnectedness of everything—the sky, the ocean, the waves, the sand, the energy emanating from the lunar surface, the hard, cold, slightly wet bench that poked a bit into my back, my friend's gaze—and smile—as she shared the experience with me. It was a felt sense of intimacy, of oneness. Words, which had been the focus of our experience for the past few hours, seemed, all of a sudden, unnecessary. I was content.

Then there was a shift. I looked down at my feet and noticed that they were shaking; they were vibrating back and forth at a very high frequency, even though the rest of my body was seemingly still, my heart calm, my mind relaxed. Barbara noticed my anxious feet as well. "What's that about?" she asked. "You seem relaxed . . . but your feet are pretty active down there." She chuckled and didn't seem overly concerned, but I was now focused on my "anxious feet" and the mood, in my body and mind, had shifted. The moon was gone and there were only feet—sand-covered toes that, like overactive children, seemed to refuse to sit still and take in the view.

At this point, you are probably wondering why I am sharing this little beachfront vignette with you. Well, as you may have surmised, or you will certainly see by the time I'm finished telling the tale, the subject of the story is not really Barbara and me, or Florida beach walking, or even moonlit evenings; it is "focus." The third tool in our tool set for transforming fear is what I call "refocusing." Like recognition and responsibility, it too comes in a paired set, for together with reframing, it takes you deeper into the energy of the dance I wrote about in chapter two, of attention and intention. As you read through the rest of my little story of a very special, yet ordinary walk on the beach, think about your own experience with focusing. See if you can remember and reflect on moments like the one I'm describing, where the subject of the conversation may have been your "lack of focus" or "need to focus" or perhaps you were feeling "unfocused"—yet, lo and behold, you were focused, at all times and in all places, on something. That, as we shall see, is the core myth about focus, for even if we don't think we are focused, we are.

Let's return, though, to my toes. My antsy toes just didn't seem to get the moment. They refused to be calm, to quiet down and take in the moon, the waves, and the grace of the exquisite scene before me. And in that moment when Barbara noticed my overactive feet and asked me, in effect, what was wrong, my mind was triggered. I started thinking—or more accurately, worrying—aloud about everything from the state of my book-writing project to the state of the U.S. economy to the state of my finances. Barbara picked up on the theme of my monologue and set off on her own version. She shared with me her frustration with the political debate since Barack Obama was elected president, her concern about job security, and whether she would have enough money for retirement. Having both recently ended difficult, if deeply meaningful relationships with significant others, we shared our thoughts, fantasies, and worries about finding the *right* partner again in the future. We both wondered aloud if the career paths we were on were the *right* ones; whether we were giving back enough to the world, living up to our full potential, and so on. You get the idea. It became a rather heady conversation, fraught with worry, concern about the future, and, you guessed it, fear.

At one point, heading off into an intellectual tangent of the highest order, I posed the questions: So what are we doing with our lives? Is this all there is? What is real? At that point in the conversation I think both Barbara and I realized that our minds were spinning out of control with all manner of dramatic worst-case scenarios. We had forgotten the beach and the moon completely, absorbed in a classic tête-à-tête with fear. We've all been there. This time, though, was different: All at once Barbara rose up off the bench and without a reply to my rather pedantic, if well-intentioned question, ran down the beach to the water. I watched from my perch on the bench as she waded into the swirling water and raised her face and arms to embrace the moonlight.

All of a sudden, my focus shifted and I was once again acutely aware of where we were, of the moon, of the water, and of how lost we had just been in the powerful pull of fear-based thinking. I quickly rose from the bench and trotted down behind her. Coming up next to her, I planted my feet firmly in the warm water, put my arms around her from behind, and hugged her close. Together we gazed up at the huge, beaming moonscape laid out before us.

At that exact moment, I became fully present to the moonlight, the warmth of the water, the presence of another heart beating close to mine, and I also felt my feet—perhaps for the first time that night—calm, relaxed, surrendering into the sand. It was an exquisite feeling of grounding, centering, and alignment. I took a long, deep breath, released Barbara from our hug, and just stood stock-still, enveloped in the awesome physical and emotional presence of the soft earth's pull downward and the moonbeams' simultaneous pull upward. I was both in and "not in" my body, seemingly at the same time. Mostly I just felt this delicious sense of presence, an awareness of the moment, with no thoughts about the past, no worries about the future, no mental attempts to understand, dissect, or judge what was happening. Barbara turned to me and, putting final closure on our earlier conversation, simply stated, "This is real." I got it. I felt it. I knew.

So what does this story tell us about the myth of focus? Have you ever thought to yourself something along these lines, "My problem is that I lack focus"? One of the most common complaints I hear from my clients, especially corporate clients or people reflecting on their business lives, is that they have trouble "staying focused." But here's the thing to notice about a story like the one above: I was always focused. First I was focused on the beach and the moonlight, then I was focused on being tired and needing to rest, then I was focused on my agitated feet, then I became focused on the future and everything wrong with the world, then I became present, once again, focused on the moment, the beach, the water, the moon, and my dear, dear friend.

In the space of two hours I went through an entire gamut of energetic shifts. The dance of attention and intention moved, often instantaneously, between the physical, emotional, and mental domains, from the past, to the present, and to the future, from an awareness of the internal mind chatter on over to a sense of interconnectedness with the external world—and back again. Focus is not something we ever lack; for although our minds will trick us into believing that we have lost focus, we are always, every moment, focused on *something*. The issue here is very similar to my discussion, in chapter three, of the myth of the symptom: We focus on the issue of "focus" but that is *not* where the trouble lies. The real challenge is to put aside our judgments about our so-called lack of focus, recognize that we are always focused on something, and become more awake to what our energy is attending to, at any given moment.

I submit to you that most of the time when we are caught up in a conversation about ourselves as lacking focus or losing focus, we are actually very focused: on our fear. We just don't know it. Think about that moment when I was talking with Barbara about our lives back in New York. It felt perfectly normal to dialogue about the future, to reflect on the past, to worry about the state of the economy—and the state of loved ones far away. We do it all the time. When my clients tell me they are worried about their lack of focus, I can easily find my own mind sliding into cahoots with this conversation, and together we are off to the races with plans of "attack" for getting focused. But, as useful as this conversation might prove to be, even I miss the point: My client *is* focused, in that moment, on his or her fear.

SHIFTING YOUR FOCUS

The dictator from chapter two—your ego—is in complete control in those moments when you tell yourself you are being unfocused or focusing on the wrong things. Think about it: Where is your attention when you are worried about your need to focus? What is your intention when you are judging your lack of focus? What are you present to in *that* moment? Fear: The fear of the unknown; the fear of not being good enough; the fear of not doing, being, or having enough. You name it. So what does it take to shift?

The answer is simple, but not easy: You need to become aware that fear is the focus of your attention (which is challenging because it will show up as a "symptom" with many different names: resistance, worry, anxiety, lethargy, and so on), and then find the trigger that brings you out of your head, into your body, and ultimately, into your heart. For this, you need to become aware, not of your thinking, but of your energy, and particularly the energy in your body: You've got to find your toes!

Whenever you feel yourself overwhelmed by a focus on fear—and it can happen at any point in the cycle of change—I heartily recommend making the effort to find your way to a beach, a river, or a lake on a moonlit night. The human body, as a complex system of energy made up mostly of water, resonates powerfully with the forces that hold together the universe. The moon with its gravitational pull on everything and bodies of water like the ocean that carry within them the energy of life—enveloping the earth like the soft, viscous womb from which we all emerged—carry powerful energetic impulses that can do wonders in helping us shift into a grounded, aligned state of presence.

On the other hand, when you're stuck in traffic or running late for a meeting, feeling out of control and unfocused (you *are* focused at that moment, remember? On your fear.), it may not be helpful to think about walking on a moonlit beach (although just having the fantasy, if felt deeply in your body—down to your toes—might be enough to create the energetic shift from dread to delight). In situations like these, however, the tool of refocusing is always available to you, but it requires that you become facile with the two key trigger mechanisms that can instantly transform your relationship with fear: (1) remembering that your internal conversation is focused on fear, and (2) shifting the energy of attention from your mind to your body.

I am not the first to study the transformational power of refocusing. Eugene Gendlin, a professor at the University of Chicago in the early 1960s, developed a method for enhancing the healing efficacy of psychotherapy that he called "focusing," which has grown into a full-fledged therapeutic technique of its own, utilized by thousands of practitioners worldwide. More recently, Ann Weiser Cornell has written a book called *The Power of Focusing* that provides a step-by-step guide to learning the skills needed for anyone to utilize focusing in their day-to-day lives. For my purposes the key elements of the focusing practice that we can draw upon to shift our experience of fear are fundamentally the same: We shift our attention from the thinking mind to the feeling body and we enter into a conversation with the body, creating a space of inquiry, openness, and curiosity. The true key to refocusing is just this: recognizing that when we shift our focus from the mind to the body, we open ourselves to a deeper wisdom, bypassing the controlling ego, listening in for a different story, a story of now.

The Inner World and the Outer World

There are basically two places on which we can choose to place our attention: the inner world and the outer world. When we are cruising along in life feeling good about ourselves and the world in general, we enjoy a harmonious natural flow back and forth between what's going on with us inside (our feelings, thoughts, and body sensations) and how we are dealing with the rest of the world (work, our social life, our relationships, and everything else that falls under the day-to-day heading: external).

This state of flow is similar to driving a car with ease, moving our gaze back and forth seemingly effortlessly between the rearview mirror and the road in front of us. Yet, what happens when we become fixated on the road ahead and forget to look in the rearview mirror? Or worse, we become distracted by something in the mirror and take our eyes off the road ahead? We enter the danger zone.

This is where focus comes in. One of the keys to staying on track as you move through the inevitable stages of every life change is staying centered. Too often, however, the dictum to "focus, focus, focus" is limited to *either* our inner life *or* the outer, so-called real world. Spiritual teachers may tell us to focus on the inner world, to step back and spend more time in contemplation and meditation. Leadership trainers and life coaches are more likely to tell us to stay focused on our goals, to stay in action and keep working at the outer edge of our experience.

The truth is that we need to be able to shift our focus back and forth in order to navigate the six stages of self-renewal. Have you ever noticed that your darkest thoughts and worst fears are triggered when you're navel-gazing or worrying about how others are judging you? The key to successful refocusing is learning how, when, and where to *shift your attention*.

One of the most common symptoms of fear is the feeling of being "frozen," incapable of action. This is a sure sign that we have become fixated, either spinning down a mental side street on a fantasy journey of our own making, or obsessed by some external scene of supposed calamity or danger. In either case, we become distracted drivers—either so lost in our internal thoughts and fears that we drive right by our turnoff, or so caught up in the rubbernecking frenzy of a roadside accident that we drive right into the car in front of us! The tool of "refocusing" helps us to check our lenses and recalibrate our attention—moving from an overemphasis upon the external to attending to the internal world, and vice versa as needed.

The experience of my client David, who was recently forced to abruptly shift his attention from external to internal, is a great illustration of how the process of refocusing works. In the midst of what can only be described as a midlife melt-down, David came to me with a long litany of problems: a dysfunctional marriage, a stalled writing career, a series of breakdowns and conflicts with his siblings over elder care, and a mounting pile of debt. Father to three well-adjusted teenagers and formerly a very successful screenwriter, David had lost his bearings.

When we first started working together, what was most noticeable about David was that as a writer and eloquent storyteller, he was totally caught up in the drama of his own life. Hour upon hour, he would regale me with the pain-ful stories of a wife addicted to shopping, a mother-in-law who despised him, a boss who was impossible to deal with, and so on. The focus was all external.

When I asked David how he was feeling, in his body, right in the moment as he sat comfortably with me talking away, I noticed that he would become agitated and confused. Focus on himself? His feelings? His body? He seemed almost constitutionally incapable of self-reflection, self-monitoring, or self-observation. Here the tool of recognition—becoming awake to the present moment in the body, heart, and mind—was the first order of business. Yet, in the process of recognizing his tendency to focus almost exclusively on the external story of his life, David would quickly become overwrought with emotion, anxiety, almost panic. Recognition brought him to an awareness of how far outside himself he had ventured, to the point where refocusing on the internal was all but impossible. To deflect feeling overwhelmed, he would shift immediately back into the story, focusing away from himself and on to the drama unfolding all around him.

Fortunately, when the evidence began to pile up that he needed to shift gears and take a U-turn off the victim highway and focus on himself—his feel-ings, his fears, and his fantasies—the universe offered David a gift. One day he called me and said that he had twisted his neck while shaving (!) and, having pinched a nerve or something similar in his vertebrae, he would have to stay in bed for a while, moving as little as possible.

Of course, in his drama of a world out to get him, he saw this as another example of how he was doomed to misery, and although I felt a great deal of compassion for his plight, I recognized the opportunity being handed him. Days turned into weeks of resting, reflecting, and with the help of exercises and a journal for refocusing, David was finally able to simply chill out. It was perfect timing. The universe—and perhaps my emphasis upon refocusing— took him down a different road from the one he had been tearing up for years, a road back into himself where he could explore his feelings, his symptoms, his thoughts, and his own internal drama.

A few weeks later, healed of the neck pain, rested, and more relaxed than I had seen him in many months, David returned to work with me a changed man. With a newly found focus on his own internal experience, David began to move toward self-care, healing, and restoration. Refocusing brought him back to himself—with a little help from the universe.

❁　❁　❁

Let's close out this chapter by circling back to my story with Barbara on the beach. Now that you have a sense of how refocusing works, think again on what happens when we shift our energy from a focus on fear—externalizing, fantasizing, worst-case scenarios—to a focus on the present: What happens to our story about ourselves in those delicious moments of awareness? A new story emerges, sometimes seemingly out of nowhere, and we find ourselves seeing, feeling, and understanding our sense of self, our identity, quite differently. Refocusing prepares the way for the ego to soften and for a new story, a story of possibility, to emerge from your soul.

Barbara even went so far as to suggest that I was "channeling" when I spoke during that sacred moment, as we stood together in the waters of the earth, basking in the light of the moon. I remember the essence of the experience as if it were happening right now. I found myself thinking aloud: "Relax. All is well. You are right here, right now. You are exactly where you are supposed to be. All will unfold as it is meant to unfold and you need not worry about anything. You are not alone." These simple phrases and thoughts swirled through my mind and came out of my mouth but they didn't feel like they came from an energetic space of "thinking." And they certainly were not reflective of the person I typically know myself to be—headstrong, analytical, intense. They came from a deeper place, a deeper voice, that seemed to come up from below, almost as if my toes, which had just a short time before been vibrating with the energy of anxiety, were now softly listening to the earth and sending signals up through my center, to my heart, and on into my mind. It was like a reverse feeling of osmosis: My ego was not running the show and the words were simple, grounded, not based in fear but in love. I felt safe. So who had spoken these words? Well, our egos have such a difficult time recognizing the existence of a parallel *being* within us—a knowing source of creativity that I call the soul—that when we "come out" of experiences like this one, we are apt to dismiss it by calling it "channeling" or "woo-woo" or otherworldly.

It is none of these things. It is simply a wiser, deeper part of us that sometimes breaks through the chatter of the ego and has its say. The goal of refocusing, and all of the practices in this book, is simple: to shift our energy of attention and intention from the egoic stance of the dictator, who regularly clamps down in fear, to open up, embrace, and listen in to the voice of the "other" within us, the voice within who knows the truth in the present moment—that all is well. This voice is always available and accessible with a simple shift of focus—ready to remind us that we *are* the beach; we *are* the ocean; we *are* the moonlight. We are not separate from these things. We are born of them, part of them, steeped in them.

We have these amazing energetic capabilities of awareness and cognition, which are gifts unique to our system but that come with a price. So talented are we at projecting outward into the unknown horizon beyond ourselves—in space and time—that we sometimes forget where we are, forget what is happening right in front of us, and falsely find ourselves in a dark, empty, and unsafe world of our own making. In those moments, we are simply lost in the anxious overwrought story of fear generated by ego. By learning to refocus, with physical, mental, and emotional practices that shift our energy flow from mind to body, we begin to access the ever-present wisdom that emerges from a different place—a place of soul. And we can come home again.

Life-Shifting Action Step: The 360-Degree Eye Exam

This practice is ideal for when you find yourself caught up in anxious or repetitive thinking. Like a jolt of light breaking through the darkness, it will wake you up to your current energetic state, shifting your focus out of your head and your ego, and into your mind and heart.

Here are the steps: Whatever you are doing right now, stop. Look up from this book and gaze straight ahead. Take a long, deep breath. Now turn your head and move your gaze around you until you find the object that is farthest away in your line of sight. If you are looking out a window, find the farthest object and focus on it. If you are in a walled room with no windows, look to the farthest wall and focus on an item there—perhaps a knickknack on a shelf or an image in a painting. Fix your total attention on this far-off object. Notice its color, texture, location, surroundings. Take in as much detail as you can. Then slowly, very slowly, bring your gaze back toward yourself, taking in every object and sight that lies between the farthest point and you. Notice how it feels to shift your attention to objects off in the distance. Did you notice anything different that you may not have seen before? Perhaps you noticed colors or textures—flecks of paint on the wall or a photograph you had not looked at closely for years. Or if looking outside in the yard, perhaps you noticed a particular flower or moss on a tree, or even gazed through a neighbor's window. Do you notice how enjoyable and easy it is to become engrossed in the details of the outside world?

Now do the exact same exercise in reverse. Stop and breathe. Focus your attention on your breath and the sensations in your nose, throat, chest, as you breathe in and out. Shift your attention to your abdomen, to your lower body, feeling the sensations in your legs, ankles, feet, and toes. Slowly, very slowly, move your attention back up through your body until you settle your attention on the sensations just behind your eyes. Feel yourself blink. Breathe. Notice what happened as you moved your gaze from the external world to the internal world. Did you momentarily forget about the outside world? Did you get stuck along the way, either by something pulling your attention on the outside or the inside? Notice how your thoughts followed the attention of your inner and outer gaze. Notice how grounding your attention changes the way you feel from one moment to the next.

Whenever you feel anxious or distracted, seemingly unable to focus, stop whatever you are doing and allow your gaze to shift, first out beyond the horizon of your current space to a point far away, and then back onto the close-up physicality of your own body. This exercise can be done pretty much anywhere, at any time, even while driving or sitting on an airplane. It can help you become aware of your place of focus and your ability to *choose* where you want to fix your attention; it can support you in becoming present to your mind's chatter—and the symptoms of fear that may be clouding your vision—and bring you back to the present, grounding your attention in the "real" world—not in your fantasies of disaster.

Life-Shifting Action Step: Be a Tree

In this practice, we focus our attention on the energetic connection between our bodies and the earth. The idea here is for those of us who tend to be constantly in motion—always running, moving and doing—to learn to become more aware of the ground beneath our feet. The ideal way to shift our attention and to become present to our center and ground, is to practice focusing our attention on our feet, feeling the energy flow between the soles of our feet and the floor, ground, or earth that bears our weight. You can begin to practice the experience of grounding by sitting quietly, even for a few moments, and focusing your awareness on your feet. Planting your feet on the ground, without shoes or socks, take time to feel your toes, the balls of your feet, and the heel. Wiggle your toes, shift the bottoms of your feet just a little, and feel the energy that flows through your feet. Notice if you find yourself feeling jumpy or anxious. Notice if you find it difficult to sit still and hold your feet still. Breathe deeply and just feel the ground beneath your feet. Relax your foot muscles and luxuriate in the connection to the earth.

Once you have become more practiced at grounding your energy in your feet, and becoming focused on the earth connection, try the following balancing/grounding yoga pose: Stand straight and tall, ideally barefoot, in the center of a room. Allow your hands to fall gently to your sides, shake out any excess nervousness or anxiety that you are feeling by doing a mini-version of the "moving energy" exercise from chapter two. Now breathe deeply and begin to raise your arms above your head slowly. Bring your hands together, palm-to-palm and straighten your arms above your head. Keep your head straight and your eyes focused on a fixed spot on the wall or outside the window that lies directly before you in a straight line of sight. Begin to lift one leg off the ground, staying balanced on the other leg, and place your foot as high up on the other leg as you can. You may be able to lift your leg as high as your opposite thigh, or perhaps place your foot against your other knee or shin. It doesn't matter how high you lift the leg, the key is to stay standing straight upright, focused, and breathe steadily while holding your arms above your head and the foot of one leg is pressed gently, but firmly, against the other leg. Hold this position for as long as you can, all the while breathing deeply. Feel your foot on the floor, and try to maintain a straight up and down posture. Then gently lower your leg and reverse the practice using the other leg. This pose is called "tree pose" and is a great practice for shifting your focus out of your mind and into the present moment, learning to balance and ground yourself into the earth, like a tree.

{ Chapter Four }

THE TOOL OF REFRAMING: REWRITE YOUR STORY

"You can avoid having ulcers by adapting to the situation: If you fall in the mud puddle, check your pockets for fish."

—AUTHOR UNKNOWN

There you are, happily cruising along, when suddenly, seemingly out of nowhere, another car is coming right at you or a truck is barreling down the road behind you or a van abruptly switches into your lane without signaling. This experience is so common, there is even a word for it: blindsided. Life is like that at times: The job disappears, clients decide to end their engagement, partners up and leave you, or perhaps illness strikes just as you were getting back on your feet.

When you've been blindsided, it's easy to slip into victim mentality and look around for someone, anyone, to blame. Yet, as I've said before—and will say again!—life is *not* something we can control. The journey is made up of twists and turns and unexpected events, all culminating in a series of cycles of beginnings, middles, and ends. Everything, no matter how wonderful, is transient, and with the powerful tools of refocusing and now reframing, even the victim stance can be temporary.

In this chapter, we will add the tool of reframing to our tool set. Reframing comes on the heels of refocusing because, once again, they fall into the category of partners in the dance of attention and intention. Refocusing, as we discussed in the last chapter, helps us to recognize that we are always focused on something and when we lack focus or feel lost in a sea of confusion—or despair—most of the time our focus is on our fear. With practice refocusing—becoming aware of our tendency to get caught up in our thoughts, our emotions, or our physical symptoms—we can take the energy of our response to a deeper level, shifting our attention to a nurturing, empowering space.

REFRAMING OUR PERSPECTIVE

Once we become aware of how and where we are focusing our attention, the story running in the background may not automatically shift. As you will remember from chapter two, learning to dance with fear requires that we perform the two-step with regard to our energy systems and this pairing; the second step involves not only shifting our energy, but peering more deeply into the frame of our story, to explore how we see ourselves in the moment life throws us a curve. Reframing is our opportunity to reevaluate the impact of fear and change on our story of identity and ask: Who do we want to be in the midst of this event or series of changes? Are we truly innocent victims? What parts might we be playing in the scene and what meaning are we attaching to the outcome? Are we missing an opportunity? Is there a deeper message to be heard than the message of fear and dread that our egos want to cling to?

If you remember, the core theme of life-shifting starts not with fear or change, but with an awareness that we are not concrete "selves" in any way, shape, or form. We are all made up. The self is a story that we tell ourselves and the world. It is constantly being buffeted by the winds of change from the outside—or blindsided by bad drivers!—and also being shaken up from the inside, with desires, passions, movement, and a need to grow. Let's look at an example where reframing a situation by reinventing the story of "why this is happening" can help us not only transform our fear of change but reignite our passion for it.

Not all corporate executives think of themselves as leaders. In fact, my friend Susan, who has a senior role in human resource management with a global health care firm, has always been hesitant to call herself a leader. With over fifteen years' experience in the corporate arena, she is a highly paid senior officer who has a wide range of talents and capabilities in everything related to talent management, from executive development to recruitment, succession planning, and organization development. She is a primary contributor to a number of highly visible corporate policy teams and is held in high esteem by her colleagues. Recently she turned down a couple of opportunities to move even higher in her organization. She recognized that the higher she goes on the corporate ladder the more people she will have to manage and the more political and visible the role becomes. She loves working with people, but she just doesn't see herself as a leader in the corporate sense of wanting to hire, direct, or control the activities of large numbers of people.

Taking herself off the "race to the top," as she might call it, has its fallout. She can feel the pinch of disappointment from her superiors; she can feel the possibility of being out of the running for new jobs that might come up, and most disturbing, she can feel the energy of the recession—cost containment and cutbacks—possibly coming back to bite her. She's worried. She knows that something probably will change in her work landscape and she knows what she doesn't want, but not what she does. She finds her mind wandering during working hours, and in the midst of those moments of lost focus she scans the online job ads.

Susan, having reached a cruising altitude in her successful career, is in the midst of a shift from the realization stage of her career into the next rupture. She is aware of the impending shift, but as we might expect—and would all feel under the circumstances—is resistant to it. She worries about her finances and the need to save for retirement. She occasionally berates herself for not wanting to climb to a higher rung on the corporate ladder, but she knows at a deeper level that corporate leadership beyond her current level is just not where her passion lies. But what to do?

Being a fairly balanced type, with equal access to her emotional, physical, and mental energies, Susan has committed to a yoga practice, is a fairly regular meditator, and actively looks to create space for her fears to shift and for the messages from her inner self—her soul—to emerge. She is open and receptive to putting aside her ego and loves to nurture her intuitive side, by engaging with practices some of us might consider "way out," such as tarot readings, practicing with a pendulum, or seeing a psychic. For Susan the issue is not whether the practice is scientifically sound or *proven*—what matters is that she connects to a different source of insight and energy within herself. These modalities offer her the possibility of breaking through the ego's rational stance that her corporate environment would hold as normal—and listen to her soul.

The trouble is that when Susan has recently been reaching into her favorite tarot deck for a message about her future, she keeps getting the same card over and over again: *leadership*. Hah! But, she keeps asking, how can that be? She doesn't see herself as a leader. In fact, she shared with me that when she pulls this card from the deck, she recoils, for in her mind this card represents the exact opposite of what she really wants. She feels called to serve in some way, but not to lead.

When I listened in to Susan's concerns about the *leadership* card, I couldn't help but hear the resistant and hesitant energy of fear creeping into her voice: Is she making a mistake to take herself off the corporate ladder? Should (there's that word again) she keep climbing up those innumerable rungs? During a recent phone conversation, I asked her to describe to me what was on this infamous leadership card. I wanted to see and hear not just the words on the card that were preaching about leadership, but the images. I asked her to share with me the visual, aesthetic manner in which this tarot deck was envisioning leadership. She described something along these lines: "There is a ladder—like a corporate ladder, I suppose—that runs in a twisted formation from the lower left corner of the card to the upper right. Funny, because I now see that the ladder is twisted like a strand of DNA. . . . Oh, and the ladder has a pair of beautifully sculpted hands placed on it opening in an upward movement, as if the hands are climbing the ladder, and at the top of the ladder, enveloped within a blue-sky background, is a shining full moon with piercing white light that radiates out over the whole card. Under the moon, just near the final rung at the top of the ladder, is a white dove-like bird."

She finished the description with these words: "I suppose the bird might symbolize peace and serenity; it is quite beautiful."

"Ummm . . . delicious," I thought to myself. Not very corporate-sounding, this card called "leadership"!

Of course, even after she had described it to me, Susan was immediately aware of how I might respond. She was way ahead of me. "Maybe I need to rethink this leadership thing," she said.

"Yes," I added. "Maybe your definition of leadership, and your story about what it means and how it is applied, is quite narrowly focused on the corporate world. Are there ways that you might reframe the story that this card is telling you about leadership? Perhaps you are being called to lead, but in a new context, in a way that is more nurturing to your soul, more connected to your essence." In that moment, I could feel the shift, even over the phone, as Susan's voice relaxed and the energy of fear dissipated. There was a message here for Susan, about the way she was holding the story of what it means to be a *leader*, and about the way she was holding her story about her self.

There is no doubt in my mind that Susan is a leader and that she is being called to craft a new story, one in which she will lead her life—and others—in a way that, like a dove in the moonlight, brings greater harmony, peace, and serenity to the world. Ultimately, it may not matter whether she leads in the corporate world. The gift of Susan's leadership is not confined to the box of identity we label "corporate America," for her offering will be much bigger, deeper, and broader than that. Leading for Susan is all about who she *is* in the world, not what she does. She simply has to see the true qualities of leadership that she embodies, embrace them, and bring them to wherever her heart leads.

Reframing our story is so simple and so profound at times that we may have a tendency to dismiss the signals that show up, in the form of tarot cards, a call from deep within our hearts, or feedback from a loved one. Of course, the simple act of reframing may be very threatening to our ego; it is perfectly normal for us to become comfortable with a particular story, to settle into a way of being, thinking, and showing up in the world. We all become, to a certain degree, habituated to the labels and roles that we come to think of as *normal*, and it can be jarring and painful to consider giving up on a way of being that has served us. Key to the shift, though, is recognizing that it is our fear that is the real signal that change is afoot. Reframing is a tool that along with refocusing offers up the opportunity to change our perspective on what is happening, to turn the story upside down and see the gift inside the pain.

STORY REPLACEMENT SURGERY—WHEN WE LOSE CONTROL

Sometimes, however, when the fortress of identity built by our inner dictator is not so easily penetrated—by a tarot card or a good friend's advice—we may need to undergo what I call "story replacement surgery," or SRS for short, in order to hear the call from our soul. SRS is my term for when something major—a physical illness, job loss, or other calamity—comes along to disrupt our lives when we least expect it. At times like this, it can be extremely difficult to find the silver lining in an otherwise difficult or painful experience. But it is in there. As the old adage goes, the universe moves in mysterious ways.

As we will explore in more depth in part three, the cycle of change, growth, and renewal that is always running in the background of our lives will at times require us to experience the literal or metaphorical ending of our story of self. If you've ever gone "under the knife" and had surgery for a minor or major ailment, you know what is involved: You are asked to surrender completely into the hands of caretakers—doctors, nurses, family, and friends—and you may be literally put out of consciousness for a period of time while the *invader* is removed. Surgical procedures are designed to remove the demons of illness from our physical bodies. SRS occurs in a similar way:

We are felled by the arrival of a foreign invader—an illness, an accident, a depression—and at some point we are taken down, forced to retreat from our workaday, self-assured, and active life—to stop, rest, and give up our sense of control. At those times, the universe seems to pull the rug out from under us. It may feel like a part of us is dying, and there is often some element of truth to this experience, but there is always, every time, another story waiting in the wings to be born.

Let's look at how story replacement surgery occurred for one of my spiritual mentors, a wonderful minister at the One Spirit Interfaith Church in New York City. Reverend August Gold tells how, after reaching a dark, fearful moment in the building of her church, the universe—or God or spirit, whatever way you want to describe fate—came to her aid, in the form of a major car accident. It was during a time when the early, fast-growth days of the church's first few years had stalled. Reverend Gold was working harder than ever, teaching classes, giving Sunday sermons, leading all sorts of extracurricular church groups, and yet, despite all of her hard work—and the work of many volunteers—the church community seemed to have reached a plateau at about two hundred members.

Then one day, as she was rushing to get from teaching class to a counseling appointment, while trying to navigate her way across Fifth Avenue and Eighty-Third Street, out of nowhere came a large red truck. Swerving to miss a bicyclist and traveling way too fast for this Manhattan side road, the truck charged right into her. Knocking her off her feet and headlong into a car parked alongside, Reverend Gold ended up unconscious, bleeding, and severely hurt. Days in the hospital and weeks in convalescence ensued. Her busy schedule became a rather moot point: She couldn't get out of bed. During this time she went through a wide range of emotions: anger at the young man driving the truck, grief at her loss of mobility, fear that the church would disintegrate in her absence, and even a few moments of gratitude that she had somehow survived and would recover.

What actually happened during her convalescence is this: The church was forced to ask other ministers to come in and preach, teach, and help out. As a result, the church no longer just had one overworked minister; it had an entire corps of fresh ministers to give it new energy. With months of time on her hands, Reverend August wound up writing a series of reflections on the experience, returning to the idea she had had many years before of writing a children's book, and becoming deeply committed to her meditation practice. Despite, or perhaps in response to, the calamity, the church started growing again.

pon her return, the church was much bigger, much stronger, and Rev-Gold was more willing to share the load of responsibility. The accident forced her to reframe her sense of self as the Lone Ranger in charge of the success or failure of the church. Ultimately, she came to see the accident as a gift, an opportunity to reframe the story of who she was in the world, to surrender her need to control and always be responsible, becoming a collaborator, part of the team that would take the church to a whole new level of success and prosperity.

○   ○   ○

The question we have to ask is this: Is the experience of sudden loss, dramatic endings, or seeming calamities something we see as good news or bad news? The first, obvious response will usually be bad news—after all, it's hard to perceive something that causes loss or pain in our lives as a source of joy. Yet if we stop and reflect for a moment on the truth of the impermanent state of all life, as the Buddhists point out, we are left with one crucial choice: We can craft a different story.

The tool of reframing is exactly that: a way to rewrite the narrative, reinterpret the way we grasp what happens in life. There is no one inevitable *truth*. At the end of the day, how we frame our sense of identity, how we describe the way we experience life, is really just a story. The one choice we always have available to us is this: We can reframe the story and explore how life may be happening *for* us and not *to* us. As we venture forward through the cycle of renewal, reframing becomes a powerful tool for shifting from victim to victor, from being a casualty to the empowered protagonist of our own life story.

Life-Shifting Action Step: Road Rage

Think about the last time you got angry or upset at another driver or found yourself irritated by a customer service representative or shop clerk. Have you ever been "cut off" by someone trying to race past you on the road, or had someone cut in front of you in a checkout line? Have you found yourself creeping up on someone and frustrated that they wouldn't just get over and let you pass? Has someone zipped in out of nowhere and taken the parking space you had your eye on? Think of an example of feeling upset at someone else's bad or aggressive or idiotic behavior and run the scenario through your mind's eye. How did it make you feel? Did you feel thwarted in your desire to accomplish some goal? Did you feel that this person was doing something to you personally? Did you feel perhaps a bit judgmental? Superior?

Now ask yourself this question: What if this person was doing this horrible thing not *to* me, but *for* me? How could I reframe my story about the situation such that the overall experience was a gift to me? If you have a difficult time with this exercise—sometimes it is difficult to see the blessing in the supposed idiocy of others, right?—try reframing any experience where you have or hold a complaint about another person, or life. You may not find a silver lining right away. Take time to reflect on the situation and your reaction to it. Journal your thoughts about what it would mean for you if this event were reframed to reflect an opportunity or blessing. What could you learn from it? What is the story you are telling yourself about the world, and about your self, that might have to change? What inner demon might have to be removed from your ego's war chest in order to shift your energy—and your story—the next time something bad happens *to* you?

Life-Shifting Action Step: The Gift of Pain

This practice is ideal for anyone who tends to be highly active or athletic. It can be conducted through simple reflection, but it is more powerful to journal your thoughts as they come up or to share the practice in dialogue with a close friend or supportive partner. If you are currently experiencing any physical breakdown—a pain or illness of any kind—the practice can be a powerful way of reflecting on the present moment, to open to messages that may be coming directly from your body to your soul. If you are feeling good overall at this time, then practice by reflecting on times during the past when you have had physical pain or experienced a sudden illness, accident, or breakdown.

Start by sitting upright in a comfortable position, with your back supported and feet planted firmly on the ground in front of you. Take a few minutes to settle into the position, close your eyes, and begin to relax your body. Take a few deep breaths through your nose. Now begin to scan your body with your mind. Move your attention through your entire body very slowly, feeling the sensations and pulses of each part. Now think of a time when you were in pain or experienced an illness that struck a particular part of your body.

Focus your attention on that part of the body that is either experiencing current pain or has felt pain or suffering in the past. The body will remember. Breathe deeply while focusing your attention on this specific body part. As you are feeling the sensations and thoughts connected to either current pain or pain from your past, ask yourself these questions:

- How would I describe the experience of pain?
- How does/did my mind and body react to the situation?
- What was the source of my pain? How might my pain be a blessing?
- What story about myself was/is being altered, removed, or dying during the experience of this bodily pain?
- How might this pain be a gift in disguise?

Take time to breathe deeply and bring yourself back to the present moment. As you close this practice, even if you only did it for a few short minutes, take time to thank your body for bringing you through the pain, for being the support system that keeps you alive and breathing, even in the midst of pain.

Chapter Five

THE TOOL OF REALIGNING: SYSTEM TUNE-UP

"Fear is just your feelings asking for a hug."
—DANIELLE SANCHEZ-WITZEL
AND MICHAEL PENNIE

Often, when we look to self-help books or guides to help us move through fear and other unpleasant symptoms that accompany life's changes and upheavals, we find that the advice focuses on one small part of our lives. For instance, we'll be told that the problem is all in our head—change our thoughts and we'll change our lives. Or we read that the problem lies in our need to trust our intuition: Become more in tune with your inner voice, listen to your gut, and you'll be able to move out of your self-imposed rut. Or we're advised to feel our feelings—feel the fear and do it anyway—to tune in to the emotional body. Or we are cajoled into taking on an exercise routine and getting in shape, hoping that by tending to the physical body we'll feel better and the symptoms will disappear. All of these can work. So which one of these guideposts is the right one?

They *all* are. We need to pay attention to our thoughts, our feelings/intuitions, and our body. The key to transforming fear is not to be found solely in the mind, the heart, or the gut, but in the alignment of all three together. The problem with advice that overemphasizes one domain—the feeling/intuitive, the thinking, or the physical body—over another is that since each of us has a predisposition and an affinity toward one or two of these modes of human expression, we are very likely to choose the guide that focuses on the one we do best, or at least the area we are most comfortable with. Unfortunately, the area in which we are most comfortable is very likely *not* the one that we need to work with. The thinkers need to get in touch with their feelings; feelers need to reconnect to their mental and physical capacities; somatic types need to step off the treadmill and listen to their intuitive, mental, or emotional intelligence. The voice of soul may arrive through any one channel, or it may sing its song in all three domains.

The key is to turn inward, to become aware of our tendency to focus on one domain over the others, to even be fearful of the suppressed parts of ourselves. The tool of realignment focuses on aligning the three domains together, for we need to listen to them all. Only then may we rediscover what we all knew as kids: that we each are a whole big ball of emotional, mental, physical, and psychic energy; that insights and inspiration can come from a wide range of playing fields both inner and outer. The key to realignment, once we've honored that change is in the works, and fear is bubbling to the surface, is to listen in for soul, wherever it may be found.

A LIFE OUT OF BALANCE

We met at a small, intimate vegetarian restaurant in the East Village, far enough from his office that Josh was fairly certain he would not run into any colleagues. The fact that he didn't want to meet at his office should have been my first clue that something was awry. But when he showed up looking fit and jovial, speaking in rapid bursts about the benefits of a macrobiotic diet, I was initially quite impressed. Here was a mid-forties, successful surgical products company executive with a big title, a big job, and a whole coterie of assistants, secretaries, nutritionists, and fitness trainers, all effortlessly orchestrating his high-powered life.

Given his rosy appearance and jocular demeanor—as well as the penchant for health food and fitness—it was easy, at first, to overlook the bags under his eyes, the haggard droop of his chin, and the manic pace and tone— the edginess—in his speech. On the surface, Josh appeared well-balanced and self-assured. Yet as we munched on tahini-drenched raw carrot salads and he shared with me bits and pieces of his crazy work life, which, as he described it, demanded twenty-four-hour availability to his clients, I began, literally, to tremble. I had seen this movie before. I, in fact, had lived it.

Josh's supervisor, a well-intentioned, observant, and supportive operations vice president at the manufacturing firm where Josh is a top marketing exec, had asked me to see Josh about what he called "an anger problem." According to his boss, Josh was one of the superstars in the firm, who over the past four years had successfully brought in more clients, more revenue, and more staff than just about anyone else in his peer group. But recently, as he put it, "Josh tends to fly off the handle with people. He just doesn't have any patience or willingness to listen to the viewpoints of others. He is very smart, and quite often right, but people have become intimidated and frightened around him because you never know when he might blow up and dress someone down. He never used to be so judgmental and edgy. I want to promote him, but unless he learns to be more of a team player and tames his ego a bit, it just isn't going to happen."

In the wake of this description of Josh's behavior, I was ready for anything. So you can imagine that I was a bit taken aback when the man I met for lunch was friendly, upbeat, and cordial. A consummate political animal, Josh was on his best behavior when we first met, although he let slip that he "didn't trust his boss" and that he (the boss) was the one who really needed a coach.

Despite the well-oiled social skills and the appearance of at least a balanced diet, something wasn't right, and I recognized it right away, for sometimes old clichés hold true: It takes one to know one. Looking across the broccoli and tofu spread before us, I gazed into Josh's sad and tired eyes. In them, I could glean a familiar landscape—a visual reflection of something—*someone*, I should say—I hadn't seen in over ten years: my old corporate self. I knew then, with the shudder of recognition from my own past, that Josh was in deep pain; fear was the farthest thing from his mind but his closest companion.

His inner life was a walled-off, isolated, and lonely room, surrounded by the colorful and resplendent trappings of external success: money, spacious apartments, fancy cars, fast women; Josh's was a life filled with, as they say, "wine, women, and song." But there was very little singing. In fact, in Josh's black-and-white world of work, work, work, there was very little music of any kind to be heard. The trouble was obvious but hidden in a dark corner of his psyche: Josh's life was seriously out of balance.

According to the exalted values of our capitalist meritocracy, Josh was at the pinnacle of his success, but below the surface jocularity, he was an exhausted, suffering soul, whose deep-seated fear of being a fraud—of being found out as the lost little boy who had somehow fooled everyone into thinking he was smart and confident—lay just below the surface. In the instant I recognized his pain I also felt a rush of compassion for Josh. I had walked in his shoes and knew where he was headed: off a cliff.

It feels like eons ago now, but in reality it was 1995. I was a senior human resource executive with one of the most prestigious management consulting firms in the world. Like Josh, I was always tired, always on edge, always on the lookout for the next political or competitive salvo from a rival down the hall. My boss, although very supportive of me, was the worst kind of role model, for he worked even harder than me, was emotionally volatile in the extreme, and was prone to angry outbursts that upstaged even my edgy repose. Surprisingly, like Josh, I was health-conscious in the extreme, watching my diet, working out at all hours of the night, yet sleeping less and less as the years went by. As a thinking-type, and a voracious reader of nonfiction—at that time mostly books on leadership and business—I was obsessive about being at the top of my game physically and mentally.

Ultimately it was my body, that powerful messenger from the soul, that knocked my ego off the crest of my wave of corporate excess by providing me with severe lower back pain, and ultimately, hepatitis A. Having never taken a sick day in over fifteen years of working in the corporate world, suddenly I found myself taken down for the count: six weeks of bed rest. Of course, it was a gift in disguise, and truth be told, perhaps even the genesis moment of the book you hold in your hands. For only when my ego was broken apart, my body torn asunder by complete and utter exhaustion, did I come to look in the mirror of my own soul and recognize the truth: I was lost. I had lost touch with my emotional, intuitive, feeling body. I had forgotten how to feel just about anything except anger, irritation, and frustration. I had stopped dancing with life and started barking orders. Success, at least for me, was supremely toxic, for it led my ego to just consume me, to become the arrogant, pompous dictator par excellence, lauding over body, mind, and soul.

Yet I was fortunate, as Josh will surely prove to be, for though the soul may be forced underground by a strident and winning ego, at least for a while, the deeper desires of the psyche to grow, live, and love will always win out. In the throes of illness, I was forced to rest, to literally do nothing—no exercise, no work, no thinking—just sleep. In the middle of this severe rupture stage, big change was in the works, and I can clearly remember the moment I made the shift—from rupture to release—when the defended walls of my identity as a superhero came tumbling down.

You might be tempted to think that the illness was the trigger that woke me up to what was really happening. You would be wrong. The physical breakdown was certainly a big upset for my ego, but I was determined to fight it—to get back in the game. No, my back pain and illness were primers for the truly transformational moment, which arrived in a subtle but potent form, as the universe is wont to do: in a poem.

One night when I was particularly feeling frustrated, irritable, and as I can see now in retrospect, quite angry at myself for being unable to slough off the debilitating effects of hep A, I reached for a book that had been sitting on my shelf for many months. Written by a deeply insightful and wonderful poet named David Whyte, the book, *Fire in the Earth*, was a revelation. In it, no joke intended, there is a poem called "Revelation Must Be Terrible" that shook me to the core.

Reading this poem, I felt something much more intense than any virus or bacteria or back pain: I felt my heart break. Tears, long repressed and shunned, flowed out of me in a torrent of feelings—sadness, grief, loss, loneliness, and mostly, *fear*. I realized, in the flood of feeling, that something had to give, that I was seriously out of alignment, that change was in the works—and I was afraid.

It took a long time for me to move through the release stage—to grieve for the corporate identity that had outworn its useful life—and to move into a new, reinvigorated stage of revival and rehearsal. But the turning point came when the song of my soul broke through the hardened walls of my seemingly impenetrable ego, in a poem. This is why I now believe that when I hear my clients speak of needing to focus on their "work/life" balance, I recognize the cover-up.

We all know the truth at some deep level—there is no such thing as work/life balance: Work is life, life is work. More often than not, when we feel out of balance, the need is not a greater balance between our work and our life, but a renewed alignment between the energy systems that make up our sense of self. Some part of our being—physical, emotional, mental, or spiritual—is out of whack.

Halfway through our tofu salads, Josh confessed to me that he felt "stressed" and needed to find more balance between his work and his life. He longed for a relationship, to get married, settle down, and maybe even have children, but never had time to "go online," as we do these days, and meet a potential soul mate. He rarely took any time off from work and even when he did, was on his BlackBerry and e-mail—work always only a phone call away.

As I write this, Josh and I are still working things through. He is struggling a bit with the tool of realignment, for his ego still wants to defend against fear. He has conceded the need to rest—and a vacation is in the works. The access route to his soul's desire has yet to emerge, but it will. At some point, and likely soon, the projected frustration, the irritability, and the anger will turn inward and force him to stop. Then his job will only be to quiet the chattering mind, relax the overworked body, to place a tender ear to his heart, and listen. His soul may speak to him through poetry, music, dreams, or some other language, but it will speak. This I know from experience. And Josh will shift, his identity as a corporate scion will break open, and something new will be born.

We all go off track now and then, as the cycle of self-renewal will pull us in one direction or another. In every change process, no matter how small, the voice of new ideas, rebirth, and possibility needs to be heard above the din of the emotional flood, the fear of endings, and the logistical nightmares that clog up the system. Just as your car will occasionally start veering toward the right or left side of the road, indicating that you need to stop and get the wheels balanced and aligned, the symptoms of fear—anxiety, stress, worry, anger, to name a few—are usually a sign that our own internal wheelbase is out of whack. The tool of realignment is designed to reestablish a straight-line connection between the head, the heart, and the gut, to help you tune out the ego-mind and tune into your soul.

Life-Shifting Action Step: Nondominant Handwriting

This exercise is easy to do and takes minimal time commitment. It is similar to the automatic writing exercise that I offered for the tool of recognition. This time the idea is to experience a form of communication with your conscious mind that breaks through the normal, energetic pathways—literally sidesteps the neural network—of your patterned thinking. If you have reached the point in these steps where you are aware of a lack of balance or alignment in your emotional, mental and physical energies, this practice can give you access to wisdom from those parts of you that may be blocked or shut down by fear.

Get out your journal or a blank piece of paper and start by writing a question at the top of the page. The question should be connected to your inquiry about being "out of alignment" or "off balance"— use the words and phrases that resonate most deeply with you and your own situation. There is no right or wrong way to phrase the question as long as it connects to your sense of being "out of tune" with your self. Once you have the question formulated and written down, you may want to meditate for a few moments—just sit quietly and take a few deep breaths. Allow your mind and body to relax and connect to the sensations of energy as they flow through you.

Then pick up a pen or pencil and place it in your nondominant hand (the left one for righties, and the right one for lefties) and start writing whatever thoughts come to your mind with regard to your question. You may find that it is quite difficult to write this way, but just take it slow, don't judge the quality or look of the writing—just slow down and allow words, however stilted or choppy, to come. What you compose on the paper may give you access to a voice from deep within you—an intuitive, knowing, visceral voice, and its counsel to you may be profound. Be cautious as you come out of the exercise and watch if your "normal" mind patterns reemerge and start to judge. Just breathe, relax, and let the message sink in.

Life-Shifting Action Step: Rebalancing Act

For this exercise you will need a blank sheet of paper, a pen, and some music. Choose something that is either meditative or gently rhythmic, the kind of music you listen to when you want to relax. This exercise is best done while alone and without interruption. It can be done in as little as ten minutes (using two- to three-minute intervals) or as long as thirty minutes. If you have the time, indulge yourself in the full thirty-minute version.

Think of an important question you have been dwelling on lately, one that is generating some level of anxiety, fear, or worry, and to which you do not readily know the answer. Write this question at the top of your paper. Put on the soothing music and lie down with your paper and pen next to you. Close your eyes. Place your hands on your forehead gently and take a few minutes to listen to the music and reflect on your question. Stop the music. Turn to your paper and write the first words that come to your mind in answer to the question. Do not censor yourself. There are no right answers, no right words, and no right sentences. Write whatever comes up. Write a few words or a few sentences, whatever comes to mind.

Stop after a couple of minutes and lie back. Put the music on again and take a few minutes to listen and reflect, while placing your hands on your heart. Stop again after a few minutes and write whatever words emerged from your heart. Feel the feelings associated with touching your heart and allow the words to flow from there.

Stop after a few minutes, put the music back on, and lie back again. This time reflect while gently placing your hands on your stomach. What stirs in your core as you reflect on your question? Stop the music after a few minutes and again write what emerged from your reflections.

Once you have reflected on the question and written your words based on the energies that emerged from your head, your heart, and your core, look over your writing. What words jump out at you? Are there common themes or words that came up over and over? Circle the words you wrote more than once. Write a summary statement that synthesizes the key thoughts and ideas that were generated from all three energies. Look for where the three domains are in alignment and where they may be at odds.

Chapter Six

THE TOOL OF RECONCILIATION: HOMEWARD BOUND

"Fear makes strangers of people who would be friends."
—SHIRLEY MACLAINE

Everyone has a bit of Dr. Jekyll and Mr. Hyde in them—dark and light sides of our nature. There are good things, what we like—and want others to acknowledge and celebrate—about our personalities. And then there's the stuff we would rather ignore or deny about ourselves, what Jung called "the shadow." The unpleasant aspects of our personality will often show up when we least expect them, seeming to come out of left field. We find ourselves kicking the dog, yelling at our kids, or flipping the finger to the guy who whizzes past us going ninety miles an hour. We all have within us the capacity for dark thoughts, dark emotions, and dark deeds. This ugly side always emerges from a place of fear. It may be triggered by stress, anxiety, irritability, perhaps exhaustion, but the real cause is a dread response—real or imagined—to something, someone, or some experience beyond our understanding or control.

As much as we dislike them, we need to learn to recognize and accept that these surprising and unpleasant outbursts of fear are perfectly natural. They may be irrational but they are very real and to deny them only makes them stronger. At its root, deep in the unconscious, the shadow represents a deep fear of the unknown "other"—the strange neighbor who moves in next door, the teenage daughter who suddenly appears like an alien, or the lifelong partner who remains unfathomable to us. When we look at how some groups create racial, religious, or lifestyle walls of separation and hatred to protect themselves against changes in the world, we see the unconscious fear of the mysterious "other" writ large.

The tool of reconciliation asks us to begin taking off the blinders and begin to acknowledge our unconscious fears and triggers. As we move through any cycle of change, we need to carry a mirror with us, occasionally looking with unflinching honesty at how our fears may emerge in ways we would rather not admit. But admit we must if we hope to move from dread to delight.

RECONCILING OUR DARK SIDE

Shadow work, as it is called by Jungian-oriented psychologists, is challenging for most people. It is best to begin in small chunks, examining the little unpleasant things we all do that surprise us—not so much with self-criticism as with a smirk of recognition. It is hugely important that we maintain our sense of humor regarding our human failings.

Let me take the plunge and share with you a personal example of how this kind of reconciliation works. As much as I would love to deny it, somewhere along the way in life I seem to have picked up an irrational phone phobia. In this high-tech age of Internet phones and cell phones and wireless communications, we all use the phone as one of our main points of connection to each other. Yet, as wonderful as it is to be able to talk quite inexpensively to friends, family, and loved ones all over the world, the newest systems and latest and greatest gadgets are not without their glitches.

Unfortunately, dropped calls, bad connections, and sporadic cell service bring out the worst in me. You would think that I would be accustomed to hearing into that empty void that emerges as you drive down the highway and your cell service hits a dead spot. Not me: I find myself infuriated every time. And worse, I am constitutionally incapable of being put on hold.

Close friends and loved ones who benignly take "call waiting" and promise to be "back in a second" suddenly become evil incarnate. Of course, in the moment, my self-righteous anger feels justified, for they are never "back in a second." But who am I kidding with my irrational indignation? One day my dear friend Gary—who lives in Florida and conducts most of his relationship with me by phone, all the while answering numerous calls along the way—called me, literally and figuratively, on it: "You know, Jeff, I think your reaction to being put on hold, or a dropped call, is way out of proportion to what is happening. At those moments, you get so triggered and irrational. I think you have a problem." Yikes. Me?

Well, after spending a great deal of energy trying to convince him—and others—that it was all in their heads, not mine, I finally relented. I do have issues with phone snafus. I do, at some deep, unconscious level in my emotional system, feel abandoned, hurt, and fearful when the phone goes dead. In fact, when I stop and reflect a bit, taking a moment to trace the history of this pattern back to its roots, I remember how nervous and fearful I was when, as a young boy of eight or nine, I first started using the phone. I don't remember any one particular incident (of course, I've probably blocked it out!) but I'm sure there was an incident—perhaps calling up a girl to ask her out and getting rejected—when I experienced what at the time felt like deep humiliation or trauma centered on phone communication.

Of course, the past is the past. But as we discussed in part one, looking in the rearview mirror is key to shifting out of our irrational fears and triggers. By seeing how these unpleasant tendencies got started, we raise our fear awareness, recognize the source, and ultimately develop the capacity to respond more effectively to the trigger in the present moment. Today, when the phone goes dead, I can step back, take a deep breath, and rather than bludgeon myself with self-criticism or slam my phone mate, I (usually) have compassion for myself—even humor—about the situation: Thanks, AT&T! Here we go again!

Now you may ask: Why is he making such a big deal out of something so trivial? We all have our tics and peeves, about ourselves and others, right? True, but big or small, irritability and overreaction to something seemingly benign hurts others and ultimately hurts us as well. The "shadow" thrives in these kinds of situations: small moments of disdain, criticism, disgust, most of which are ultimately targeted at the self, but all too often get projected and displaced onto others.

PROJECTING OUR FEARS ONTO OTHERS

It is helpful to begin our conversation about the "shadow" and its relationship with fear, by peering under the covers of our psyche just a bit, and laughing at our foibles. This lighthearted approach gives us an access route to what is actually the most challenging and sophisticated form fear can take in our minds and hearts. For Jung, the shadow represented the archetypal pattern most deeply hidden in the human psyche, the place where evil itself is born and bred—in the dark recesses of our unconscious. For the most part, unfortunately, we deal with our shadows—and the deep-rooted, childlike fears that birthed them—by projecting onto others. Yet, the harsh truth is thus: It is our own shadow material that generates the "us vs. them" approach to the world, that oppositional and judgmental stance toward others that can sometimes lead to grandiose proclamations about entire groups of people as "evil empires" or to politicians brandishing an oxymoron such as "war on terrorism."

Think about it: Isn't the energy of war born of disdain, fear, and a desire to destroy others? We might like to assuage our hearts by believing that we are acting in self-defense or just trying to "protect our soil," yet, at a deeper, more irrational level of human functioning, all acts of aggression are born of fear. We make ourselves feel superior and in control, by denigrating, attacking, and, in times of war, trying to destroy the unfathomable "other."

I recently had this point brought home to me in a gentle but provocative manner. A Buddhist teacher was lecturing a small group of devotees on the subject of fear and aggression. She brought out a videotape with a short clip that showed a large, vociferous group of social activists engaged in a rally against violence, hatred, and war. We watched the scene unfold before us—a large crowd of boisterous, passionate, and enthusiastic people, all shouting and waving placards that called for peace, nonviolence, and freedom for oppressed people everywhere. At first glance, it was a moving testament to the positive energy of possibility that a group of well-intentioned individuals can generate—a compassionate community in action. But then our Buddhist teacher rewound the tape and played the video again, this time without the sound. She asked us to look closely at the faces, movements, and actions of the crowd. She wanted to know what we saw.

It was a revelation. Looking closely, without the impassioned vocal exhortations of peace and justice, the faces in the crowd looked, well, how can I say it? Angry. The protesters were passionate yes, but also aggressive, hard-edged, rigid, and even a bit self-righteous. The point was clear. Even lovers of justice and peace, when committed to incite action and change, can be motivated by the very same energy they detest: fear. The shadow lurks behind the "call for action" in subtle and disturbing, and mostly unconscious, ways. It is a difficult foe to face—for it lies waiting to emerge and run amok in a crowd of even the most well-intentioned and seemingly loving of us. To reinforce the point from the example above, the teacher went on to show us something, in the context of our discussion of fear and human nature, truly appalling: On that same videotape, the crowd, incited to action by a charismatic speaker with a blowhorn and a thirst for change (blood?), actually burned in effigy a dummy of a corporate CEO. Peaceful protest? War on terrorism? What is going on here?

In times of great suffering, when we truly are victimized by acts of great cruelty and attacks by others, we may feel justified in exacting revenge, or building up walls—and nuclear arsenals—to keep the bad guys out. It may be human nature, as many would say, to come out fighting when our worldview is threatened, but an "eye for an eye" is not the only approach to the perils of life.

USING OUR GIFTS TO UNCOVER OUR WEAKNESSES

People like Gandhi, Martin Luther King, and the Dalai Lama have pointed a different way toward a just, peaceful, and compassionate response to the evils—really displaced fears—we see all around us. By stepping back, looking within, and recognizing that there is a murderer hiding out in all of us—and accepting this dark truth about humanity—we may come to see the "other" with different eyes, with compassion, even nonviolence. The work of reconciliation starts within each of us. We create the enemy. And the enemy, as Jung long ago tried to get us to see, ultimately lies within. This is why reconciliation, on a community, national, or global level, is so difficult to achieve. It is also why I have saved the tool of reconciliation—and your own confrontation with the shadow—for last in the sequence of tools.

If you're with me so far, you may be wondering how to get started down this royal road to the unconscious: How do we begin to confront the shadow? It may strike you as odd, or ironic, but a good place to meet the shadow is in the light! Think for a moment about the yin/yang symbol that we all recognize from the Eastern traditions of Buddhism or the martial arts. In this ancient symbol of wholeness, the dark side of our nature enfolds naturally into and out of an equal amount of light. Without light, there is no shadow.

We can actually begin to welcome the shadow aspects of our nature by becoming aware of our gifts, or put another way, the access route to our liabilities may be found in our strengths. Take a few moments to reflect on your best attributes: What are you really good at? What do you take pride in doing well? If you have a difficult time coming up with anything—or get caught up in self-deprecation (there's the shadow of self-criticism alive and well, no?)—you might ask a significant friend or partner to casually rattle off what they love and admire about you. Don't be shy. Getting in touch with your gifts is a key to unlocking the door of your fears. Once you have identified three or four of your best traits, ask yourself this rather jarring question: How can these very same attributes be my biggest liabilities? Or put another way: How can my strengths actually show up as weaknesses?

Let me share with you a quick example of how this process of self-reflection can give us access to the shadow, shocking though it may be. My friend Pam and I once had a casual conversation about the idea that we all have a shadow; that we all have parts of ourselves that we have relegated to the dark corners of our psyche we would rather not see. I asked Pam what she thought her shadow contained. She became a bit flustered and said something to this effect: "As a spiritual person, I really try to be compassionate and thoughtful and considerate with myself and others. I'm not sure that I actually have a shadow." Really? Of course, she was being honest. The shadow is hidden from view for most of us—and for people like Pam, who really are generally compassionate and loving souls, the dark side is easy to dismiss, or deny. Yet, once we dug a little deeper into her resistance to the idea that she might have a shadow, she owned up: She sometimes has little patience for people who are not spiritual, religious zealots, or people who have a fundamentalist view of right and wrong. "Where is their compassion for others?" she found herself asking.

"And where is your compassion for them?" I found myself thinking out loud. Of course, this revelation became a "moment of truth" for Pam, having to see that her own attachment to a "spiritual" way of life could actually predispose her to judge others, be impatient, and even at times project a dismissive tone onto those not like her.

Even spirituality can become a source of judgment, which is why it is often a loaded term in conversation—and a starting point for conflict. I've even caught myself at times, in dialogue with my left-leaning pals, decrying the level of "unconsciousness" in our culture, in the media, in the political sphere. But does that make me "conscious"? What does it mean to be conscious, or spiritual, anyway? All of these labels, to which our egos get attached, may on the one hand represent a shift toward a more developed, or awakened state of being, but they can also be used to place us above others, to separate us from the fray, as it were, of those lowly and unenlightened brothers and sisters in our midst. Yet, when Pam or I, or anyone else for that matter, takes up the banner of being enlightened, or more spiritually aware than someone else, the shadow quickly crosses over into the light: The very thing that marks our gift becomes our burden. And this burden is born of fear.

○　○　○

Now comes the tricky part. Recognizing that we all have a shadow, and that our greatest strengths may become our greatest liabilities, especially when the gift is threatened or attacked as unworthy, does not give us permission to judge ourselves as "bad." The opportunity here is to circle back around to the core premise of this book: to become more aware of our fears and accept them as the keys to transforming our deepest dread into delight.

At its deepest level, reconciliation in this context is a tool for self-forgiveness, for acknowledging that we are human and therefore imperfect and flawed. It is important that we honor and integrate—reconcile—those dark aspects of ourselves and embrace ourselves as fully human. The recommended practice in this arena of reconciliation focuses on self-acceptance, moving us from denial to embracing all aspects of our humanity. Only by bringing these aspects of ourselves into conscious awareness, acknowledging and reconciling with them, can we be free of their potential to emerge when we least expect it, causing harm to others, but most important, to ourselves.

Life-Shifting Action Step: Facing the Inner Demon

This exercise is designed to help you access denied or hidden fears—very likely connected to the past—that may be blocking your emotional system. By taking time out to sit quietly and feeling into the deeper truth that the "monster" lies within, we can shift gears—even in moments when we feel the energy of anger—and begin to withdraw our projections, coming to own, accept, and have compassion for the dark side of our nature.

This practice requires you to have a pen and journal or blank piece of paper and set aside ten to fifteen minutes to sit quietly to go within. Find a comfortable sitting position and relax. Ground yourself with good back support and plant your feet firmly on the floor. Close your eyes and allow your focus to shift to your breathing. Once you settled in and feel yourself becoming present and calm, allow the following image to begin to form in your mind: You are in a wide, green open pasture. The sun is warm and you are walking calmly through the natural scene. There is a path laid out before you through the glade. Take your time to visualize yourself walking through this field, strolling happily along the path. As you walk through the grass along the path, notice a building emerging at one end of the field.

Walk calmly down to the path and into the front door of this building. It may appear to you as a house in the suburbs or a castle or a barn. Just let the images come. As you enter the building, notice that it is extremely dark inside. Notice the lack of light and feel yourself entering into the darkness. Breathe deeply and allow yourself to walk into the building, feeling whatever comes up as you enter the darkness. Ahead of you is a door. Walk to the door, open it, and see a flight of stairs going down into the basement. Breathing and feeling whatever comes up, open the door and walk gently and carefully down the stairs. At the bottom of the stairs you find yourself in total darkness, except for the glow of a small candle lit to one side.

Before you, in the dim glow of candlelight, is a figure enshrouded in a black cape. Allow yourself to feel whatever emotions emerge as you move closer to this dark figure. Allow your vision to evolve and evoke whatever wants to appear before you. Allow the face of this dark figure to appear to you. Allow the image to morph into whatever comes—a monster's face, someone you recognize, or even just a dark swirl of energy. Allow yourself to feel the emotions that this dark image brings up in you. Breathe deeply and just feel the feelings—of fear, recognition, sadness—whatever comes.

Take a few minutes to just be with this image; ask it if it has a message for you. Allow yourself to silently speak your feelings to the image and see what occurs. After being in the presence of this dark figure for a few moments, visualize yourself backing away from the image and walking away and up the staircase that you came down. Go back through the dark house and out the door, into the light.

Find yourself back in the sunlight, in the field, surrounded by flowers and grass and blue sky. Allow yourself to feel the energy shift from the darkness to the light. Feel the warm glow of the sun beaming down on your skin. Breathe deeply a few times, and when you are ready, gently open your eyes.

Pick up your pen and journal and begin to draw the image that came to you in the basement of the house. Whatever comes—a face, a monster, a swirl of dark clouds—just allow it to flow out of your pen and on to the paper. This is not the time for being artistic, just allow the image, words, or symbols to flow freely onto the page.

When you have drawn your image, allow yourself to sit back and just reflect for a few moments on the following questions: What does this image evoke in you? How did it feel in your body to "be with" this image? What part of yourself is reflected in this image? Does this image make you think of someone that you know or someone that you have known during your life? What is it about that person or about yourself that is being symbolized by this image? What message about your fear, your anger, your shadow, might it be offering you?

Life-Shifting Action Step:
Collaging Dread/Delight

This exercise is ideal for those of us who find it difficult to sit quietly or to visualize imagery. It provides you with an opportunity to access both your inner critic—and shadow material—and to evoke the VOR (voice of reverence) that I spoke about in chapter six of part one. For this practice you will need four items: a journal (or two blank pages from an 8½ x 11-inch notepad), a stack of old magazines, a pair of scissors, and some glue or tape. Write in big letters at the top of the left page in your journal "DREAD." On the opposite page, write "DELIGHT" at the top. Go through your magazine stack and cut out images and words that resonate for you the two opposing aspects of this emotional/mental experience. As you page through the magazines, ask yourself: Which words/images make me feel fear/dread in my body? Which images bring up feelings of joy, calm, serenity, and peace? Make two stacks of cutouts from the magazines and then begin to create a collage on the pages. Take your time with the exercise and have fun. Allow yourself to play with words, images, and symbols as they resonate with your own feelings of fear and joy, dread and delight. Once you have completed an arrangement of the cutouts on the pages, glue or tape them. Creating a collage is a fun and powerful form of active imagination—you can do this alone, with a partner, or with your children.

When you have completed the creation of your collage, look at the juxtaposition of the two sides of the emotional coin and reflect and journal on these questions:

- How does it feel to see the images/words about fear/dread and joy/delight side by side?

- What was it about these particular images/words that drew you to cut them out?
- Do you recognize how you create the dark and light images and feelings within yourself?
- Can you feel how they are a reflection of your inner world—both dark and light?

Feel how you respond to the two different energy flows and how easily you can move from one side to the other. Allow yourself to meditate on the images and play with the energy of "shifting" from dread to delight within your own energy system.

You may want to post these pages on your wall—or have them readily accessible to you whenever you are feeling stuck, or fearful. They symbolize the power of self-acceptance: These dark and light energies are both in you, at all times and in all places. Accepting this deep truth about your humanity, and recognizing your freedom to choose to shift your attention from one side to the other and back again, will help you "lighten up" and gain some distance from the overwhelm of the darker emotions—all fear-based—when they show up.

PART III:
LIFE-SHIFTING 103

The Process:
A Journey through Change

INTRODUCTION

"I have accepted fear as a part of life—specifically the fear of change. . . . I have gone ahead despite the pounding in the heart that says: turn back."

—ERICA JONG

Let's look at where we've been together thus far, and set the stage for the next part of our journey—through the full cycle of self-renewal. If you've approached this book with an all-American, task-master mentality (we all know the drill: "Step one, step two, step three. Stay in line. Don't color outside the lines"), then you've been good students and have diligently read and digested parts one and two.

Perhaps you have gleaned a few nuggets of gold from part one:

- *Our solid, authentic, or real self is anything but;*

- *The story of our identity is constantly being written and rewritten throughout our lives;*

- *The nature of life is constant change;*

- *Moving through change with agility and ease requires more than just positive affirmations or "changing your thinking"; it requires the full engagement of our mental, emotional, and physical vitality;*

- *The doorway to life shifts, true acts of transformation and renewal, is entered through a two-step dance of attention and intention;*

- *Much of the time our symptoms of malaise—worry, anxiety, anger, depression—are not diseases in themselves, but signals that change is in the works;*

- *Striving for eternal bliss—happiness—in the form of comfort, structure, and stuff, is often misguided and fear-based;*

- *The soul, if we deign to hear its call, longs for something more than a big house and an SUV; it longs for connection, creative expression, depth, and meaning;*

And most important, the conflict between our soul's deep desire for us to grow and change and our fierce protector of the status quo—the dictator par excellence, the ego—is fraught with fear. Fear is, in essence, the roar of our protective life force when the vehicle of self gets stuck. If you've ever driven a stick-shift car and accidentally pushed the gear shift into neutral and pressed the accelerator, then you know of what I speak. The engine literally howls at you: "Varoom! Get me in gear, you idiot!"

And so, we left off part one with an admonition to never drive alone, to be sure you have wise and supportive companions along for the ride. You've also been handed the key that ignites success: Be gentle with yourself. We all get stuck in neutral at times; we all have a loud, self-critical VOJ ready to dress us down when we are frozen in fear. We need to approach the endless twists and turns of life change—and the call of our soul to dissolve the hardy and hardened boxes in which we construct our lives—with reverence: "Go gently, my dear ones, into that dark night."

In part two, we jumped into the dark depths of fear together. I hope by now you've tried out a few of the tools in the tool set, discovering along the way something new about your particular dynamic in navigating fear. Maybe you think you are a cerebral type, yet while meditating immersed in a deep pool of warm, enveloping water, you found yourself having a good cry. Or perhaps you've always been a "doer," one of those high-energy worker bees who keep the engine of production humming in your business, your family, or your community. Suddenly, after dismissing the very thought of sitting still and just watching yourself breathe for five minutes, you sat down, took a deep breath, and melted into the floor—hearing your heartbeat, your back pain, and your stiff neck calling out to you: "Slow down, give us a break. You can relax. There is time. In fact, there is *nothing* but time. Listen to us. We're here *for* you."

Or perhaps you've gotten all the way through part one and most of part two of this book and have been slyly thinking/feeling a bit smug and self-confident, wondering when I would get to the punch line. You are a self-help book reader par excellence, a student of your feelings, awake to your fears, one of the fortunate: You recognize your soul's call loud and clear when it pounds its way through your chest. But do you listen? Perhaps you've read a surfeit of self-help books and think you know the "secret" or at the very least you've had a bout with therapy, have analyzed how your parents screwed you up, and have enough fear awareness to recognize when it's time to "let go."

And yet, will you tremble, just a tad, when I ask: Are you done? Is it enough to read the literature and hire a coach, cry a good cry, and just get on with it? I don't think so. No matter how in touch you may be with your feelings, your physical energy, your thoughts, fantasies, and soulful yearnings, you bought this book for a reason. Something remains hidden. Someone is hiding. Your deepest fear may be thus: that you read all the right books, participate in personal growth workshops, backpack through Africa, and meditate in an ashram, and still, and still, and still . . . the heart longs for more. The voice within calls you deeper . . . but to where?

Perhaps you'll go back, own up that you didn't do any of the practices in part two because, as a well-read, well-studied, feeler type, you know the drill. I know the type and can call your bluff for one reason, and one reason only: I am you. So do me a favor, and pick up a pen and chicken-scratch some thoughts with your nondominant hand, reflecting first on a rather benign question like, "Who am I?" You may be surprised to discover who, in you, is really watching, witnessing, waiting to be born anew.

I remember the first time I tried writing with my nondominant hand. It was painfully frustrating; it slowed my chattering mind down to a snail's crawl; it was a jarringly knife-like killjoy to my overeducated ego. In a word, it was humbling. But it was something else as well: profound. The three words that I wrangled out of my right hand (I'm a leftie) were barely legible. These three words were scrawled so large across the page that it looked like a billboard drawn by a monkey, and so it was. The question I had asked was this: "What am I supposed to do with my life?" The answer I received was this: "*You are enough.*" Well, that stopped me dead in my tracks.

So, I hope by now, even if you skipped around (which I am all in favor of) and read, dabbled, and experimented with your thoughts, feelings, and physical reactions to the ideas, practices, and themes I've explored in parts one and two, that somewhere along the route, you've heard a voice bubble up from within that you maybe didn't recognize; one that offers you a bit of counsel, support, and wisdom, reminding you that you are on track, in the groove, on the move—*shifting*, literally, before your very eyes. This voice, when it pokes through—in a meditation, visualization, in the midst of a story, or on the other side of a beaten-to-a-pulp pillow—is your guide, your soul mate, your lover for life. Welcome her into your world. She's there for a reason: to get you up out of that chair, out of that office, out of that story that binds you like glue to a life that may appear "happy" yet feels unfinished, incomplete.

THE HEALING WISDOM OF AFRICA—
FROM GRIEF TO PLAY

I feel blessed to have had the opportunity to meet and work with Malidoma Somé. As some of you may know, Malidoma is an African shaman, whose mission is to heal the isolated, lost souls of the Western world: i.e., *us*. Born in Burkina Faso and raised by his clan to be a teacher and healer, Malidoma was sent to France and then to the United States (he has innumerable PhDs) to be an emissary for his people's offering to the world: the gift of community. The elders of his tribe sense that something is amiss in the world; that as the Western ways of individualism and capitalism encroach on their communitarian, earth-centered way of life, the gulf between the planet and we who rely on it for our very existence is widening. A bridge toward healing, wholeness, and remembrance is clearly needed. Malidoma has been sent to the West to build it.

Malidoma has written many books about the shamanism of Africa, and along with his former wife, Sobonfu, he leads rituals, shares stories, and passes on the teachings of his tribe all across America and Western Europe. Synchronicity brought me—and fifteen or so lucky pals—to Lake Tahoe for an encounter with Malidoma that changed our lives, forever.

While traveling with a troupe of spiritual seekers on what can best be described as an "intentional vacation" (i.e., a bunch of us gathered from all parts of the United States with the idea of resting, relaxing, and exploring the idea of "community"), one of my close friends, who had worked with Malidoma in a yearlong shamanic training program, noted that he lived only a few miles from where we were staying. As luck would have it, Malidoma was home that week, and very generously offered to come up to the lake and spend a day, offering us a real-life experience of African ritual. For me, and most of the other gatherers, many of whom are steeped in the mindfulness practices of Buddhism and other teachings from the East, the opportunity to be in the presence of a spiritual teacher from Africa was exciting and a bit intimidating.

After arriving late the following evening and politely gorging himself on two huge steaks and massive amounts of red wine (after those of us who, quite wrongly, prophesized about what an African shaman would eat and had prepared a huge green salad, tofu, and nuts. Not!), Malidoma told the troupe to gather at dawn the next morning in the living room of one of our rented homes, by the side of the lake, and to "be prepared to do ritual." I'm sure that many of us did not sleep much that night, giddy with anticipation that we were soon to have "ritual" done to us. Nevertheless, I remember the sun just poking up across the horizon of the spectacular blue lake, when I yanked myself awake and slogged, sans caffeine, my way downstairs to find my compadres already huddled together in clumps on the array of sofas, chairs, and ottomans that would compose our "ritual space."

Soon enough, Malidoma and his lovely female assistant arrived. He sat silently in a distant corner of the room, not speaking at first, just sitting with eyes closed. I assumed he was calling forth the earth spirits, but more than likely he was just getting comfortable, grounded, and centered for what was to come. After a few minutes of silence, during which I became wide awake, Malidoma brought out a drum and gently began to beat it. The sound was soothing, rhythmic, and haunting. I found myself falling into a light trance, not quite dozing off, just breathing and connecting with the energy of humanity that surrounded me, the view of the lake, and the gentle *thrum, thrum, thrum* of Malidoma's drum.

After what seemed like a long period of time, he stopped. Slowly, haltingly, he started telling a story. I don't remember the details, but the gist of the tale was about a long-lost tribe of people whose villages had been destroyed by a devastating series of hurricanes, fires, and earthquakes. They found themselves homeless, wandering in an arid, desert landscape—bereft and alone. They were beside themselves with fear and worry, feeling as though the world was about to end, for in fact, theirs had. I don't remember any more of the story, for at a certain point, as Malidoma spoke softly, deeply, and with fervent if elusive meaning, one of the women in our little group started to cry.

Patricia is a big woman, a boisterous soul. Normally full of joie de vivre, she is the kind of person who is always the first on the dance floor. Yet, here on a sunlit morning at the edge of Lake Tahoe, while cuddled up together waiting patiently to have our "ritual" done to us—she sobbed. Soon, she wailed. It was eerie, almost creepy at first. Something had touched her deeply in Malidoma's story and the tears just came. Then, lo and behold, I kid you not, one after another the rest of the troupe started crying. A dark, deep cloud of sadness seemed to enshroud the room.

Malidoma stopped talking and sat in silence. He could no longer be heard above the din of sobs, wails, and sniffles. Cerebral to a fault, I was shocked at first by the sight of so many of my friends in tears. But it didn't take long before I too was pulled into the swirl of what can only be called thus: existential grief. At the sight of so many tear-streaked faces, I remember reaching out to hug a dear friend and, holding him tight, feeling him sobbing into my shoulder, my chest heaved. It seemed like a flood was occurring. Years and years of pent-up sadness, loneliness, separation, and fear—all burst forth in one gigantic tsunami of despair.

Hours or maybe minutes later, when the wailing had started to subside, Malidoma spoke. His statements were simple and direct, and went something like this: "My first engagement with groups of Americans always involves a grief ritual. This is what we've done. You Americans have lost touch with your ability to grieve, to feel the very real loss of connection between your-selves and the world. Everything dies, and you are all dying as well. But you deny it. You avoid, deflect, and numb out to the reality that life is a circle of beginnings, middles, and ends. Watching television, surfing the Internet, working like maniacs to pay the bills, you have lost touch with life. My people come together and grieve, really grieve the end of every season, the end of every year, the end of every life. It is the starting point for healing, the starting point for rebirth, and the starting point for saving this planet."

I was profoundly moved by the ritual (although it still felt like he had not done anything *to* us) and deeply touched by his words. And as I sit here today, reflecting on my support of clients and executives in the midst of their own life shifts, Malidoma's message still speaks loud and clear: The ultimate signpost of "downshifting" is grief. We can spend hours dissecting the symp-toms of fear—anxiety, depression, anger, stress—but when a true shift is in the works, and we are moving down the path from rupture to release to retreat—the downshifting half of the cycle—it is always deep sadness that replaces our fear. In fact, for some, it may be grief itself that we most fear. But it is in there—and it must be honored.

Letting go of an identity, whether it be as simple as "I'm no longer an autoworker" or as profound as "my time as a mom is done"—*the shift*, the true transformational shift that leads to renewal, requires some part of us to die. So here is the bad news: If you have reached this far in reading this book and have yet to feel, and I mean really feel, a deep sadness for the way your life is shifting, transforming, and yes, dying, right before your eyes, you've got work to do. As we move through the final section of this book together, and I share the deeply transformative stories of clients who have truly let identities die so that amazingly new ways of being can emerge, watch for the sign called *grief*. Allow it to show up wherever and whenever it will. Don't be frightened by it, and if you are, that's OK, too.

If your heart feels heavy, your breath starts to quicken, and you feel yourself holding back tears, let it be. Go back to the tool set and practice refocusing. Allow yourself to feel whatever you feel and just tend to the sensations gently. Reframe whatever feels bad as a gift and accept its arrival. Downshifting—and grieving—is a normal, natural, and wonderful moment in the journey. Allow yourself to have it. Give your ego a hug, set it aside, and allow the feelings, thoughts, and sensations to flow. Your soul will know what to do. I promise.

My opportunity to be with Malidoma Somé on that beautiful day was a blessing of gigantic proportion, for unlike any psychological theory I might have learned in graduate school about how human beings learn to adapt and grow, the truth of the matter is simple: All change involves loss. And loss brings with it sorrow, as empty space takes up where some part of who we know ourselves to be dissolves, takes its leave from us, moves on. We need to learn not to fear grief, but to welcome it, to acknowledge its necessity—not as a concept—but as a very real part of every life shift.

Once the grief ritual was over, and the tears wiped away, Malidoma led us out into the sunlight, onto the lawn of the suburban lakeside dwelling that had been our temple of despair. He directed us to gather bundles of stones, leaves, and grass—which would symbolize the burdens we had just literally released with our tears. We completed the grief ritual in the blazing sunlight, by forming a line in front of a makeshift altar compiled of smooth, round rocks pulled from the lake. One by one, we marched forth, and bowing in gratitude to the divine spirits who had reached into our hearts and pulled out our sorrows, we buried our burdens in the brown, rich earth.

As we each let go of our symbolic packet of woes, the energy shifted again, the grass positively glowed with vibrancy, the lake shimmered in the sunlight, our bodies revived with the energy of life. Soon, after a short, restful nap in the sun, Malidoma himself was up on his feet, stretching, disrobing, and suddenly, he dove into the lake. The signal was clear: It was time to play. For me, the sight of half-naked bodies flinging themselves in the lake brought on my second dose of the terrors that day. After dancing with my fear of looking silly if I let myself cry (absurd, considering that everyone was crying!), I clearly remember my first reaction to the idea of skinny-dipping in the icy pond:

"Whoa! Wait a minute here. You want me to strip down in broad daylight and jump into a liquid glacier? Yeah, right. OK. Take a breath. There's Pat, who was just a few hours ago wailing about the end of the world, now jumping up and down in her bra and panties, breasts and tummy jiggling and jumping, dancing—playing!—in the nectar of the gods. Who am I to hold out on the game of life that we had all signed up for?" So there you have it: fears dismissed. Dropping drawers with the rest of them, I held my nose, closed my eyes, and took the plunge. It was glorious. This time I know it lasted for hours: the water, the sun, the playmates—and the play. It was the perfect antidote to the morning's funereal rite; a baptism that would put the Vatican to shame.

Later, Malidoma spoke to the group once again, this time as we all baked in the sun spread out on our "Tahoe is for lovers" towels, giddy with joy. His words, as best as I can recall, were about the other side of the tragic American narrative that needs to shift: "As Americans you think you are a happy people. But you have forgotten how to be happy. You buy lots of toys—cars, gadgets, and boats. You visit artificially created play lands like Disney World, and you wander the globe taking pictures of life lived elsewhere. But what do you do in your own backyards? Grill burgers and scarf down potato salad? Buy a six-pack and watch sports on television? If you're lucky to have kids, the younger the better, let them teach you, once again, how to play. Playing is simple and it requires no toys. Nature is the ultimate playground, as the child in all of us knows. So always remember: Grieve the sad truth that your life is dying and then play full-out in the bountiful, beautiful splendors of nature. If you learn to play on Mother Earth, and grieve her—and your own—passing, maybe, just maybe you will finally come to treat her with respect. In return, she will provide you with the ultimate gift of reciprocity: You will be reborn."

With these words, Malidoma brought our ritual day of sorrow, and joy, to a close. In just one day, he had led our group through an entire cycle of self-renewal, leaving each of us reinvigorated, revitalized, down- and upshifted to the max, born anew. He had demonstrated, in real time, something I've experienced over and over again with hundreds of clients: True transformation does not have to take years or months; it can happen in hours, even minutes. The arrival of symptoms such as anxiety, anger, and most often depression may signal that change is in the works. But in order to not get lost in translation, you need to give yourself permission to feel the deep, unavoidable sadness that is the hallmark of every ending. You must open up your mind, heart, and body, face your deep fear of change, and walk down the path toward the unfathomable depths of your grief. But there is also good news: The aftermath of grief, the upshift period that we will soon explore—the revival, rehearsal, and realization stages of your journey—inevitably arrives, expands, and takes flight on the wings of play.

I apologize if this story has frightened you into thinking that you will need to bawl your eyes out in sadness or freeze your butt off in a frozen lake in order to remake your life anew. Not every road trip through self-renewal need be so dramatic or shocking to the system. On the other hand, I need to be honest with you. Too many self-help books these days, especially those steeped in the trendy happiness, now and forever, lexicon that is all the rage, truly miss the mark. Surely it is important to focus on the positive, to get in touch daily with gratitude and nourish our systems—physical, emotional, and spiritual—with healthy ingredients. But the wisdom of Malidoma and the message of his ancient people cannot be denied: Life involves death. Endings, of all stripes and colors—death of a pet, loss of a loved one, the dissolution of an identity—are a natural part of the mystery of living, as is rebirth.

So as you venture forth with me on the journey through the six stages of self-renewal, be on the lookout for the hallmarks of transformation: *grief* and *play*. Be awake to the downshifting part of the cycle and watchful for thoughts of loss, feelings of sadness, and symptoms of distress that may be grabbing the limelight but covering over both. This is just fear.

I once had a client who spent many months in a lethargic, depressive state, able only robotically to go through the motions of work, feeding and tending to her kids, avoiding her friends. At one point, I remember asking her if she ever allowed herself to just feel the great sadness that was writ large across her furrowed brow, to allow herself to cry. I hate to say it, but I think her response, heartfelt yet fearful to the core, might reverberate just now through millions of American households, caught up as we are in the throes of an economic recession (collective downshifting on a massive scale), whose medicine chests are chock-full of antidepressants and other anti-grieving meds: "If I let myself cry, I just might never stop." But you will. We always do. Just as the sun always rises and the rain always ends. Cliché as it sounds, it is true.

And so it goes in our just-get-a-job-and-get-on-with-it American drama. But what about the American dream? We fear grief like the plague. Yet it is the plague of fear—that we desperately need some downtime; that we might not look upbeat for that job interview; that we might disappear into the quicksand of sadness—that keeps us stuck, that has put the fabled dream of America's renewed promise on hold. Likewise, we may go on vacation (i.e., *vacating* our work-obsessed lives for a few days), BlackBerry and laptop in hand, but do we truly allow ourselves to unwind, to frolic, to get down, dirty, naked, and play? Rare indeed. Yet, grieving and playing, as we will see, are the two crucial turning points on the road to real self-renewal, for each of us—and the world.

As we now enter part three of this book and gear up to venture with a few companions across the rough-and-tumble terrain of a complete cycle of self-renewal, be watchful, awake, and listening, not just for the story of fear that will surely arise and make itself heard, but for transitional moments when sadness pulls on your physical, emotional, and mental space and threatens to "take you down." Welcome it. Don't push it away. Get support. Ask for help and allow the feelings to come. On the other side of the hill, the silver lining awaits—a story of possibility, creativity, and love (for self and others). The song of your soul is just *dying* to get downloaded onto your iPhone: It wants to play!

PREPARING TO EMBARK

In this section of the book, I want to deliberately walk—or better, drive—you through the full cycle of change that I outlined in chapter five of part one. Each chapter in this section describes what I have found to be the key characteristics of each stage in the cycle, including the mental, emotional, and physical shifts that are likely to occur, and most important, the particular *dread* that is likely to accompany you at each stage of the journey.

If you complete the diagnostic exercise at the end of this chapter, you will have a fairly strong sense of what stage of the cycle you are in, depending upon which domain—career, relationship, family, community, self—you may have chosen to examine. With this in mind, if you find that you are *not* in the rupture stage (stage one) of the cycle, you may feel a pull to skip ahead and plunge into the chapter that resonates with where you are in your own life. That's OK. The good news is that you will not be going on this pilgrimage alone. Since some of you may skip ahead, I want to take a brief moment here to introduce you to your three willing and exemplary traveling companions—a doer, a feeler, and a thinker. Originally, they were clients of mine. Today they are, all three, dear friends. I have changed a few of the details to protect their privacy but what matters is this: They are real people; people who have completely reinvented their story of themselves; people who have faced their fears, engaged with their egos, grieved the loss of ways of being that no longer served, and heeded the call to play, listening in for the childlike stirrings of soul.

One of them is primarily a somatic type, although he would never have guessed this when we first met. In our work together, he discovered how to listen, learn, and break through his self-imposed box of identity through his physicality. By tuning in to his body, and listening in for its wisdom, he ultimately heard the call of the awkward sprite of youth that was pushing to break out of his encrusted fifty-year-old story.

Our second passenger on the good ship *Life-Shifting* has probably never sat down long enough in front of a television to watch a soap opera, but when you meet her you'll think: dramatic. As a consummate feeler, she brings tears, laughter, a biting wit, and fierce passion to everything she does. The trouble is she does too much. With a to-do list that might as well include saving the world and everyone in it, she came to me overwhelmed with the burden of taking care of everyone in her large circle of coworkers, a househusband, three young children, and a surfeit of friends. There was only one problem with her well-intentioned to-do list: She herself wasn't on it. Her ego, as we'll see, was a trickster of the highest magnitude, for she knew how to access tears, how to cry and grieve for the sorrows of the world, just not for herself.

Our third companion on the trip is a type with which many of us are quite familiar: a high-achieving, goal-oriented thinker par excellence. Arriving on my doorstep with an Ivy League MBA, a long résumé of achievements, and "I've got it handled" stamped on her forehead, she was wilting under the weight of her own success. Today, when we reconnect, I don't even recognize her. She appears twenty years younger, is twenty pounds lighter, and most important, dances with life—bedecked in pink and purple beads and bangles—in a way that even she would have thought impossible just a few years ago.

It is my hope that as we travel together through the six stages of transformation with these three amazing individuals and learn about their trials, tribulations, and triumphs along the way that you'll recognize yourself in one, two, or maybe all three. So pack your bags, bring plenty of Kleenex, and let's go!

PART III:
LIFE-SHIFTING SELF-RENEWAL
DIAGNOSTIC #2

INSTRUCTIONS FOR TAKING
THE DIAGNOSTIC EXAM

Identify an area of your life in which you may be in the throes of change—and fear. The following list of life domains may help you determine the frame of reference you want to examine: work/career, family/relationships, community/social life, or simply self/life. For one domain at a time, reflect on the following questions and rate them on the scale as follows:
Always/Regularly: 10, Often: 7, Occasionally: 3, Rarely: 0

Scoring the Exam

If your total for any one set of questions is between 70 and 100, this is likely the stage in which you may be currently experiencing a life shift. If your score for one or more stages is between 30 and 70, you may be in transition between two stages. If your score for a stage is below 30, you are not currently in this stage. Take this diagnostic as often as you like, using different or the same domains depending upon your life context. You may be in different stages at the same time for different domains of your life. This is OK, even normal.

I. Stage One: The Rupture

How often do you:

- *Feel bored, listless, or lethargic?*_____

- *Feel restless, anxious, or uncomfortable in your own skin?*_____

- *Feel lonely or disengaged even when you're with other people?*_____

- *Experience unexplainable physical pains, such as headaches, backaches, or nausea?*_____

- *Feel tired, exhausted, or worn-out?* _____

- *Feel frustrated or overwhelmed by life?*_____

- *Feel yourself losing interest in what you are doing?*____

- *Have trouble sleeping—either falling asleep, staying asleep, or sleeping too much?*_____

- *Find yourself daydreaming or fantasizing about being somewhere else?*____

- *Experience difficulty with focusing or paying attention?*____

Total for Stage One: _____

II. Stage Two: The Release
How often do you:
- *Feel like something in your life or sense of self is shifting, outdated, or obsolete?*_____

- *Feel distracted, unable to focus, or out of control?*

- *Feel regretful?*_____

- *Feel like something or someone is missing?*_____

- *Have feelings of sadness?*_____

- *Want to cry?*_____

- *Feel yourself letting go of something or someone?*_____

- *Feel a sense of loss?* _____

- *Feel like something in your life is completing or finished, over?*_____

- *Feel a desire to let go of something/someone?*____

Total for Stage Two: _____

III. Stage Three: The Retreat
How often do you:
- *Feel a sense of emptiness?*_____

- *Feel confusion or lack of direction?*_____

- *Feel like you do not know who you are—lacking a sense of self?*_____

- *Feel a yearning to just stop and rest?* _____

- *Feel tired of feeling sad?*_____

- *Feel calm and quiet?*_____

- *Yearn for solitude and/or time alone?*_____

- *Long to be in nature?*_____

- *Feel a desire to pull away from the world, from others, from work?*_____

- *Feel contemplative and/or reflective?*____

Total for Stage Three: _____

IV.   Stage Four: The Revival
How often do you:

- *Feel like you're waking up from a long sleep?*_____

- *Feel moments of excitement and anticipation?*_____

- *Feel awkward, vulnerable, and/or self-conscious?*_____

- *Feel a renewed sense of possibility?*_____

- *Feel like you are being judged?*_____

- *Feel raw and unskillful?*_____

- *Feel a renewed energy for work or relationships?*_____

- *Feel creative and generative?*_____

- *Feel inspired by those around you?*_____

- *Feel like trying something new?* _____

Total for Stage Four: _____

V.   Stage Five: The Rehearsal
How often do you:

- *Feel a renewed commitment to something/someone?*_____

- *Feel frustrated with your lack of skill?*_____

- *Feel self-critical about your inability to "get it right"?*_____

- *Feel motivated to practice something over and over?*_____

- *Feel like what you are working on is worth it?*_____

- *Feel like you might fail?*_____

- *Feel a sense of meaning in your life?*_____

- *Feel excited by all you have to do?*_____

- *Feel impatient with your progress?*_____

- *Feel a nagging sense of not being good enough?*___

Total for Stage Five: _____

VI.   Stage Six: The Realization

How often do you:

- *Feel a sense of "having arrived"?*_____

- *Feel a desire to celebrate?*_____

- *Feel a sense of gratitude and peace?*_____

- *Feel a strong sense of self?*_____

- *Feel like giving to others?*_____

- *Feel relaxed and grounded?*_____

- *Feel wary of being "too happy"?*_____

- *Feel undeserving of your success?*_____

- *Feel anxious about meeting the expectations of others?*_____

- *Feel uncomfortable with your achievements?*_____

Total for Stage Six:_____

FINAL THOUGHTS ON THE DIAGNOSTIC

As you read through part three, and take time to reflect on the questions and suggestions at the end of each chapter, notice what elements of each stage resonate for you. Be gentle with yourself as you shift from one stage to another, or change focus from one life domain to another. Take time to go back and work with the action steps in part two that you found most helpful, especially if you find yourself feeling stuck, moving backward and forward along the path, or spending too long in any one stage.

Remember: This is just fear. Recognize when it arrives (and it will), accept and give it space. Take time to refocus, reframe, and realign as needed. Practice reconciliation—self-acceptance—all along the road, and soon enough you will notice yourself in transition, moving forward, on to the next stage.

Keep in mind: The path is a circle; there is no final destination or ultimate stopping point for any of life's domains. You are never finished. So when you feel like you've been through an entire cycle, making each shift along the way, accept the inevitable: Soon enough you will find yourself back at the beginning. Welcome back! This is just nature's way.

{ Chapter One }

THE RUPTURE:
LOST IN A DARK WOOD

"The only difference between a rut and a grave is their dimensions."
—ELLEN GLASGOW

No matter how many ruptures I support my clients through, or how many upheavals, bad breaks, and bouts of illness I experience myself, the rupture stage remains a mystery. Sometimes it arrives in the form of internal upset, when the song of our soul decides that it has waited long enough to be heard and it simply pops through our overinflated sense of self. Sometimes, though, the universe, seemingly out of left field, hands us the grenade and yanks off the safety latch, and just as we run for cover, we get taken down—and lose our job. Other times, the rupture is seemingly gentle, arriving through the mouth of a dear friend over an innocuous lunch date. Yet, however it shows up, the rupture stage is more often than not an unwelcome visitor, as we suddenly find ourselves standing at a fork in a road we didn't even know we were on.

With the onset of change, in the form of a rupture, rut, or upheaval, there are only two things I know for sure: that pain, in all its forms, is most often a cover-up for fear, and that somewhere, somehow, someplace, there is a *gift in the shift*. Something blessed, meaningful, and profound is pushing through the walls of our heavily fortified ego, and as I have said many times before in this book, our challenge, and choice, is to learn to dance with our fear—and change.

HAL: THE SUFFOCATING SIDEKICK

"Buried alive," he mumbled softly. "That's how it feels to me. Like I'm suffocating, the walls are moving in on me, the air gets stifling hot. I feel like I am going to pass out. I . . . um, don't know how else to describe it. It feels like I am being buried alive." I will always remember the first time I met Hal. Not because he is a particularly unusual guy. He's an average Joe in many ways: a good-looking, Irish, corporate CPA, otherwise known to the world as simply "an accountant." No, it was not Hal's personal demeanor, credentials, or résumé that was remarkable but how his soul, in its endeavor to be heard, broke through the walled-off fortress of his comfortable life.

I have experienced stories from clients before about feeling "suffocated" and "buried alive." These are not uncommon symptoms of anxiety for many people and are fairly common in men: Your breathing becomes shallow and labored, your palms sweat, and your chest feels like a weight has been dropped on it. These, unfortunately, are also primary symptoms of a heart attack—anxiety writ large—so they are best not ignored. What was unusual about Hal's symptoms was where they occurred: at thirty thousand feet. In midflight, as he traversed the country attending high-powered capital invest-ment conferences, he would often have panic attacks in which he felt like he was being pushed six feet under, not floating above the clouds. The soul stirs in mysterious ways.

The good news is that Hal was not having a heart attack. In fact, he was in picture-perfect health, according to his doctor, and there was no medical explanation for his anxiety attacks. When he found his way to me, he was unaware that I was trained in Jungian psychology, hence always on the look-out for the symbolic meaning behind the symptom. He, like most of us under similar circumstances, was looking for symptom relief. He simply wanted to be able to fly again, to buckle up, taxi down the runway, and lift off, relaxed and in control of his straight-line, upward flight to success.

The High-Flying Rupture

At the time, Hal worked as COO for a multinational home decorating com-pany. He was second in command at the firm, managing the day-to-day opera-tions of a far-flung empire of factories, distribution centers, and retail outlets. The company was quite successful, and besides the small detail of having an abusive, dictatorial, micromanaging boss, Hal appeared happy.

In our early work together, Hal was a bit dismissive when I asked him to tell me about his work life, his personal life, and his childhood. He wasn't looking for "therapy," for he had "been in counseling mode," during the long, drawn-out process of divorcing his first wife. Fear, in the form of resist-ing change, was the farthest thing from his mind. Like many of us, when the symptoms of the rupture appear, Hal was initially unaware that major change might be afoot.

The first intimation that Hal's life was on the cusp of breakdown—and breakthrough—showed up in his fantasies, dreams, and visions of running his own firm, of meeting the perfect woman and being married again, of having children and a family of his own. Yet, like so many of the hundreds of corporate executives I have worked with over the years, Hal dismissed these dreams, considering them fanciful and silly. He simply wanted to get back on track, feel confident in his blue suit, starched white shirt, and red tie, and wow the clients with his financial prowess. And what, you would be right to ask, is wrong with that?

The answer, of course, at least as a starting point, is *nothing*. But there is a reason why Hal found his way to me on that fateful January day when the plane of his ego's flight to material wealth came grinding to a halt on the tarmac. He was fooling himself, and his body, that finely tuned instrument of soul, knew the truth. Hal was not really happy. He disliked his job; he felt stifled by the work environment, exhausted by the endlessly long hours, and suffocated by the heavy-duty responsibility of constantly cleaning up after his boss had made a mess of things by screaming at the workers, firing people indiscriminately, and mishandling the finances.

He knew, deep in his heart, even if he was reluctant to admit it, that he was a far better, more talented, and more compassionate leader than the guy he worked for. Yet, he was stuck, or so he thought. There was a deep recession on, so the logic goes, and he needed the job, needed the paycheck, and most important, seemed, at some deep level, to need to be forever the side-kick underling to an authoritarian boss.

Iceberg Ahead: Navigating Through Choppy Seas

By now, perhaps you've gleaned the essence of why I have chosen to kick off our adventure through the vicissitudes of the rupture stage with Hal's story. Hal is a classic Everyman, living, as the famous quote states, a "life of quiet desperation." He works hard, plays by the rules, does his homework, and makes a good living. But, just as with every individual who appears to have it all together, there is much more to the Hals among us than we usually care to admit. If he had simply hopped in the ambulance and headed to the emergency room, cauterizing his pain with the anti-anxiety medication that our current medical model would prescribe, Hal might be happily back on that plane—ouch—a heart attack in the works. (Mark my words: The soul *will* be heard!) Fortunately, a voice inside Hal spoke to him with a call for something deeper, more exploratory, and more soulful than the "let's pop a pill," fix-the-car-and-get-back-on-the-highway approach to suffering we have come to consider normal.

Harkening back to my discussion in part one of the myth of the symptom, Hal's anxiety attacks, in essence, were the tip of a very big iceberg—of fear. At midlife, he had constructed a story of self that looked as clean, polished, and shiny as the surface of his gleaming sailboat. But whether he sailed off into the sunset or took off into the clouds, the box of his identity—successful, oppressed sidekick (SOS!)—was like an ever-expanding balloon, ready to pop. Perhaps it was the thin atmosphere high over Chicago that ultimately sucked all the hot air out of Hal's high-flying story, but regardless how his ego got deflated, a new story deigned to be told.

It wasn't but six months later, after recognizing his pangs of anxiety as fear, and resistance to change, that Hal's dreams began to take flight, at least in his heart: to be in the pilot's seat of his own business, to have a loving companion as his copilot, and to fill the plane with loyal, supportive colleagues—a compassionate, hardworking team where everyone would feel at home. Of course, it would take a few more stages, and the release of more than a simple fear of flying, to ultimately recalibrate Hal's story so it could take wing, in real time. But by looking beneath the symptom and being willing to read the banner that said "you are about to change," writ large across the sky, while listening deeply and with humility to the pounding in his chest, he was on board for the trip.

THE SOMATIC SELF

As I wrote in the introduction to this section, it may come as a surprise to hear that Hal is a somatic type; he is more attuned to the sensual and sensory than the mental or emotional aspects of life. As an accountant, one might think "cerebral," but as with most things about Hal—and many of us—the surface reality belies the deeper truth. He is not a big reader; he is empathic and collegial and compassionate, but his language of choice in describing himself, and others, is not flowery or dramatic or laden with affect.

Hal, though not an athlete by any stretch, is a physical guy—a lover of water, a swimmer, a consummate skin-diver and adept sailor. His favorite vacation takes him to the far-flung outcroppings of coastal reefs, where fifty or so feet below the surface he can escape the onslaught of his boss's (and his mother's, as we will soon learn) harangue, where he can float with the fishes. Here is a man who feels "buried alive" in the compartment of an airplane at thirty thousand feet, but whose soul becomes unfettered and free in the depths of the sea.

Many of you may relate more to the learning styles of our next companions, the feeler and thinker. But somatic types like Hal are more common than we think. As Hal's story demonstrates, you don't need to be a type-A, action-oriented person or a high-powered athlete to have your body be the access route to the soul. All of us, to a certain extent, can derive meaning, messages, and intuitions by listening to the signals from the body. Whether we are somatically, intellectually, or empathically inclined, when the body speaks, with symptoms of depression, anxiety, or worse, our billboard of self gets "taken down," our ego humbled, and very often, if we can be open and receptive, our soul's deep yearning may be heard.

As we now know from research into early infant development, the brain goes through stages of growth that begin at the level of pure, physical sensation—and need—and ascend gradually over two to three years with the development of the amygdala (limbic center: emotional) and prefrontal cortex (cognitive) as it assimilates the uniquely human capabilities of awareness and self-consciousness. But the body—and soul—remain resonant from birth, with inherent, intuitive wisdom. Ultimately, it is in the domain of physical sensation where the deep echoes of passion and desire—those instinctive, animal stirrings of soul—are most likely to be found.

CAROLYN: THE CARETAKER

Studies have shown that there has been a huge shift in the economic landscape of America and the industrialized West over the past forty years. While over 80 percent of all married households in the sixties had one breadwinner, the man, today the statistics have reversed. By 1990, in over 80 percent of all households both the husband and wife were holding down jobs. But today, the even more startling statistic is this: In nearly half the married households with children in America, the woman earns more than the man. The stereotype of a woman "wearing the pants in the family" has become a norm.

So it was of no major surprise to me when I first met Carolyn and heard of her struggles: She is the main breadwinner for a family of five, including her husband. When we first started working together, she was already in the throes of deep change, as her fourteen-year, seemingly happy and comfortable marriage had ruptured into a war zone, with each party taking up arms, staking out his and her respective "no-fly" zones: the playroom for him, the bedroom for her, with the kitchen/dining area left as the only demilitarized zone in which civility—over a family meal—might reign. It was not a pretty picture.

Feeling the pressure of working long hours to take care of her three kids, one of whom was on the delicate cusp of adolescence, Carolyn was a poster child for worry, overwhelmed and frustrated by the never-ending pressure to pay the bills, keep the kids in Nikes, and push her husband, who somehow himself got stuck in adolescence, to play his assigned role, as dad. It was not that he didn't work. As a computer programmer, his work life was mostly ad hoc and part time; he attempted to make up for this scattershot lifestyle—which he actually enjoyed immensely—by being a good househusband, chief cook, and bottle-washer. Yet, as we all know, the days when you can raise three kids in a suburban, middle-class lifestyle, replete with after-school activities, computers, and fifty-inch flat-screen TVs on less than two stellar incomes are long gone.

Carolyn's job, as a human resource manager for a major telecommunications company, was the ticket to a three-bedroom house, an SUV in the garage, and a fridge stocked with steaks. Carolyn was fortunate in one respect: She liked her job, and she was good at it. With a naturally participative and empathic leadership style, Carolyn was ideally suited for her role in HR. She is a good listener, a collaborative and collegial partner to colleagues who struggle with paperwork, the endless politics, the pain of cutting costs—and employees. Playing referee to her litany of bosses, who are spread out across the globe, and to her triumvirate tag team of kids, who are often anything but "collegial," Carolyn has talents as mother, leader, and wife that are legion: She appears to take care of *everything*, with ease.

The Rupture from Hell

Arriving on my doorstep feeling overwhelmed and stressed out by the endless needs of everyone around her, as I have just described, it might have been a fair diagnosis to see the symptom of Carolyn's rupture stage as simple: *exhaustion.* But that, as the good book says, would only be half the story. Aware of her feelings of irritability and edginess, Carolyn was wise to ask for help, for as we all know, the universe is anything but predictable, and the real rupture was yet to arrive.

Soon enough, however, it did, in the form of the all too common badge of recession these days: the pink slip. It's not that Carolyn hadn't worried that she might lose her job. The country had been in a recession for more than a year, and her company, whose profit relies heavily on buyers from Wall Street and London, was belt-tightening to the point of corporate anorexia. No, Carolyn, as a manager who had actually been overseeing cutbacks within her own ranks for many months, was not surprised. Nevertheless, she was shocked, angry, and hurt.

THE EMPATHIC SELF

So, my empathic readers, can you feel Carolyn's pain? I hope so, for it was very real for me when I heard the news that she had lost her job—palpably intense. I remember feeling my own anger rise and my heart break with compassion, as I listened to her story. It is such a common and misplaced gun that fires on so many tireless, committed, and loyal workers these days, leaving them unemployed, with families to feed, and bills to pay. Carolyn was luckier than many; she got a decent severance package and an early bonus payout. She was also eminently employable, with skills and experience that any number of good companies might want.

But before she could recognize the opportunity *to shift* that this untimely rupture was handing her, before she could even begin to get in touch with her fear, she had to face down the antagonist that sneaks up on many of us whose default setting is *feeling*: anger. As I discussed earlier in this book, anger is a formidable foe. For feeling-type individuals, anger, irritability, and edginess may be the surefire signals that change is in the works, that some story of identity to which we cling in fear, is about to come undone.

Anger can be a tough nut to crack, though, for in the midst of a conflict with our boss, or a breakdown with a partner, for which we, at least initially, see ourselves as an innocent victim, our ire inevitably feels justified. We may want to lash out, scream at our kids, or hire ourselves a lawyer and get back at the lousy bastards who would disrupt our lives. Yet, we do all of the above at our peril. The damage is done, and acting out in self-righteous indignation is likely to just make matters worse.

Unfortunately, anger unchecked, and fear unrecognized, may drive a wedge between us and our loved ones, thereby making the pain of our victim stance even worse. We all recognize this downward spiral of suffering; it is where the great dramatic tragedies find their martyrs. But we also know something else: Life doesn't have to be tragic; we just have to surrender our need to know, to control, and most fundamentally, to be right. Would you rather be right, as the saying goes, or content?

Whether truly a victim of circumstance, as she initially thought, or the recipient of a much-needed gift—of rest, time, and freedom—that she desperately needed (which I may have intuited but wisely kept to myself), Carolyn felt anger that was real, intense, and quite dramatic. Fortunately, we had only just begun to work privately together, so she had an alternative to taking her vitriol out on the kids or her wary husband. Wisely, she chose to vent in the safe cocoon of our sessions together. By pounding pillows, screaming at the top of her lungs, and moving energy with intensified breath practices and body shaking, Carolyn was able to move through the anger phase of her rupture and begin to create space for the deeper feelings—of sadness, loss, and, finally, fear—to emerge.

If you are an empathic, emotional person, and you have a tendency to feel frustrated, irritable, or angry when change is afoot, take heed and take heart: You are not alone. We all have a self-righteous ego at times and we all get pissed off at life. When life throws you a curve, the key to life-shifting, as we will see with Carolyn, is to release the fire energy of anger as quickly and safely as possible (think: punching bag!), to prepare the emotional ground for transformation—to get in touch with your fear, and ultimately, your grief.

It's all in there, and just as a forest fire is nature's way of clearing out the debris so new growth can emerge, so too the seeds of rebirth lay waiting to be germinated beneath the flames of your anger. So let it out, shake it out, and shout it out. Whatever you need to do—get it out and prepare to ground, center, and move inside, out of your head, into your heart, and onto the landscape of soul. This, as we shall see with Carolyn, is the pathway from victim to victor.

MARIE: THE COMPLIANCE OFFICER

When I met Marie for lunch on that fateful day in late 2005, it had been five years since we had last been together. Back in the boom years of the late 1990s, Marie and I had partnered on a variety of leadership development programs. She had been a senior executive for a major Wall Street bank, and my partner and I, running a training and coaching firm, had supported Marie in corralling her forty talented if sometimes recalcitrant financial managers into a high-performing team. During our lunch, she recounted for me how the company had been taken over by a European banking conglomerate; she had moved on to a lesser, and less stressful, compliance job with another bank, and completed the long, arduous process of ending her twenty-year marriage.

Despite all the change she had been through over the years during which we had lost touch, she seemed sanguine, relaxed, and as she put it, "just feeling peachy" about her newfound freedom and her less than thrilling yet secure job. But something wasn't right. I could feel it. I remembered Marie as a passionate leader, a visionary, if a bit cerebral, whirlwind of energy and drive. The woman who sat across from me now, however, chomping on Asian chicken salad and speaking haltingly of her triumphs at work and home, seemed—how can I put it? Bored.

It was true, as she admitted, that she had "put on a few pounds." It was also true that she had stepped off the ladder of leadership and was working in a purely administrative role, as backup to the "guys at the top." It was also true that she wasn't dating—"hah, not ready for that, Jeff. The last thing I need right now is another man in my life. I've got three arrogant, needy bosses to deal with, and a son to get through college. That's quite enough male energy for my tastes at the moment, thank you very much."

And so it went, that lengthy, laborious lunch date, as Marie droned on in monotone about her routine: early train to work, long day at the office, a couple of glasses of wine and a bit of TV, then off to bed. Today, only a few short years later, we laugh together as we recall how it ended: I handed her my card, told her to stay in touch, and chided (trying to be pointed but gentle) that she might want to "do some personal work," if she could "fit it in" to her strict routine. We debate about whether I actually spoke the words to her, but I do remember thinking, "Marie, you are depressed."

In any case, regardless of whether I made the pronouncement or not (I think not), she got the message. Within a week she was in my office, perusing the stacks of self-help books and asking, "Is there anything in here that tackles boredom? Seeing you last week reminded me of how much fun we had together back when I was managing a team. I used to work out in the mornings, work hard all day, and still have the energy to go to the theater—in London, Hong Kong, and New York. I loved my crazy, busy, harried life. What happened to me? I'm feeling so—how can I say it?—settled."

The Mild-Mannered Rupture

And so began the odyssey with Marie that would see her through an entire cycle of self-renewal, a journey we undertook together as she clawed her way out of complacency and reclaimed the inner voice of her passion, her creativity, her insight, and her leadership. Not all ruptures are dramatic. In fact, truth be told, most of the time when we wake up in the rupture stage of life change, we might not initially even notice that something is amiss. Marie was not feeling particularly anxious, nor was she on the cusp of losing her job or dealing with crisis. But she was also not feeling very alive either, not experiencing any vitality, passion, or drive.

Fortunately, she was open to feedback, and with a history of being adventuresome, inquisitive, and thoughtful about how she lived her life, she was willing to look in the mirror and see the truth: Depression had struck. The light of her soul had dimmed, drawn down to a mere flicker in the vacuity of a monotonous life, in which there was little fresh air to keep it lit. But, and here, of course, is the almighty BUT: The winds of change were beginning to pick up. Transformation was in the works.

At first, much like Hal's onslaught of anxiety, or Carolyn's initial rage at *the man*, Marie's symptom of depression was not, at least noticeably, a harbinger of fear. Yet fear, as she would soon discover, was the real source of her ennui. Rational to a fault, Marie had constructed a sturdy life story for herself, with a fixed routine, a comfortable home, and a well-thought-out explanation (i.e., rationalization) for her lack of energy, spontaneity, and fun. Yet, it was her fear of change, not her depression, that was really holding her stuck. As in the famous fairy tale of the three little pigs, fear was the glue that held the bricks of her not-so-happy home together, keeping the wolf of change, and transformation, at bay.

THE CEREBRAL SELF

I'm eternally grateful for the prefrontal cortex. If it weren't for the amazing cognitive and rational abilities that we humans have developed over the past few thousand years, you would not be reading this book. The gifts of the cerebral self that most of us have become conditioned to consider "normal" are legion. Science, medicine, technology, much of what we take for granted as responsible for giving us longer and healthier lives, greater creature comforts, and the immeasurable pleasures of entertainment, worldwide travel, and instant communication, are all the result of our amazing ability to think.

But rational thinking, like just about every aspect of human nature, is, at its core, paradoxical, and not without its shadow. The gift that we modern, educated readers have for logical, deductive, and inductive reasoning is also responsible for our tendency to dismiss and ridicule as mostly frivolous the bountiful, creative expressions of our humanity—of music, poetry, dreams, art—that give life meaning. If you doubt me on this, just look at the way we spend our hard-earned tax dollars, at least here in America. The budget for the arts is outnumbered by the budget for the sciences, and the military, by about twenty to one for the former, and seventy to one for the latter. The total federal government allotment (that's our money, by the way!) for all things related to creative expression, outside the realms of technology and science, is smaller than the entire annual budget for Rhode Island.

I'm grateful for the medical researchers who have learned to tinker with the machinery of the body, able to miraculously return our vehicle to the road after even the most devastating accident or disruption to self. Yet, some of those very same, well-intentioned scientists do irreparable harm as well, by dismissing the very idea of soul, reducing love itself to a biochemical reaction in the brain, and believing, quite falsely, that the "cause" of everything will one day be summed up simply in a genetic, molecular formula.

Life itself, and death without doubt, is a mystery. That is why, when I work with cerebrally oriented clients like Marie, who remind me of myself, I am always on the lookout for what is left unsaid. Our work with journal writing, body movement, visualization, and imaginal dialogue—just to name a few—is designed to dive below the rational explanations and excavate the meaning behind the symptom. For us thinker types, our rational capabilities are what often get us in the deepest trouble, for we can easily dismiss the symbolic, subtle, and gentle urges that show up when our soul attempts to break through the walled-off fortress of the mind.

I also find, not surprisingly, that thinker types, whether intellectual like Marie, who is highly educated and a big reader, or simply those of us who are biased toward seeing the world rationally, are the most likely to experience depression. This finding points at another of the great paradoxes of our time: We have, fortunately, come to recognize depression—lethargy, lack of interest in life, boredom, low vitality—as a debilitating demon that attacks a large percentage of us at some point in our lives. However, with our conditioned tendency to reduce every ailment down to its biochemical or genetic cause, we have also come to dismiss therapy (as taking too long and being too expensive), focusing instead on how to ward off the pain with pharmaceutical intervention.

As I have stated before, I'm not against using medication when we simply can no longer function in the world. Yet, the pharma fix is both a blessing and a curse, for far too often, it may help us get back to work, but it also provides the rational ego a convenient excuse not to look under the hood and explore the deeper questions at hand. We alleviate the symptom, at least temporarily, but muzzle the soul.

So, if you are a thinker type, and many of you are, my suggestion is thus: If symptoms of boredom or depression arrive on your doorstep, and the unwelcome visitor seems unwilling to leave after a few days or weeks, don't hesitate to ask for help. See your doctor and listen with respect to his recommendations. But, at the same time, be your own healer as well: Take time to reflect, write in a journal, and explore the potential meaning of your malaise. Get in dialogue with someone you trust and ask for honest feedback. Most important, be on the watch, night and day, for dreams, visions, and fantasies. Don't ignore, dismiss, or discard them, for that, my friend, is *resistance*—and fear.

The rational ego will have a tendency to be arrogant, righteous, and dismissive, so you must be vigilant, open, and flexible if your soul's extraordinary vision of your future expression of self has any chance of seeing the light of day. Be gentle with yourself as well, and just listen. You don't have to change your life, quit your job, or leave your spouse. But, if a true rupture is in the works, you will move more quickly through the transition to release and be much more likely to arrive at a destination I call renewal, if you are at least willing to consider that there may be another, wiser, more loving "you" whose call is being muffled by the heavy blanket of depression.

MAKING THE FIRST SHIFT: TRACKING RESISTANCE

As you read through the stories above, did you notice anything that Hal, Carolyn, and Marie had in common? It may seem fairly obvious. When symptoms of rupture arrived on their doorstep, in the form of anxiety attacks, pink slips, anger, and even simple boredom, the last thing on their minds, at least initially, was fear. Given our cultural tendency to want to simply relieve the symptom, and get on with life, *as it is,* the possibility that major change might be in the works is something we typically ignore, avoid, and most commonly, *resist.*

Resistance, as I explained in part one, is the crucial fear factor that marks the arrival of the rupture stage. Yet, it is also true that not every ailment, virus, or attack of the lazies signals a rupture, or a call to change. Sometimes a cold is just a cold. The arrival of a true rupture, a disruption in the habituated pattern of our lives or a noticeable dissatisfaction with the pattern itself (two sides of the same coin), is something that only you can discern, in deep dialogue with your self.

With all three of the individuals described here, what was most noticeable to me was the more prescient, if hidden, symptom that lay below the surface complaint: a lack of passion, energy, and vitality for life. Hal, Carolyn, and

Marie were all frustrated, unhappy, and discontent with some aspect of their lives, and at some level of awareness—perhaps below their immediate focus on the ailment and disruption at hand—they *knew* it. I could feel it. Their stressed bodies, low energy levels, and negative attitude toward life—all sang the siren song of resistance: *I want to change yet I don't want to change.* My job, and the real job of any good therapist, coach, or dear friend, is to hold up a mirror for them and get them into a deeper dialogue with themselves.

If a true rupture is in the works for you, at some level below the surface of symptoms and your ego's story of "woe is me," there is likely to be another voice speaking within you, however softly at first, calling you to change. But only you can know when the winds of change are blowing. The practices for recognition and responsibility from part two can support you in the exploration. Using all kinds of writing exercises—journaling, automatic, nondominant, or poetry—and also practicing meditation, connecting to your deeper physical energy through yoga, or conducting a dialogue with images from your dreams and fantasies, you may cut through the mind's incessant chatter (resistance) and create space for the wisdom of your soul to speak. Only then may you discover whether there is a deeper story of self that might need to be recalibrated, reinvented, or discarded. Only then will perhaps the energy of resistance make itself known to you, allowing a doorway to the soul to open and the crucial question to be heard: *What am I afraid of?*

Fear, as I have said many times before in this book, is not the enemy. It is a signpost, a signal along the highway of life that it is time to shift lanes, turn around, or take a side road into unknown territory. This is why it is so important, when even what appear as minor symptoms of frustration, worry, or angst show up on the GPS system, that we, at the very least, pay attention, and get into dialogue with ourselves. Our greatest risk is not that we will mistake a mere headache for a rupture, but that we will ignore the tiny irritants that signal "change is afoot"—and resist the dialogue with soul that can propel us quickly and effortlessly to the next miraculous creative expression of our souls, as the next great story of self gets told.

Life-Shifting Reflection Step

If, after reading this chapter and taking the diagnostic exam, you discover that you may be in the rupture stage in a particular domain of your life, take time to practice with the tools of recognition and responsibility. Give yourself space to breathe, get present, and listen in to your heart, your mind, and your body. When you feel ready, shift your attention below the symptom and connect to your fears, real or imagined. Reflect on the following questions:

1. What is/are the symptom(s) you are experiencing?

2. If the symptom is pointing to a deeper meaning for you, what might it be?

3. Where in your life do you feel disappointment, unhappiness, or discontent?

4. What fantasies, visions, or dreams of possibility are showing up, however faint and unclear?

5. What habits or patterns do you find yourself repeating over and over? Why?

6. Do you feel change in the works? If so, where—in your body, mind, or heart—do you experience resistance? What might you be resisting?

7. What are you afraid of?

Chapter Two

THE RELEASE:
PUTTING DOWN YOUR BURDEN

"All changes, even the most longed for, have their melancholy, for what we leave behind us is a part of ourselves; we must die to one life before we can enter another."

—ANATOLE FRANCE

We have now reached what I consider to be the most important leg of our journey together. If you remember the earlier discussion of my particular use of the word "shift," then you'll understand when I say that it is here, in the release stage, that we are most likely to get *lost in translation,* shifting the outer circumstances—ditching the boyfriend, quitting the job—but not truly letting go of what no longer serves: the underlying story of self. The reason the release stage is so important, elusive, and at times tricky to pin down is that letting go of our deeply held stories of identity requires that we look behind the walls of our ego, that we dive below the surface story of fear—and anxiety, depression, and all the rest of the symptoms—and flush out the emotional, physical, and mental plumbing called "the self."

There have been, and continue to be, many books written on the subject of letting go. Many of the most deeply moving poems I have read, by Rumi and Rilke, among many, tackle the subject of surrender. The challenge with this theme is that, like falling in love, it can be a sly trickster, prompting us to lose ourselves temporarily, but not breaking us open to a deeper level, to a level that breaks down our defenses, bringing us to the soft, vulnerable story of self that has, like an old gas-guzzling station wagon with wooden side panels, simply outlived its usefulness.

Some of these poems and self-help tomes are beautifully written and profound, but to my mind, many of them, especially when they focus on letting go of fear, miss the real bull's eye—our identity—thereby unwittingly setting us up for a fall. Letting go of our fear at a transitional moment in the cycle *is* important, for as our fear subsides, we may let down our guard and trust that change is happening *for* us, not *to* us. In that moment, we can make the shift to the next stage—and move forward. However, becoming "fearless" in a world where real danger still exists, and where death is inevitable, although a laudable spiritual goal, is *not* the key to the kingdom of self-renewal. The real gold lies buried beneath our fears in the beliefs and stories about ourselves to which we stubbornly cling; stories that keep us stuck in neutral or worse—repeating self-destructive patterns—stories that prevent us from the lifelong possibility of renewal.

As you listen in to the stories of release from our three traveling companions, pay attention to your physical, mental, and most important, emotional reaction to their flashes of insight. You might want to read through the questions for reflection at the end of this chapter in advance, and if you feel your heart stirring with sadness, your chest becoming heavy with fear, or your mind challenged to stay focused—take heart, you're on track. You may or may not be in the release stage yourself at this time, but your ego will sense what it will be up against when you are, and it may resist.

Be gentle with yourself. Go back to practices in part two that helped you stay centered, get present, and feel grounded. Listen in to your body, heart, and mind, for your own story of self. Allow your identity, whatever stage in the cycle you may find yourself, to become more fluid, permeable, and moveable. Whether in down- or upshifting mode, the more willing we are to see ourselves as "in process" rather than fixed, the more likely each transition will occur with less effort and more ease.

HAL'S *SHIFT:* SO LONG, SIDEKICK

Like many guys I know, Hal has a fondness for vehicles—cars, boats, planes. So it was no surprise to me that when he had his major transitional moment, into the full release stage of our work together, he was sitting in his car. If you remember, we left Hal learning to stretch, breathe deeply, and focus on the physical sensations in his body whenever his anxiety would rear its ugly head—as he faced off with his boss, or settled into his seat on the airplane. As Hal became more adept at listening to his body, feeling the fear that was running the show, and not judging but just being with the feelings, his anxieties diminished. He started to talk more openly about his desire to change, to get out from under the weight of his boss's abusive style, to consider other options. It was around this time as well that he started to remember his dreams.

One day, when he could only escape to his car and talk to me from the underground parking lot of his office building for fear that his boss might "need him"—since *everything* with his boss is an emergency—he shared with me the following dream:

> *I am a small child, maybe five or six years old. I am lying in a black box, probably a coffin, and I'm trying desperately to get out. But I can't move. Something is holding me down. I can barely breathe. I'm shaking with terror; I'm stuck in this box in a hole in the ground and calling for help. But no one comes. Then I see a dark figure, a lone woman, dressed all in black, with a black shawl covering her face—I don't recognize her— but I feel like I know her. She comes up to the edge of the hole and peers down at me. I'm beside myself with fear, shaking, crying, terrified. She smiles at me, a sneering, unadulterated look of disdain, and begins to kick dirt into the hole, onto my body. I feel myself being covered over with dirt. She is laughing now, kicking dirt on me, and I feel like I'm about to pass out. Fortunately, at that moment, I woke up, shaking, covered in sweat, my heart pounding in my chest as if it might burst.*

Then, with a chuckle, Hal blurted through the mouthpiece, "I know you're not a big fan of drugs, Jeff, but thank God for the Klonopin my doctor gave me, I needed it last night. Otherwise, I would never have gone back to sleep."

"Ha ha." I laughed out loud. "I'm not against the meds, Hal. They can be a lifesaver at times. Don't criticize yourself for needing help. But let's talk about this dream. What do you think it is trying to tell you? Who, pray tell, might be this dark female figure, who would bury you alive?"

And so, with the trigger of a powerful dream—in truth, a nightmare— arriving at a crucial moment of vulnerability, Hal let down his guard and began talking about his childhood and the fearful, anxious mother under whose oppressive, if loving, regime he had grown up. His mother, it turns out, is a super-strong, opinionated, and formidable presence in his life. From a very young age, Hal felt more like a husband, confidant, and therapist to his mom than a kid. She was constantly fretful, worried, and anxious, relying heavily on her only son to be the "rock" that held her world together. She would often tell him, as he hesitantly, with great emotion, recounted to me, that he was "everything to her," that he was her sole source of happiness.

"Even today," he continued, "when I talk with her she rarely lets me get a word in. She goes on and on about her troubles, complaining about every ache and pain, regaling me with stories about how the world is out to get her, how the waiter at the restaurant screwed up her order or the police officer was just waiting in his car to nab her for speeding."

"It's always all about her," he said with a sigh. "Then she asks me how I'm doing, listens for half a minute, tells me she loves me, and hangs up. I always feel drained by these phone calls. Yet, ironically, she will e-mail me the next day and say how great it was to hear from me, how she feels so much better after we speak. Ugh!"

Just at that moment, our own phone call was abruptly interrupted. His boss was on the other line. When he came back to me a few moments later, his voice had changed. Strangely, he sounded out of breath. I could feel the anxiety rising in his shallow breathing, his curt tone. "Sorry, Jeff, that was my boss again. Something about needing to fire my . . . you won't believe it . . . *my* secretary! He wants me to fire my own secretary. I just don't know if I can take it anymore."

There was a long, deep silence on the line. I could hear Hal breathing, haltingly; he was clearly upset at this phone interruption—and the dream. I told him to take deep breaths, to focus on his body sensations and my voice, to be with me. I wasn't going anywhere. He was not alone.

Moments later, when I could sense that he was a tad more present and grounded, I asked the simple but obvious question, bringing the elephant, finally, into the room, or should I say, car: "Do you think there is a connection, Hal, between your boss, your mom, and your dream?" He was way ahead of me. I could hear the tears coming.

Hal was on the verge of seeing, perhaps for the very first time, that the deeply held narrative of his life—the burden he had carried around for many decades—was a story of "being the lackey" to someone else's needs. He was his mom's loving sidekick, just as he had become his boss's second lieutenant, and though he was paid off for doing the job so well—with kudos from Mom and big paychecks from the boss—the real Hal, the one with his own needs, his own dreams, his own passions, got buried, parked in the back corner lot of his own psyche.

This wasn't the last time Hal and I would discuss the story of his identity as "second fiddle" to Mom, nor did he waltz back into the office, throw a temper tantrum, and quit his job. But it was a momentous occasion: It was the time, place, and event in which the shift from rupture to release took place, as

Hal, once and for all, began to grieve the story of a little boy who was forced to grow up way too soon; to grieve the loss of the man who, deep down, knows he has the talent to step into the CEO's office and take his seat at the head of the table. Buried, literally and metaphorically, in fear, Hal had protected himself, and survived for decades, by handing over the wheel of his vehicle of self to Mom, then a former wife, and now his boss. It was time to reclaim his voice, to climb out of the backseat and into the driver's seat of his life.

CAROLYN'S *SHIFT*: PUTTING SELF FIRST

The irony of Carolyn's transition from the rupture to release stage is that it wasn't in the least bit dramatic. Accustomed as she was to feeling intense emotions of anger, sadness, and disappointment, Carolyn's challenge, as she struggled to take the focus off of her life's external upheavals, was to turn inward and connect to her fear. Fearless to a fault, her conditioned tendency was to banish all traces of self-pity and get valiantly back in the game. Keenly aware that she was in the midst of major rupture, she was determined to bypass any further roadblocks or detours on the path that would return her to the corporate world. Given her natural ability to emote, and her easy access to tears, it wasn't always easy for me to convince her that "getting back in the saddle" might not be the change for which her soul was yearning, or the gift of renewal she so ardently sought.

Grieving, for emotional types, can be a tricky translation tactic, especially for those with responsibilities for others at home and bills to pay. Carolyn's journey through the rupture stage would often appear in a form most of us would call grief—with buckets of tears and sobs of concern for the welfare of her children. I felt a great deal of compassion for her plight but would often notice that as she wove her tale of woe, she would leave herself out.

"I have to find another job, Jeff, and soon," she would lament. "My husband does his best, but he just can't make enough to cover our expenses. I have to keep the kids in good schools. I am sick with worry about my older one. She's so troubled by all the disruption at home." At times I would pointedly say, "Carolyn, stop for a moment. Take a deep breath. What exactly are you afraid of?" The answer would always come in familiar flavors: She was afraid that her kids would not turn out OK, afraid that her husband would leave, afraid that she would never find another job.

On the surface, Carolyn was aware of her fear, aware of her grief, and awake to her pain. But since her fears and sorrows were always related to someone else, or something else—her kids, her job, her livelihood—the story of who she was, in the midst of all this turmoil, somehow got lost in the shuffle. If you remember the very first chapter in this book, I discussed a key component of any true life-shifting process: a dialogue with self. At some point, we all have to turn away from our responsibilities to others, and to the world, look in the mirror, and face off with our own complex, sometimes terrifying, internal world.

For Carolyn, the *shift*—from rupture to release—occurred in the midst of a simple exercise, one that I highly recommend you do for yourself, if any aspect of her story resonates with you. I asked her to bring to one of our sessions some photographs of herself as a child—at a variety of ages. It was a simple request, yet given her inability to focus on herself—to feel her own inner fear and connect to her own story—it took her many months to fulfill it. One day, seemingly out of the blue, she walked into my office and rather haphazardly flung a large manila envelope onto my coffee table.

So it began, finally, a journey with Carolyn down memory lane, and the unmistakable fact that in every photo where she wasn't arm in arm with a brother, hugging a grandparent, or kissing her mom, *she wasn't smiling*. In photos of her sitting alone on a stone wall at the delicate age of maybe four or five, she looked awkward, strained, at the very least, uncomfortable. In later solo shots, from grade school and college, she looked positively pained, almost panicked to be caught by herself. I was struck by the extreme contrast in the images. The change in her demeanor when she was with friends and family—upbeat, rosy, and cheerful—versus when she was by herself—sullen and stone-faced—was just too big to ignore.

I remember the moment well, for it wasn't dramatic and there were few tears, but the shift in energy in the room was palpable. After pointing out to her what I couldn't help but notice in the photos, she sat quietly for a long time, gazing at each photo, of herself alone as a little girl, of her smiling with friends and family. Then softly, ever so softly, she began to cry. When the words came, they were profound; they felt like they emanated from a different place in her body than I had seen or heard before, a deeper place that had until now been hidden from view, perhaps even from herself.

"I don't like to be alone," she whispered. "I never did. I was always at the center of everything as a kid, orchestrating the family, keeping my dad happy, keeping my brothers and sisters in line, doing the cooking, cleaning, and fixing that my mom would throw my way. I never complained. I guess I just thought that was my role . . . to be the one that held it all together. I never thought about myself much. That would have been, well . . . ummm . . . selfish." And with those words, using the pronoun "I" more times in one paragraph than I had probably heard in a month, but with few tears, Carolyn's *experience of Carolyn* shifted forever.

Selfish. That was the word she used: *selfish*. Her biggest fear, if you can call it that, was that she would get caught putting herself first—a fate worse, really, than death, or losing a job, being miserable in a marriage, or not sending her kids to the right schools. It just wasn't done . . . until it was. Carolyn's deeply held story—that her own needs didn't really matter—was finally, literally, out on the table. There was no going back, no more hiding, no more blaming the boss, the husband, or even Mom and Dad. And most of all, there would be no blaming herself, no retribution, no recoiling from the truth. Carolyn's moment of vulnerability was poignant and perhaps repugnant to her ego, but she held on to those pictures of a forlorn, lonely, separate little girl, and finally seeing into her own eyes, she held the gaze, felt the fear, and welcomed the call from her soul, which ironically softly whispered in her ear that day, "I want you back. I miss you. I need you. *You* matter."

For those of you who are caretakers in your families, professions, and communities, who feel deeply the call to serve the planet and make a contribution to others, as do I, the tendency to put yourself last can be quite easy to miss. The possibility that we might be "selfish" is antithetical to our story of being good little boys and girls. It is the Achilles' heel for professional caretakers, therapists, coaches, nurses, firefighters, and the like that we wind up angry at the world—and thrown a curve by it—when, according to our ego's story, all we want to do is "help." But the truth, which sets us free, is this: Selfishness, in the sense of taking care of one's own needs *first,* is a sign of self-love, self-care, and maturity. And so, with the release of her story of "never being selfish," Carolyn began to reframe her situation, until one day, soon in fact, she came to see that the universe had handed her a pink slip, not just for the nine-to-five job, but to the identity called "caretaker." And this, as she would surely acknowledge today, was a gift.

MARIE'S *SHIFT*: OFFICER DISMISSED

When I first ran into Marie again after a five-year hiatus, it wasn't lost on me that her current job title, "compliance officer," seemed apt not just for her work life, but for her whole life as well. In fact, if I remember correctly, during the six months or so of our early work together, Marie was committed like a good soldier to her regimented routine. She would head off in the early morning hours to her employer's secret data storage warehouse, where she single-handedly rewrote, rewired, and reconfigured the company's entire disaster recovery plan. The universe is so precise in its outer reflections of our inner world that, not being attuned to subtlety, most of us rarely even notice when it comes knocking—or should I say, mocking—at our door. Marie, hard at work in the bowels of her company's data storage vaults, was in parallel mode in her own life, inching her way down a dark, hidden path within her own psyche, where the lost database of her own soul—her passion, dreams, and talents—lay waiting to be restored.

Given that Marie was a highly functioning, rational individual, even when depressed she would go through the motions of her life. Like the Energizer bunny, she kept on going. It wasn't enough for her to "change her thoughts" or practice "positive thinking," nor, as I have stated innumerable times before, do these kinds of brain shifts, however pleasant-sounding to the ego (read: quick fix!), typically result in actual changes to our behavior, our circumstances, or our inner lives. The access route to Marie's soul would not be through reading self-help books or posting affirmations on her laptop, but only through new practices; practices that would, as the cliché states, get her out of her head, and into her heart.

For many of my mentally focused clients—and for me as well—the practices that work best are meditation and journal (or automatic) writing. In fact, if you are a bit like Marie in the sense of living a cerebral, habituated, somewhat regimented lifestyle, I highly recommend the approach Marie took to these practices: She took them on with a vengeance. Starting small, by simply meditating five minutes each morning and writing in a journal whatever thoughts came up as she rode the train each morning, she simply, and with discipline, incorporated these new practices into her routine.

Within a few months, the five-minute meditation had grown to twenty, and the journal, which she had purchased reluctantly, began to fill up as she wrote and wrote and wrote, literally whatever came into her head/heart, as she rode that fateful train to the disaster recovery site each morning at 6 sharp. Little did she know at the time that she was already hard at work, by 5:30 a.m. on the meditation cushion, conducting her own internal disaster recovery program.

Soon enough, Marie started writing down her dreams, which having disappeared from view for years, began popping up and finding their way rather serendipitously into her journal each morning. She started drinking less, eating less, sleeping more, and waking up feeling more refreshed. Most important, and this is a key marker for those of you in a depression-style rupture, she began having visions and fantasies again—of doing something different with her life, of *running* something, perhaps a nonprofit or another business enterprise, and of maybe even—yikes, I said it—*dating*.

Now, it would be many more months before Marie would put on her dating shoes, but as she recounted her dreams to me, recorded her story in her journal, dug up her past, and became present each morning to her heartbeat, her breath, and her lost vitality, she started to recover her voice. Soon enough, with a little prodding from me, she started complaining about her cadre of bosses—"those three white dudes who run the show"—who, although she considered them friends and colleagues, never really listened to her.

She started reminiscing about her long-lost days as the head of a global team, remembering her passion, talent, and successes as a leader. She, as I had witnessed firsthand, was capable of pulling off something that eludes even some of the best international managers: making a virtual, far-flung gaggle of culturally diverse people from all over the world feel like a team. She was *that* good. Yet, in the wake of her divorce, the trauma of 9/11 (where she was near Ground Zero at the time), and long-lost years of self-doubt, somehow her inner leader had gone underground, and an obedient, loyal, *compliant* backup player had taken charge.

The Obedient Daughter

As with Hal, Carolyn, and just about every person I've ever worked with, at some point along the path of excavating Marie's lost "self," there came a time when, rather innocuously, I asked her to reflect on her childhood, to see if the key to unlocking the mystery of her sudden loss of passion and joie de vivre might be found buried in a hidden vault left untouched since she was a little girl. "How," I asked her, as I discussed in chapter six of the first part of this book, "might the past still be present?"

The question didn't come to me just casually, or out of left field. In fact, Marie had been dreaming about little girls—fascinating, if completely haphazard dreams—for weeks. Early on, in the dregs of her lusterless state, she had sloughed off talk of her childhood as banal, useless, a waste of time. I had heard that many times before, so I didn't press. Yet, with the arrival of childlike dreams, suddenly there were also memories, and, as the universe often helps out, familial triggers in the form of challenges with an ailing mother and siblings.

The stories of Marie's childhood were not particularly dramatic; there was no child abuse or violence; there was, in fact, little conflict at all in the well-orchestrated family constellation of Mom and Dad and three younger siblings. Marie's most prevalent memory was of her mom always being on time for every-thing—the meals, the cleaning, the laundry—and her dad, ex-military, loving but strict, always looking at his watch and smiling, rather cunningly, as every-thing ran like clockwork. Except, of course, when it didn't, and there was hell to pay and punishment (not physical but psychological) to dole out.

The stories of Marie's childhood were not filled with tabloid-level drama, but, as the oldest child of four, and her mother's loyal assistant and dad's compliant snitch, there was a consistent theme: Marie herself *never* got in trouble. She always did what she was told, always led by example for her younger siblings, always toed the line—and got rewarded with those two pre-cious hours of television. She never broke stride, never wavered in her com-pliance with the rules, never made waves—and as she could now plainly see for herself, she still didn't.

"But when," she would blurt out to me one day from behind the furrowed brow and frumpy black turtleneck designed to hide those extra layers, "when did I ever have fun?" Long silence. "I remember," she finally spoke softly, more to herself than to me. "It was in college, I ran off to Paris. I got away from the goodie-two-shoes life that I had been stuck in. I had a blast. I was pretty naughty, now that I think of it. It was fun." And then the tears arrived, slowly at first, then like a flood. In between sobs and sniffles, she cooed, "Where did all the time go, Jeff? Where have I been all these years? I miss myself!"

I knew then, as the inner and outer conversation between Marie and Marie shifted from head to heart, that her well-constructed, if resistant to change, story of the mind was about to undergo radical surgery (remember: SRS!). I also knew that built around Marie's strong-willed ego, and intellectual rigor and vigor (much more vital than her physical systems at this point), her iden-tity shift would reconstitute itself in short order, and that, although the walls of the fortress had been penetrated, something more, something embodied and physical—something where her mind would meet the formidable foe of her heart and body—would be necessary for a true release to occur.

ABORT THE TRANSLATION TRAIN: ENGAGE THE BODY

For those of you reading this who are cerebral types, this is a crucial moment in the process, when you wake up to the dead zone in your story and begin to feel the fear, in the form of sadness, loss, and most likely, self-criticism. I must reiterate: You will not break out of your self-imposed box of identity simply by reading books, or writing in a journal. Not that these access routes to your identity, and your fears, are not helpful, but they are also, unless the body gets engaged, rarely enough for deep, transformative change to occur. More than likely, you will wipe away the tears, feel immeasurably better for about a day, and reconstitute your story of self right back to the way it was before: *translation time.*

Here's the rub: If those of us who are mentally inclined truly want to break through the stuckness of a rupture, moving through our fears and our resistance to change, we must bring the full force of the vehicle of self into the game: *head, heart, and body.*

The Posse of Patriarchy, Deposed

So it was with Marie. The transition from rupture to release may have begun in my office, but she wouldn't get the breakthrough that her soul most desired until she stepped full on into the boxing ring with her ego. I remember the moment like it was yesterday. In a personal growth workshop led by two of my dear friends and powerful teachers, after moving energy (See Part II Chapter 2 for the example) and meditating, Marie's prep work complete, she got called on the carpet, literally. For weeks leading up to this workshop, she had been contemplating (note key word—*contemplation*: what thinking types will often do in anticipation, and often, avoidance, of *action* and release) walking into her bosses's offices, where there were not just one but three hungry wolves just waiting to eat her lunch, and have her say. Of course, to date, she had done nothing of the sort.

In the workshop setting, where I thought she would perhaps be able to shift her energy from tearful rupture to full-on release, the opportunity would arise for her to get off the sofa, into her body, and into action, or at the very least rehearsal. At her own request, the facilitator offered Marie the opportunity to practice her speech, to role-play the scene in which she would face down her bosses, who were ostensibly relegating this talented, high-powered leader to the back of the class. Standing in the middle of the room, Marie found herself facing off against three tall, foreboding white guys who had volunteered to behave, much as her bosses were likely to act, in an arrogant, dismissive, even condescending manner.

Marie was clearly beside herself with fear, as she stood alone in the center of the room facing her three fake foes, encircled by the rest of the participants, including me, as a loving and supportive cheering section, poised to make her pitch to be heard, to be seen, and to be counted. At first, the back and forth between her and the acting triumvirate went smoothly, if tempered. She stood her ground, looked at them directly, yet quite impishly, and started to "tell them off." Knowing full well how to act like arrogant white guys—kings of the world—the three stand-ins did their best to give Marie the brush-off.

"Get back to work," one of them stated sarcastically. "Don't you have some paperwork to fill out, or coffee to make . . . haha!" In the face of their derision, Marie faltered, but droned on. "You guys totally underutilize me. My talents are being wasted here." This went on for about ten minutes and Marie's tone, shrill and forceful one moment, defeated and drowned out by their endless affront the next, just wasn't penetrating the fortress I'd call, perhaps a bit tongue-in-cheek but poignantly, *a posse of patriarchy*.

We seemed to be getting nowhere fast. Suddenly I felt the urge to push her; I knew from our work together that she was more than just a frightened wimp who was resistant to the sound of her own voice: She was angry. But where was the vehemence, the roar of that inner lioness that yearned to be heard across the street, and across the globe? So, with a nod from the teachers, and no further prompting, I stood up, gently pushed one of the actors aside, and jumped into the role of head honcho—his name was Bob—myself.

"Give us a break, Marie," I heard myself shout at her. "You're wasting our time and yours! You don't have it in you to lead. You are in *compliance*, for God's sake, for a reason! Haha!" Surprising myself at how good an actor I could be, I was almost sneering now. "You couldn't lead your way out of a paper bag. You're better off in the back room, filing the compliance papers, and keeping your mouth shut . . . or else!" Marie didn't respond. She just looked at me. There was a dead pall of silence. We all felt the shift in the energy in the room. Suddenly, as if an earthquake were rumbling up through the floorboards, a mammoth voice emerged from Marie—passionate, powerful, huge—unlike anything I had ever heard before or since.

"Fuck you, Bob," she shouted. "I can run circles around you and your cronies. Everyone in this damn office comes to me for advice. They come to me for decisions. They come to me to complain, to vent, and to get support. I'm the one who really runs the show here, and I'm sick and tired of you getting all the credit and all the money. I've had enough of this bullshit. I'm twice the leader that you'll ever be. And we both know it, cuz it is the truth!"

And so there it was: The roar that shook the room, shocked me, and stunned the troupe of workshop companions burst forth from Marie and, most important, rocked her inner world. At that, she slumped to the floor, heaving, crying, almost hyperventilating. For a few moments, I thought I had pushed her over the edge, worrying that perhaps this role-play thing had been too much for her, that she wasn't ready for release. Yet, these fears lasted only a moment, and they were mine to own, having nothing to do with Marie, because soon enough, very soon in fact, Marie looked up, and turning to me (I was still standing there in full patriarch stance, in shock) she smiled and began to laugh. Tears kept coming. Grief poured out of her as she shed years of pent-up anger, sadness, and self-deprecation, but she was smiling through it all—and the joy, right beside the pain, was palpable as well. She had broken through.

Funny, unlike our fiery companion Carolyn, whom we might have expected to experience her breakthrough to release with a flamboyantly staged drama, it was mild-mannered, cerebral Marie who only finally swam across the river of her own resistance—to accessing the lost voice of her passionate soul—with a splash so loud it flooded the room. I was, in truth, not surprised. For thinker types, whose lives are lived mostly in the mind, a truly transformational downshift often requires the full-on engagement of the entire vehicle of self in full motion, pedal to the metal.

Of course, Marie, like Hal, did not summarily stroll into her bosses's offices the next day and give them a piece of her mind. She didn't throw a temper tantrum or dress down the men in suits who paid for the workshop. The role-play was a dress rehearsal, not for a showdown with her bosses, but for act two of her own internal drama: the face-off with an identity—the compliant, good little girl—whose execution day had arrived. It was bloody dramatic theater, and I was blessed to play my part, but the main event occurred between two sides of Marie herself: her ego and her soul. And fortunately, at this gunfight at the OK Corral, her soul won.

MAKING THE SECOND SHIFT: TRACKING GRIEF

For those of you who spend your personal development time reading books on the so-called secret to endless happiness (i.e., thinking positive thoughts and holding positive intentions; sorry to give it away, but now you can save your money), this chapter may be a difficult pill to swallow. I wish I could make it easier on you, but I also believe that self-help books, if they are to really *help*, need to get real and be more honest. At the end of the day, as much as I might like to join in the chorus of blogs and books that regale you with "five steps to happiness," I think they skirt the dirty truth: *Transformation is hard work*. Real personal growth, the kind that takes you up to the edge of who you know yourself to be, and flings you over the side into the abyss of the unknown, requires something to occur that everyone in our culture, including self-help gurus, is conditioned to avoid: *death*.

Some part of your story, of how your dictating ego has deigned to construct the box of your identity, must dissolve, be murdered, maimed, and killed off, or, as in Marie's case, at the very least, shouted down, in order for you to learn once again something you knew how to do with ease as a child: *to dance*. Life can begin again, over and over in fact in every domain—career, relationships, family, community—but the birth of something new requires the dissolution of the toxic waste from the past, and the clearing of a space. This cleared field must then be tilled, so that into the soft, vulnerable folds of soil, the seeds of a new you may be sown.

So if, as you read this book, you find yourself in a place where the *jig is up* on an old, outworn story of self, don't waste your precious time wishing, affirming, or positively thinking away your fear that an ending, yes, *a death of sorts*, may be near: Welcome it. Let it come. Let the sadness and grief express itself and be heard. It won't kill you. It will revive you. No matter what the self-help gurus may tell you, life is not about always being happy. It is much too precious, too important, and too short for that. Life is an amazing series of cycles with twists and turns and periods of calm and periods of major upheaval, and loss. You may not know what is seeking to be born in you, what flash of creativity or insight or manifestation of your singular, amazing gifts might want to break through to the light of day. But you will never find out, if you don't let go, release the past, grieve the endings, and make room—create space—for the best of you yet to be born.

Life-Shifting Reflection Step

If, as you completed the diagnostic at the beginning of this section, or after reading this chapter, you find yourself feeling heavy, confronted, upset, or just sad, take time to be with the feelings. Don't push them away. Get support from a professional or a loving confidant. Take time for yourself to journal, to practice with the tools for refocusing, reframing, and realignment in particular, keeping these questions in mind:

1. What part of your story has outworn its useful life?

2. Do you feel an ending approaching? If so, what needs to end?

3. What is your worst fear about endings?

4. Who will support you as you grieve?

5. What are you most sad about?

6. How have you handled endings—and loss—in the past? How did you move through it? How might you do it differently this time?

7. Can you be gentle, loving, and supportive . . . of you?

{ Chapter Three }

THE RETREAT:
EMBRACING THE DEAD ZONE

"Nature herself has never attempted to effect great changes rapidly."
—QUINTILIAN

A message from the universe, in the form of the following poem, blew across my desk this week, just as I was preparing to write about our next stop on the path of self-renewal: the retreat stage. Long buried in a pile of papers from a series of workshops I participated in over a decade ago, it is a powerful reminder of the importance of patience, downtime, and repose that is called for in the wake of a life-altering release. The writer, a spiritual teacher and philosopher I had the privilege of working with in the wilds of Vermont, Toni Stone, is a generous, wise woman—a truth-telling soul. I was moved by her and her work. I think her poem beautifully captures the essence of what I mean by *retreating.*

The Mess in the Middle
Possibility
exists as seed.
Resting is required.
Seeds are small,
falling apart happens.
Process unfolds,
stories are told.
Arrangements
CHANGE,
some things are
eliminated.
Ideas become
OUTCOMES.
Simple becomes complex.
Union is a FORCE.
Old makes way for new,

seen is not all there is.
Things are setting up to
HAPPEN.
Possibility exists
as seed.
Resting is required for listening
and growth.

TONI STONE WONDER WORKS STUDIO, 1995

The retreat stage is a paradox. In the wake of grieving an ending—of a relationship, a career, a way of knowing yourself that no longer serves—the idea that you might need to rest, to take time away from routines and action-packed days to integrate the changes that have occurred and are likely still under way, somehow just makes sense, no? Yet, this stage, as far as I can tell, is the one most often left out of the books on change. It is that reflective, quiet period—an in-between time of limbo, unknowing, waiting—that most life coaches, career counselors, and well-intentioned significant others rarely understand. "Get on with it," we hear them admonish us, however lovingly. "You've had your cry. Now get out there . . . and get a job, get a new partner. Get a life."

Spending time in retreat, waiting mode, or downtime requires a level of courage and fortitude that is generally antithetical to our action-oriented culture. *Doing nothing*, even for a few hours or days, let alone months (which is often what is called for) is considered by most people a sign of weakness, not strength. But, as much as we might like to skip this stage, it is a crucial time; a time for stepping back and reflecting on our journey thus far; a time for taking care of what is very likely a body drained of emotional, physical, and mental energy. It is a time for self-care, and most important, *rest*. If we jump back on the rails—whether by rushing to send off those résumés, hopping onto every Internet dating site, or jamming our calendar with networking events—too quickly, the rebound reflex may have its way with us, sending us right back to ground zero and another rupture stage. You know the drill: "Go directly to Jail. Do not pass Go and do *not* collect $200."

One of the fear factors we have to face in recognizing the value and necessity of the retreat stage, no matter how truncated, is that it may *feel* like a rupture of sorts, like a bottomless pit of empty space, a hole from which we might never emerge. Yet, just as bears surely relish yet resist the end of those final days in the sun before they step into the cave and hibernate for the winter, nature does know best. Rest, time for reflection, time for new ideas to percolate, especially in times of great change, is necessary, nurturing, and, you guessed it, *normal*.

MY LIMBO LAMENT

I remember, all too well, the highs and lows of my own major foray into the retreat stage, which arrived soon after I walked into my boss's office on August 1, 1995, and announced that I was resigning. I had already spent the prior two weeks on a beach, grieving and releasing the fears, anxieties, and *the story* that I had been resisting for months, if not years, that corporate life was just not me. Given that I had offered up my resignation of my own, some would say crazy, volition, I walked without severance, bonus, or even much of a cheerful send-off. I think my boss was still in shock during my going-away party. Many of my colleagues were aghast, muttering to me more with sympathy than kudos, "Wow, Jeff, I could *never* do that. Just up and leave my job. You're either strong, courageous, or mad."

And so it went, my step off the corporate ladder and off into the limbo land of unemployment. I had a bit of savings in the bank—enough to get me through a few months—and a vague, faint inkling of starting my own business, but truth be told, I had no plan. In today's current climate of global recession, I suppose my release and retreat stages would appear almost otherworldly, at the very least sophomoric, naive, or stupid. And there were times, during the "messy middle" when, in mid-October I was still floundering, not feeling motivated, fearful that I had made a big mistake, anxious to find the path toward happiness again, or at least to a well-paying job! Only years later, in retrospect, did I come to see the real gift of that time, of waiting, watching—and growth.

The truth is that even though I was certifiably unemployed, I was always busy. I reconnected to my body and began running, swimming, and working out again. I reconnected to my creative side and began writing again—this time not those dreaded PowerPoint presentations, but poems, journal reflections, and essays. I learned to meditate, initially by sitting, breathing, and staring at my cat, who is a feline Buddha, for hours on end (we would challenge each other to see who would blink first. I always lost!). And then by going on my first Vipassana meditation retreats, where I had an opportunity to really learn what it means to be present, in the moment, in the body. My retreat stage was not wasted time, and that is why I place a great deal of emphasis on this stage for my clients and give it the room it deserves in this book.

HAL'S RETREAT: SAILING SOLO

Once Hal had woken up, broken open, and started listening to the call of his soul—for change—rather than tuning in to the self-negating rant of his boss and his mother—the universe, in the form of expense cutbacks and the demand that he take a huge cut in pay, offered him a gift. He decided, with great courage given the foreboding drone from CNN of impending recession, to go one step further and quit. Like I had done a decade earlier, with a bit of savings in the bank and no immediate plan, Hal called his boss's bluff and walked.

We had discussed the need for him to take time for himself, in the wake of his breakthrough—and release—and given that he had long ago mapped the escape route to his own personal nirvana, Hal knew what to do: go sailing. The problem was that in recent years, as he had avoided the gnawing ache in his heart—and body—by not wanting to be alone, his sailing adventures had mostly been, shall we say, disappointing. Choosing to bring along a string of Internet dates for day trips, overnights, and God forbid, weekend sojourns up the coast of New England, Hal had actually begun to dislike his own sailboat. It seemed that every time he brought a new woman along for the ride, he'd end up with a drunken passenger vomiting over the rail, a nonstop talker who drove him batty, or a neophyte sailor who, much like his boss and his mother, would sit back and bark commands, demanding that he cater to her every whim.

So when I casually suggested that this time, out of respect for his need to rest, reflect, and rejuvenate, he sail solo, he initially balked. "The boat is too big, Jeff. I can't sail it alone. I love sailing but I'd be lonely and anxious and just feel guilty about quitting my job the whole time. I'm not sure that sailing off into the sunset, without at least a hot babe to keep me warm at night, is such a good idea."

"How about hiring a small crew to go along?" I gently suggested. "Maybe pay a couple of young people who want to learn to sail to come with you, to work the riggings, navigate, and most important, *take care of you*, instead of the other way around."

"Ummm, interesting idea." Hal relented. "I do like the idea of being the guy in charge for a change. Maybe playing teacher, captain of the ship, and giving the orders would be good for me." And so it went. Off into the wild blue yonder we sent Hal, with a tiny crew of young pups who, easy to find, were keen to gain nautical knowledge and happy to be under the watchful tutelage of Captain Hal. His initial foray into the retreat stage only lasted a few days, a short three-day excursion, as they ventured out beyond the shoals of Martha's Vineyard and around the lovely beaches of Nantucket and back. But, with Hal finally in the captain's chair of his own boat, his anxiety subsided, his boss's harangue became an echo in the wind, and perhaps for the first time in many, many years, Hal rediscovered a lost voice within, the voice of guide, mentor, and teacher to a coterie of students who were thrilled to learn from this seasoned mariner and happy to serve.

For Hal, this retreat period was not only restful and rejuvenating, it was a revelation. He shared with me later the newly emergent sense of resolve that appeared, a hopefulness, an inkling of possibility, that arrived in the form of this inner voice—that had always been there but had been snuffed out by fear—that whispered to him that perhaps he would run his own company one day, that he deserved to find a truly loving and reciprocating partner in life, and that his mother, bless her heart, would get along just fine, thank you very much, without always having his shoulder to cry on.

In the weeks and months that followed this transitional sailing excursion, Hal didn't always hear the voice of hope; he sometimes found himself feeling anxious once again, fearful that this in-between state would go on forever, that he would use up his savings and have to sell the sailboat just to pay the bills. The retreat stage, as I have noted, is not without its own forms of dread, those terrifying moments when we second-guess our shift, lose sight of the horizon, or feel adrift in the current without a compass.

Funny how the universe works in this regard, because I clearly remember that on a second or third weekend sail, with his newly trained apprentice crew, Hal did, in fact, run into a shoal of rocks, getting caught too close to shore at low tide. I was shocked to hear the story, which he regaled to me while zipping along Route 95, heading back home after handling the debacle, it seemed, with aplomb. "Yeah, it was horrible," he recounted. "I heard the scrape of the rocks against the hull and thought 'Oh my God, the end is near.' Haha! Well, we survived. It was my fault, actually, and the guys were great about it. We just pulled into a nearby marina and they patched us up pronto. No big deal. Life happens. I'm OK."

That's when I knew: The retreat had worked. Hal was calm, cool, and collected even in what could have been a crisis. He reached out for help and led the boat and his crew to safety. He didn't sound anxious, or guilty, or lonely, or even self-critical. He was awake, accepting of the rhythms and randomness of sailing, and life . . . and soon, very soon, he would be on to revival. Hal—that is, Captain Hal—eyeing the horizon with gusto, vitality, and a renewed passion for life, was back in the saddle, or I should say, the cockpit, of his life.

CAROLYN'S STORY: THE FORCED RETREAT

The universe, God, or spirit—whatever you deign to call her—never fails to amaze me, working as she does in mysterious, yet loving ways. In the wake of Carolyn's release experience, totally drained of any residual energy she might have stored up in some hidden cavity of her razor-thin body, she was still unemployed, challenged by her marriage, and left with three hungry mouths to feed. So as you might expect, although she longed to take time for herself and retreat, and she was *now* acutely aware of the importance of tending to her own needs, Carolyn was anything but receptive to the idea. We talked at length about possibilities: a few days at a spa, a meditation retreat, a week on a beach. These all sounded glorious to Carolyn but, as she gently reminded me, "Just because I suddenly wake up and see that I need to take care of myself, the world that I've got constructed around me doesn't just up and float away."

What could I say? She was right. On the other hand, seeing how completely wiped out she was by the personal work she was doing, the release of anger and hurt that came with her job loss, and the lack of support she was receiving at home, I gently but persistently kept up the refrain: She desperately needed to rest. I was worried that, for someone like Carolyn who could easily become overwhelmed with worry, fear, and concern for the needs of others, by adding herself to the list, we might have made the situation worse. Without at least a tiny break from the routine, a small, even minute moment of retreat, she would be prone, at least as far as I could surmise, to ending up in some unforeseen disaster, or at the very least, caught in a new variation of full-blown rupture. As it turns out, I was not far off the mark.

During one of our sessions, when the now oft-repeated discussion between Carolyn and Carolyn (I just played referee: She was, finally, in deep dialogue with herself) was about how she could find a way to be, at least for a few days, in retreat, she suddenly burst forth with a great idea.

"I know," she declared hopefully. "I'll take the kids skiing over the holidays and when they are out on the slopes, I'll skip the lifts and head to the

hot tub. Maybe I'll just send them off . . . and head back to bed!" "Right on,"
I remember saying. "There's the ticket." And so it was secretly arranged, the
"hideout" phase of Carolyn's path to restoration. I was fine with the plan, so
long as she followed through and actually sent off the family, stayed back, and
took *real* time for herself. I knew, from experience, that it wasn't a quantity
issue. What was important was that she made good on her promise of quality
time for herself, repeating the mantra: *I take care of me.*

It was not to be. The universe, as I said, had other plans for Carolyn,
much wiser, bigger, and more dramatic than even she, with her flamboyant
flair, could have imagined. A few weeks later, in the midst of Christmas week,
when I knew she would be in Vermont with the family, I tried to reach her by
phone. When I finally got through, after a number of calls that led only to a
very corporate-sounding voice on the answering machine of her cell phone,
we finally spoke. She was, by that time, in the hospital.

I'll never forget how she broke the news to me. "You got your wish, Jeff,
haha, I'm laid up. I can't move. Doctor says that I won't be doing anything,
much less skiing, looking for work, or fighting with David (her husband) for
weeks!" Oh my God, I thought, she ignored our plan, went off skiing with the
kids, and hit a tree or something. Before I even said these words out loud (as I
remember it), she continued, "Nope, it wasn't what you're thinking. I actually
followed our plan. On the second day we were here, I told everyone that I was
done skiing for this trip, and that I would be hanging back at the condo. My
kids thought I was sick or something, but with the snow beckoning, honestly,
they didn't much care. So I sent them all packing. And just as I was about to
head back in the house for another cup of coffee, and finally, for the first time
in months, put my feet up, I saw a huge icicle dangling down over the front
door. My first thought was that this huge chunk of ice was in a precarious
spot. If it fell on one of my kids it could crack open their skull! So, you know
me, I had to fix it. It looked simple enough. I walked up to the railing, reached
above my head, and yanked on the tapered end of the ice, which was hanging about three feet down from the roof, and like a solid rock stalagmite or
whatever they are called, it wouldn't budge. So I went in the house, grabbed
a hammer, and returned to give it a nudge. Well, haha, I nudged it, all right!
I nudged it right down onto my leg, where it proceeded to make a five-inch
gash in my upper thigh. It came down like a lightning bolt, Jeff, truly. I never
saw it coming. The wound is so ugly, so deep, and so painful. But . . . it's
OK. The doctors say that I will be able to walk again . . . just not soon." I was
shocked, stunned. Not a word escaped my lips as I took a deep breath, and

she continued, "Haha (she really did laugh out loud, perhaps due to really strong painkillers?), I guess I'm going to get my wish, for a real rest, a real retreat. I just hope they keep me doped up!'"

Two months. Carolyn, the one client I knew needed to rest more than anyone I had met in years, was about to have two delicious, if a bit painful at times, months to rest, integrate, and assimilate her release. And even better: She would need to be taken care of—by nurses, doctors, her husband, and even her kids. It was a miracle, perhaps a true pain in the butt—or thigh, as she would often remind me—but still, a miracle. For the next two months, Carolyn learned how to be the center of attention in a new way; how to put herself first; how much those who loved her actually wanted to take care of her; and most important, that she and her family would be OK. Yes, they had to cut back on ski trips and other expenses, and yes, Carolyn would need to get back to work soon enough. And yes, there were times in the middle of the *mess in the middle* when Carolyn would call me and fret about feeling useless, worry that she wasn't healing fast enough, fearing that this limbo state would go on forever. Fear was still around, in spades. But it was a different type of fear, and it was a different Carolyn, who once and for all learned that putting herself first did not make her selfish, or less loving, or less capable; on the contrary, it made her human, part of the family.

RECESSION WOES: A SIDEBAR COMMENTARY

Before we shift gears and head into Marie's journey into the retreat stage, I think this might be a good time for a few offline comments about the recession and the stories I have shared so far. I'm a tad concerned that many of you, reading about Carolyn, Hal, and my personal sojourn through the cycle of transformation, may be thinking that by swallowing my prescription for self-renewal, you may be forced to experience a particularly egregious side effect: You will inevitably lose or quit your job. Nothing could be further from the truth. It turns out that the case studies I have chosen to share with you do involve individuals who have, in the wake of transformative shifts in their sense of self, decided to make changes in their career trajectory. And this, as we shall soon see, will also include Marie.

But this is not always the case, and it is certainly not a requirement for renewal. As I am writing this book, and we in the West are in the midst of a major economic downturn, I'm keenly aware that job change and job loss are rife in the atmosphere of our political and cultural lexicon at this time of collective upheaval. It is for this very reason, however, that I think case studies that involve redesigning and re-creating our work lives are most appropriate and helpful. This is not to diminish or make light of the very real pain of job loss.

But, just as our country will recover from this recession, hopefully with a reconstituted definition of our collective values, and a revival replete with a deeper, richer, more nuanced sense of what happiness means—*sometimes less is more*—my hope is that those of you who are experiencing career upheaval will find the stories here inspirational. These courageous souls, Hal, Carolyn, and Marie, have all been through the wringer when it comes to bad bosses, company takeovers, and downsizing, yet they have also used the experience as a tool for reinventing themselves, for reconnecting to a lost or covered-over part of their souls.

In essence, they have come to view the shift in their economic landscape as an opportunity for them to slow down, step off the treadmill of work as the monochromatic, monolithic path to happiness, and reevaluate who they know themselves to be. In this way, every recession, every downturn, and every icicle accident is a gift, but we have to learn to set our fearful egos aside long enough to see.

MARIE'S RETREAT: YOGA, REIKI, AND THE TRIP TO NOWHERE

Now back to our regularly scheduled programming. Where did we leave Marie? Coming out of the powerful workshop and her fictitious face-off with the triumvirate of bosses who would deign to snuff out her own valiant voice of leadership, Marie was elated. She met with me soon afterward and, gallantly reprising the entire scenario, announced that she was going to "make good" on the plan to confront the "guys," as she called them. Needless to say, I was cautiously supportive. It was clear to me that the personal work she had been doing, culminating in this workshop, was having a huge impact on her sense of self.

She was *shifting*, emotionally, mentally, even physically, right before my eyes. She looked younger—and thinner—but sounded older and more grounded. She may have been exhausted by her trip into the eye of the storm with the tyrannical tag team, but she had come away inspired, fired up, raring to go. Who was I to stop her? Who was I to remind her that rest, retreat, and rejuvenation might be in order rather than further confrontation, this time with the guys who really did hold the purse strings. So we rehearsed the scene, over and over, as she whipped herself up into a frenzy of excitement, preparing to stomp right into their offices and make good on her promise to herself to be heard.

I remember the day of her planned assault on the unsuspecting bosses well. I awaited the outcome with some trepidation, hoping the best for her, but fearful, dare I say, that she might come away disappointed or worse, fired. It turns out that I needn't have worried, for the universe, as is so often the case, had other plans. In a voice brimming with a mixture of anxiety, a bit of glee, and mostly relief, she called to report: "I did it, Jeff. I walked into the office when the three of them were all huddled together, and I stood my ground, called them to attention, and made the speech, just as we had rehearsed. I demanded that they either promote me or transfer me to a more challenging job. I told them, in no uncertain terms, that I felt like I was totally underleveraged, that I could do much more than my current job, and that I wanted a change! And guess what? They all laughed! At first I was furious, but then, when they calmed me down—after all, they are pretty good guys at heart—they told me the news: Bob is leaving the firm. The other two are getting reassigned to different jobs . . . and me, I will be moving as well, to a new role in a different division."

"Wow!" was about all I could come up with at that moment. "I'm so proud of you. You did it. You spoke your truth. That's what matters. The outcome is out of your hands." And so it was. Marie was clearly shaken by the news and unsure of whether to be happy or sad. As it turned out, the new job she was assigned to was not a whole lot different than her current role. She didn't get promoted, or demoted, just shuffled around, as is so often the case in corporate America. She didn't get fired and she didn't walk out the door, but instead she wound up with a new job that didn't require nearly as much energy or time. With only one rather benign boss to deal with, who, being based in Hong Kong, was mostly out of sight and out of mind, Marie got what I, tacitly, had hoped for: *She got time for herself.* And so began the months of what can only be called a gentle, luxurious, if occasionally tedious, retreat.

Marie was, despite this "setback," still newly energized, but rather than focusing on pushing herself forward for a leadership role, or jumping ship completely and heading off on a job hunt, she listened in to an emergent inner voice—her soul—that told her to do something else instead: to relax. She had done what she set out to do. She had spoken up, not just to the bosses, but to the universe. In time, as I reminded her, this voice would be heard. For the moment, there was nothing more to do. So she started focusing less on the demands of her job, and instead turned inward. She started taking yoga classes first thing in the morning instead of rushing to the train; she started going to meditation retreats and writing poetry, and she discovered Reiki, a wonderful form of hands-on healing that is gentle, serene, and, most of all, nurturing.

Months would pass before Marie and I would speak again about her future career, her call to lead, or even that seemingly far-off fantasy, to date. In the wake of her rupture and release, Marie finally got the message: It was time to sit tight, to wait, to be patient, and to heal. The time for action was over, at least for now, and the universe had offered her just what she needed: a less stressful job, and time to spend, not in her head, but gently mending—her body, her spirit, and her soul.

There would be moments, as I have noted in all three cases, and in my story as well, when Marie would fret about her "lack of decisiveness" or impatience to "get on with it," and fear would rear its ugly head, as she worried that she might toil away forever in obscurity, alone, becoming some sort of corporate monk. At those times, I would gently remind her that she was truly in process, and that as the weight came off, the inner self realigned, and the outer garments changed subtly from black, to blue, to purple, that one day, when the time was right, she would know what was next. For now, her job was to attend to her body, to allow herself the gift of dreaming, visioning, and percolation. Soon enough, only a couple of months later, in fact, she arrived in my office, twenty pounds lighter, bedecked in flashy, if tasteful, newly purchased accoutrement, looking positively sexy and radiant, *in pink*.

MAKING THE THIRD SHIFT: TRACKING EMPTINESS

The retreat stage, as we have seen with our travel companions, is a necessary if not always easy period, and it can, unfortunately, sometimes feel like a retread rupture. So before we skip town and head into revival land, I want to clarify the distinction for you, so that when you find yourself in the aftermath of any of life's innumerable endings—whether big or small—you will recognize the importance of slowing down, be patient with the process of germination, and heed the soul's call *to rest*.

The core difference between the rupture and the retreat is fairly straightforward. In the rupture stage you will *know*, at some deep level, that change is in the works, and you will resist it, preferring, according to your ego, the status quo. In the retreat stage, if you are being honest with yourself, you will *not know* what is happening, or where you are headed, but rather than resist this feeling, your ego may attempt to skip right over it, often foolishly revving you up for a new adventure long before you are ready. The key to success, if you can call it that, in the retreat stage, is to recognize that *not knowing* is a perfectly normal, and wise, part of the process of change, and that fear—of emptiness, immobility—is a natural companion at this juncture.

When these fears show up, you don't need to panic, or jump on the tread-mill, literally or figuratively. Just go back to the practices in your tool set that work to bring you present, focused, and aligned. Remember that life is a mystery to be lived, not a puzzle to be solved. Remember that you are in transition; that letting go naturally creates a vacuum; and that you—your ego—does not need to rush out to fill it. Trust your inner wisdom. You'll know when the time for retreating is over and the energy of revival has arrived.

Life-Shifting Reflection Steps

If you find yourself, through reading this chapter or by taking the diagnostic exam, in the retreat stage, take heart, breathe deeply, and relax. Let time weave its magic. Rest, sleep, and wait. Be patient. Consider the following suggestions:

1. If you are coming out of a major period of letting go, get lots of extra sleep.

2. If you find yourself feeling lazy, tired, or just wanting to hide out, accept these feelings as normal.

3. What is your favorite form of self-care? A massage, a hot bubble bath, a walk in nature, curling up with a good book? Whatever it might be for you, give yourself permission to have it.

4. Treat yourself gently during this time. Don't rush to make decisions. Above all, respect the process, and listen to your heart.

Chapter Four

THE REVIVAL: LIGHT AT THE BEGINNING OF THE TUNNEL

"Every man, through fear, mugs his aspirations a dozen times a day."
—BRENDAN FRANCIS

We've reached the halfway point in our journey. If you've made it this far with me and our traveling companions, having survived the rupture stage, given in to the downward pull of release, and taken at least a day or two of R & R (hopefully more), you are probably ready for some good news: It is time to play! At some point, usually when you least expect it, having perhaps come to know yourself as anxious, angry, depressed, or most likely at this juncture, *tired*, you will wake up one day feeling—well, how can I say it?—refreshed and alive. It happens, I promise. Shift *happens*.

Unfortunately, there is a reason why I left fear off the list of the negative emotional and physical sensations that suddenly, seemingly of their own accord, disappear once we've transitioned into the revival stage. Fear lingers, morphs, and like a true chameleon, reappears in a new guise, often just when we think we've got it licked, as fear of inadequacy, fear of being judged, fear of being silly. Don't be overly concerned. These fears too will pass (to be replaced with new ones in rehearsal) and they remain for a reason. As I have repeated all along, the cycle of dread, if you remain awake to its meaning at each juncture, operates, even in the incipient upshift stage of renewal, as a guide, a mentor, not a foe.

Being awake to the specific type of dread you experience, especially in the back half of the cycle of change, can be extremely helpful: It will show you exactly where you are on the road to renewal. Just as you are advised not to drive a brand-new car over fifty miles an hour for the first few thousand miles (it's true, read the manual), the revival stage is *not* the rehearsal stage, and even though you feel a sense of invigoration and vitality it does not mean it is time to "head back to work." Instead, if you can manage to give yourself even a few days of true revival energy, it is a time for exploration of possibilities, for experimentation.

Whenever I work with couples who are going through their own variation of this cycle and need to reinvent their relationship, I find that more important than getting through the rupture/release stages of breakdown, or avoiding the disaster of divorce, the revival stage is the moment of truth. For even if the couple has succeeded in moving beyond anger, blame, and recrimination for all the faults and failures of their loved one, the identity of the relationship, *who we are as a couple,* fundamentally shifts in the revival stage. It is in this stage, emerging from the dark nights of conflict, anger, and upheaval—calls from the soul to change—that couples may feel a bit calmer and more grounded on the one hand, but on the other feel as if they don't recognize their partner anymore, that this person they married, so many years ago, is a *stranger.*

When this happens, and fear of the unknown "other" appears, rather than getting pulled back into patterns of behavior that sent the relationship off a cliff in the first place, I recommend they honor the revival energy, reconnect to that awkward adolescent they may have long forgotten but who is still very much alive and hiding out in their inner community (usually holed up in a back room, terrified of the inner parents that typically run the daily show) and do what heretofore might have been unthinkable: *date.* I ask them to reconnect with the childlike, playful energy of those tenuous first encounters, to get to know each other again, to see the other, with innocent eyes, as if for the very first time.

The revival stage is an essential, if vulnerable moment in the transformation of identity, whether of an individual or a couple. It is when we must regress, at least metaphorically, and disrobe the ego's hardened cloak of "knowing" such that the innocent, some might say infantile, babe of our soul is allowed to run naked on the beach either alone or with our newly rediscovered loved one. As complicated as it might sound, there is really only one rule: It has to be fun!

There will be time for disciplined hard work soon enough, but if the unformed identity that is newly emergent has any chance of surviving, if the couple that has been through the hellfire of blazing battles between victimized egos, or the unemployed self who has lost a job or ditched a career has any chance of reconstituting itself in a new profession, the time for playing, experimenting, and just trying on the new outfit of me—or us—is fragile, ungainly perhaps, but necessary. Let me share with you a vivid and true example.

HARRY THE POTTER

Harry was a professor of philosophy at a prestigious college in New York City. Coming to me with an intellectual, heady stance on life, he entered my office on the very first day, with the pronouncement, *"I have no self."* As a cerebral count from the high courts of academia, he knew the theories, the cycles, and the epistemology of "self" better than anyone I had ever met. So when his exalted ego broke down, with symptoms of clinical depression, and his career was in jeopardy, he knew not only from the books, but in his bones, that he had to get help.

To make a long story short, we worked through the challenging stages of his rupture, release, and retreat stages together, as he slowly and painstakingly worked his way backward—not without tying me in hyper-rhetorical knots many times along the way, seeing as he could quite easily spin his own story into a web that included Plato, Marx, and the entire pantheon of Greek gods. Nevertheless, he finally did break through and connect to his deepest fear: that he would end up in the same conflagration of destruction as his mother, who, when he was seventeen, committed suicide.

When I first met him, this dramatic and horrific part of his story had somehow been chopped out of his cerebral cortex, summarily dismissed from memory, through the miraculous protective mechanism known as dissociation, or splitting-off. He had survived the loss, as a young man, by figuratively, and literally, climbing out of his own shattered adolescent body/heart and escaping behind the walls of his mind, where, institutionalized in a sense, he had escaped the pain, until now.

In any case, after moving with great pain through the grieving of the real, tragic loss of his parent, and of the inner guilt, self-recrimination, and terror of repeating the past, he, being a professor, was able to take a long summer's rest, and returned to me in the fall of 2008, revived and raring to go. Initially, what he had in mind by "revival" was hitting the research library and writing a book on the cultural symbolism of Greek tragedy; clearly a recipe for intellectual self-flagellation and *translation* of the highest order: a retread rupture in the making.

Sometimes, in the wake of a dark period of release and suffering, our tricky egos will actually endeavor to make us suffer more; it is their way of retaining at least some semblance of control, even as the ship of self sinks. Yet it wasn't to be, and on some level, I knew that he knew it (otherwise, he very likely would not have reappeared in my office after the retreat stage at all).

The antidote proved simple, if antithetical to his mighty intellect. His newly emergent, soul-infused, childlike identity had no interest in further adventures in philosophy, or anything else of the mind, for that matter. So when I suggested that he experiment, find a hobby, put down the books and *do something with his hands*, he was initially reluctant but, having trusted me this far, relented, and signed up for a class in making pottery.

It was supposed to just be for fun. Yet, as often happens in the revival stage, when unrestricted, unregimented, and accessed through play, this hobby rekindled his long-lost passion for art, for creativity, and shocking to his identity of the mind, for making things! Soon he was bringing me beautiful examples of his handiwork, coffee mugs, vases, and spectacularly inventive bowls, which he would brandish flamboyantly (and believe me, in the months we had worked together, he had never done anything flamboyantly!), declaring with glee, "I made this with my bare hands."

Today, my now former philosopher king is living in Vermont and running a high-end, organic coffee-bean roasting company. Who would have guessed? The universe and our evolving identities are unpredictable, not linear beasts. The moral of this story is not, if you are in the revival stage, that you need to run out and buy Play-Doh, but that you need to respect the process, hold off on the recommitment ceremony, and leave, at least for a few days or weeks, the résumés in the drawer. Get in touch with the childlike, playful part of yourself that has been hiding out in a dark corner of your psyche. Reconnect with a long-lost pair of ice skates or dancing shoes that you may have tossed in the back of the closet. You'll be glad you did, because more often than not, it is out on that seemingly innocuous playground, where the gold of the future career, the reinvented marriage—the jewel of a new self—will be mined.

HAL, CAROLYN, AND MARIE: AWKWARD ADOLESCENT AWAKENING

With the exception of Marie, who managed to "play hooky" on many a day throughout her revival stage, all while holding on to her job, our three companions on the journey of renewal were by now trusting if a bit skeptical of my oft-repeated mantra that the "pain of downshifting will pass." They also understood that even if the burgeoning visions and voices from their unconscious were whispering to go out and get that new job, to hang out the entrepreneurial shingle (Hal), to jump back on the corporate ladder (Carolyn), that they would be wise to take it slowly. Even though they all had begun to feel better physically, emotionally, and mentally—with inklings of hope, fantasies, and dreams of better days ahead, they listened when I suggested that, even if it meant using up a bit of the severance or racking up a bit more on the Visa bill (I'm going to hear from Suze Orman on this one), it would be important for them to take at least a short time to consider new configurations, to play with ideas, to try out new—or old—hobbies. I also reminded them that fear, our constant companion, would rear its ugly head in a new form, as *fear of inadequacy*, and that this was not only to be expected, it was a sure sign that they were on track.

Photos and Fantasies: Hal Revives

Hal's revival stage lasted about four months. His hobby of choice was photography. Having dabbled for years with a camera, he bought himself a snazzy high-tech digital contraption during a now much less anxious trip to Las Vegas. He decided to conduct a half-time revival and half-time rehearsal phase. Rehearsal, as we will see in the next chapter, is just what you might guess: time for getting in gear, rehearsing, practicing, and working toward a new level of achievement or mastery. As you've hopefully gleaned by now, I'm not linear in my view of this cycle, and I'm not attached to the time frame or structure of how we go through these stages. The important thing is that we recognize and honor their existence and their passage—how we move through them, in every case, is unique.

With Hal, we agreed that he would work on his résumé and look for a new job in the mornings, while preserving his afternoons for play, which meant roaming haphazardly, with great glee, I might add, for this middle-aged corporate suit, around Manhattan and environs taking photos. He did admit to me, during this play time, that he sometimes felt "silly" and guilty and worried what his colleagues—and his mother—would think. Yet, he gave himself permission to be a fledgling photographer and to explore his creative impulses.

Bringing the playful energy of his revival time into his job hunt, he also began exploring the possibilities of a dream he had only glimpsed during his rupture stage: being his own boss. He finally allowed himself to fantasize about setting up his own firm, an advisory for corporate restructuring (he, in fact, has come to call it "corporate renewal"!), and began scratching out the rudimentary framework of a Web site, a brochure, and a strategy—for helping organizations "release the power of their most valued asset: people."

Fear, in the form of feeling unprepared to be the CEO, and worry that this fledgling venture would never provide enough revenue to support his expensive lifestyle, was always waiting in the wings, ready to attack him—again in the form of heart palpitations and body pain. But he knew something else now: that he was strong, resilient, and capable; that this anxiety was a harbinger that change was still under way, that he would survive it; and that if he kept refocusing his energy on the present, remembered to breathe and stretch, and honor his body's needs for rest and sustenance, he would keep moving ahead, in the direction of his dream. Most important for Hal, and for the rest of you who may have lived under the harsh glare of a needy, demanding, authoritarian boss or parent, he learned to recognize that a great deal of his fear was self-inflicted by his own inner boss/mother figure, and that although he/she would never be completely banished from the inner circle, she no longer had to run the show.

Ants, not Angst: Carolyn Revives

Carolyn, having survived her forced retreat and returned, still hobbling, to her life as mom, mentor, and master of the minions, was, as you might expect, looking to "get back to work." I was OK with this idea, not only because I realized that she needed the money, but because of something more fundamental: She had changed. She was emotionally less flighty, more grounded, and calm. Having the transformational experience of being supported, and served, by her friends and family during her time of need, and come out whole, if a bit scarred, she carried herself with a new level of vitality and resolution. Most of all, the energy that replaced her apocryphal worry-wart former identity came from far on the other end of the emotional spectrum: *gratitude*.

With time in bed to reflect, she woke up to a truth that had existed all along: She had money in the bank (at least enough for a few months); she had three great kids; and she had a husband who, though imperfect, was there for her when it really mattered.

For Carolyn, the revival stage took place over a few short months, while she worked part time at a consulting gig that a good friend discovered for her (once again, help from the universe). She wasn't unemployed for very long, but better: She accepted the part-time job with a clear understanding that she wasn't ready for the next big career move; that she needed time to recuperate, reconnect to her friends and family, and to remember something she had forgotten for many years, how to enjoy life. Her revival stage took a form I highly recommend for anyone whose life includes young children.

In the three days a week she had free, she spent time with her kids and let *them* reteach her how to play. She attended their sports and after-school events, went to plays, baked cookies, and learned how to play video games. Letting down her hair, so to speak, by actually ignoring the lawn and letting the grass grow in the backyard, she substituted the mowing, pruning, and planting time with playing soccer, building a tree house, and collecting ants. (I know, it may sound disgusting, but her youngest son was studying entomology, so she reconnected to her childhood love of all things creepy-crawly and bought him an ant farm.) I remember one hilarious session with me when she explained how fragile ants really are, after her son had deigned to forget to feed them and woke up one morning to find a whole array of ant carcasses strewn across the kitchen table. "Look, Mom, these guys are all scrunched up and dying. They remind me of how you looked when you got home from Vermont last winter. You got crushed like an ant by that icicle, right, Mom?"

"Haha, that's me," she told me, flinching. "No longer master of the universe or even my own household, I'm just an ant in the anthill of northern New Jersey, Jeff, but at least I still have two legs . . . and my sense of humor."

When I casually mentioned to her that I thought her rehearsal stage, which would arrive soon enough with the full-on push to find an executive role in the corporate world, might just land her in a job even *bigger*, more global, and more powerful than the one from which she had been summarily dismissed, she initially pooh-poohed my intuition. But I knew something was brewing, stewing, and reigniting in Carolyn, something that would ultimately make her twice the leader she had been in the past. She was assimilating, as part of her new identity, crucial missing rungs from the ladder of effective leadership: compassion, for self and others, a collaborative spirit, born of recognizing the value of bringing all hands on deck—and not trying to do everything herself—and most of all, *vulnerability*, a rare commodity among business types and, to my mind, the hallmark of greatness.

Polka and Pole-Climbing: Marie Revives

"I ran into an old boyfriend, Jeff, from over twenty years ago," Marie recounted, giggling. "He just wrote to me out of the blue. I think he found me on Facebook. Can you imagine? I don't even have a picture up on that silly application—I thought it was only for kids! Out of the blue this guy writes to me, and lo and behold, he's an old flame from my college days. So guess what? We're seeing each other this Friday and you won't believe what we're going to do." Of course, at this point, I would believe anything that Marie, who was now immeasurably lighter, both in body and in presence, attitude, and tone, might be up to in the midst of her revival.

"We're going dancing!" she giddily proclaimed. And so, frumpy, heady Marie, in full revival mode, would summarily over a period of four months dance, paint, ride in a hot air balloon, and my favorite: do a ropes course. I wish I could include a photograph here, of Marie, fifty-some-odd years old, standing on top of what can only be described as a telephone pole, thirty feet in the air. She had climbed up to the top, by herself, without any support other than from the loving cheers of her safety crew (she was strapped in with ropes) and fellow adventurers. I love Marie's story of revival, not only because as a cerebral person, she really took on the suggestion that she get back in her body—with dancing, yoga, and pole-climbing—but that the rediscovered little girl in her had a seemingly endless vitality and passion for play.

MAUDLIN, MURKY, AND MUNDANE: THE MIRACLE OF HUMAN METAMORPHOSIS

Psychologists, especially those with a Jungian or psychoanalytic orientation, will often employ the butterfly as a metaphor for the process of transformation. At first blush, it is a potent image: The resplendent, colorful butterfly, as we all know, goes through an amazing metamorphosis on its way to taking flight. Hatched from an egg into a strange, almost prehistoric life form, the caterpillar, it awkwardly strides through a few days or weeks attempting to find its footing with over a hundred delicate little legs and a squat, furry, roly-poly body. If it survives this pubescent period, at some point it takes the escalator up the side of a tree, perches precariously above the ground-floor traffic, spins a cocoon or chrysalis, as the scientists call it, and hibernates. During the days it spends in deep repose, a mysterious biochemical shift occurs—one that biologists still don't fully understand—and soon enough, the elegant and delicate butterfly emerges, fully formed, and takes wing. It is a spectacular example of not only the miracle of evolutionary biology but also the fact that true transformation really does occur in stages.

The trouble is that when we try to map our own intricate human dance of change to the cycle of butterfly development, as much as we love the idea of emerging from our periods of hibernation—retreat—and bursting forth from our cocoons resplendent in the colors of the rainbow, it just doesn't happen that way. We humans are not butterflies. In fact, our cycles of self-renewal, as far as I can surmise after working through the process with hundreds of people, transform ourselves exactly the opposite way: We step forth from our cocooning phase more like caterpillars, replete with unformed limbs, awkward body movements, and vulnerable, fractured, and fragmented egos.

In fact, as much as we might prefer the idea of emerging from the retreat stage fully formed, flapping our wings of achievement, and ready to swarm the planet, we do so at our peril. The reality is much more murky and mundane. If, after a period of disruption, upheaval, or just plain, good old-fashioned change, you don't reenter the hardscrabble landscape of self with extreme sensitivity and caution, you very likely may end up squashed like a bug by the demands of the world, and unfortunately, right back where you started in full-blown rupture. So, take care, be awkward, look silly, but be gentle with yourself, and have fun.

MAKING THE FOURTH SHIFT: TRACKING INADEQUACY

The revival stage, as you may have surmised by now, is different for everyone, but one thing is for sure: It is all about energy. The energy of the divine child, as Jung would call it, must be encouraged to poke through the by now vulnerable, and hopefully permeable protector, the ego. The time in this stage may be very short—just a few hours or days—but if you hope to reinvent your marriage or your career, it is essential that you set aside a bit of money, and a bit of time—for exploration and experimentation.

You get the idea: Get out of your comfort zone and pretend you're a kid again just learning to drive. You may hit a few speed bumps along the way, but you never know whom you might meet—and just as that surfeit of self-help books will tell you, there is such a thing as the law of attraction. If you are out there having fun, being playful, and just having a lark, people will find you magnetic and all sorts of new possibilities may come your way. But be cautious and ever watchful of that insidious partner, fear, in the form of feeling silly, feeling judged, not being good enough—or being inadequate to the task. The truth is, in the revival stage, you don't need to be competent. Competence, discipline, even hard work, are for later. We will be on to rehearsal before you know it, so hang out here, reviving, as long as you can. As Susan Jeffers states in her well-known book of the same name, in the revival stage, I fully agree with her: *feel the fear and do it anyway.*

Life-Shifting Reflection Step

If, after reading this chapter and taking the diagnostic exam, you discover that you are in the revival stage in a particular domain of your life, enjoy it! Give yourself as much freedom and leeway as possible to relax, meet new people, and take a few risks. If you are a thinker type, get down and dirty with activity that gets you out of your head and into your body. Be willing to be a beginner, and most of all, have fun. Here are some questions for you to reflect on:

1. What activity would you *never* do? Why?

2. What game or challenge have you always dreamed about, but never tried? (Hint: Now is the time!)

3. What is the balance in your day between work and play? (Hint: Increase the latter.)

4. Who do you know who tries new things, learns new things, and doesn't mind playing the fool? (Hint: Hang out with that person.)

5. What was the most enjoyable activity for you as a child? (Hint: It is time to do it again, and again, and again . . .)

6. Are you willing to try something new, look silly, and laugh at yourself? (Hint: Your new self will thank you, and your ego will survive.)

Chapter Five

THE REHEARSAL:
THE *CURSE* OF ACHIEVEMENT

"Panic at the thought of doing a thing is a challenge to do it."
—HENRY S. HASKINS

Somewhere along our upward trajectory through the second half of this journey, I have a sneaking feeling that many of you may find yourselves thinking, "OK, Dr. J, we've shifted gears, released our depression, anxiety, and even our identities. Isn't it time to get back to work? Isn't it time, after all the grieving, resting, and playing, to sharpen up the résumé, and set some goals?" Well, I will equivocate, "Yes and no." By now, you've probably surmised that I'm a rather unorthodox life coach, one who would, in the face of voluntary or even involuntary job loss, recommend that my client take time to grieve, rest, and even play. Most important, I would recommend that any time you get hit by an internal or external storm or upheaval, you take time to explore *the meaning behind the mayhem*.

NO MORE GOALS!

So in keeping with what may be a rather counterintuitive and controversial stance on life change, I want to take an axe to another sacred cow and suggest that as you transition from the exploration stage of revival and take up the gauntlet of commitment that marks your transition to rehearsal, *you don't set goals!* That's right. Even in light of the harsh truth that I'm not going to earn much revenue on the motivational speaker circuit with this one, I reiterate: The rehearsal stage is not about goal setting, or raising the ante on achievement, but about nurturing with attention, intention, and patience, your newly emergent identity in the world.

It's not that I'm against goals per se, but just as I wrote about the elusive dangers of "happiness" in chapter four of part one, the trouble with goals is that they tend to concretize our experience of life. Too easily we become attached to the outcome and forget to enjoy, relish, and live in the creative process. We end up with a long list of to-do's, checkmarks on the boxes that indicate "one down, two to go," and emotionally set ourselves up for disappointment.

When the dictating ego is running the show, he will want to set goals, define the boundaries, get out the whip, and tote up your successes and failures, just as likely to flog you with self-criticism whether you do or do not make your quota. Haven't you had the experience of reaching the bottom of your to-do list, meeting all those New Year's resolutions you ardently strive for, and ending up feeling exhausted, empty, and instead of elated, wondering "what's next?" It is a common disease of our culture: *addiction to results*. The soul, on the other hand, operates on a different wavelength, deriving meaning from images, symbols, and dreams, delighting in the energy of giving, receiving, and relating, not just achieving.

Goals are great if you want to sell life insurance and tote up sales, but if you hope to extract meaning, depth, and joy from your journey—arriving at realization (yes, we will get there!) with a sense of peace, serenity, and grace—I advocate a shift in perspective on what matters, from *quantity to quality*. Far too often we live for the future and forget to be awake, alive, and present to the gift that is life, now. Just as multiple research studies have shown that happiness is not achieved by acquiring material wealth, fulfillment of our highest potential as humans is not about checking off a long list of goals.

So as we enter the time of discipline and focused action, giving your new identity a practice run before stepping out on the world stage, I suggest you take time, as much time as you can afford, to extend the reflection, play, and exploration period before taking up the gauntlet of goals. Just as it is quite possible to get lost in translation during the retreat and revival stages, and end up back in rupture, it is an acute danger at this point in the cycle.

The trouble is twofold. First, the rehearsal stage, with its focus on commitment, decision-making, and focused effort, will feel familiar to most of you. Work mode, as we might call it, is a comfort zone in our culture, and a boon to our ego, which thrives on activity, distractions, and action. Second, the bullhorn siren song from the external world—the media, the government, your family and friends—is likely to reverberate in your ears constantly with the refrain, "Hi ho, hi ho, it's off to work we go." So be cautious. As invigorating and exciting as the newly emergent energy of determination and disciplined practice may feel, fear may still be driving the bus—or about to step on at the nearest cross street.

STRAIGHT LINES TAKE YOU IN CIRCLES

Hal will be pleased that I finally got around, in the rehearsal stage, to employing his favorite metaphor for life: sailing. Even though I am an amateur on the yacht club circuit, having only been a lucky passenger on a few outings, one aspect of sailing is patently obvious: *You never travel in a straight line.* In fact, no matter whether you are facing into the wind or have the wind at your back, if you try to navigate the boat in a linear fashion, like a power boat, you will end up going in circles.

The rehearsal stage is the same. It is a time for shifting out of play mode, and making a commitment, identifying, at least in a big picture, fuzzy, dreamlike vision, a destination way off on the horizon. But it is also a time for tacking gracefully starboard and port, holding the tiller steady, and preparing for detours, setbacks, and heavy seas all along the way. If you can relax and be aware that this is how the process of "rehearsing" works, that it is not the destination, but the journey that counts, you can stay present and focused, *in the now*, an intrepid sailor on the seas of change.

Cocktails and Commitment: Hal's Rehearsal

Hal's shift into rehearsal mode took place, somewhat uneventfully, while having drinks with an old colleague. She casually asked him what he was up to, and he replied that he was enjoying life out from under the critical gaze of his old boss, reveling in a bit of play time, and pondering starting his own company. Not two days later, she called him and invited him to give a presentation on this new company, his capabilities, and his value proposition. In a full-blown panic attack, he called me, exhorting, "An opportunity has come up, Jeff. I may have a client for my consulting business. But now I have to prepare a slide show, get business cards, and make good on my vision."

"Sounds exciting," I told him. "Take a deep breath, and think of this shift in focus as a new sailing adventure. You don't have to do everything perfectly or have everything nailed down. You don't have to go it alone, either. We've been talking about your finding potential partners and friends to play with (yes, I used the word "play"). Now may be the time to sign up your next flight crew on the good ship *Hal Inc.*"

At times like these, when the shift to rehearsal mode hits full-on, the practices of responsibility, refocusing, and realignment can help you stay steady, grounded, and on track. Hal was excited and fearful, alive with the dread/delight of anticipation, knowing full well that it was time to "put up or shut up." But taking a deep breath and honoring his need for time, space, and practice, he requested and received an extra week to prepare his pitch. Then, armed with a partner and a tiny support staff, he not only pulled together a powerful and impressive presentation but also nailed the client engagement. And with that small step into the CEO's office, now *his*, Hal's new career and life as an entrepreneur was born. It wasn't dramatic or "hard work" or even, after Hal recommitted to his grounding practices of yoga, meditation, and journaling, particularly anxiety-provoking. It was, however, a revelation.

He was shocked and elated at just how different he felt, even if still wearing the same medium-sized, conservative corporate getup. The new Hal seemed bigger, stronger, more present, as he stepped up to the plate and led the charge, once and for all bidding adieu to the identity of underling, sidekick. In the months that followed, he would grow immensely as an individual, and as a leader, learning to partner with colleagues, learning how to step into the limelight (he would soon be flying to conferences, anxiety-free, and presenting to the masters of the banking world, instead of hiding out in the back).

The period of time in which he slowly birthed his business was not without its setbacks, and Hal did occasionally give in to his fear—of failing. But having learned to see fear more as a reminder of where he was on the path, and recognizing that failing was a story being perpetrated by his fractured and fragile ego, he was able to shift energy when it would hit, tack a bit right or left, and stay the course.

Vision, Vigilance, and Values: Carolyn's Rehearsal

For Carolyn, the rehearsal stage arrived, sans drama, just as you might imagine it, with her recognition that it was time to get back on the career track and get a full-time job. But something about her approach to work was different. What was most telling, more than her renewed vitality or positive attitude, was what I consider a crucial marker of transformation, and a hallmark of soul: *a shift in values*. No longer willing to be propped up, or taken down, by the outworn narrative of caretaker to the world, Carolyn geared up to look for a job, again in human resources, a field she loves, but centered, balanced, and aligned, with a clear sense of purpose and a newfound wisdom about herself and her work: to put her own needs first.

In the process of networking and interviewing, Carolyn remained vigilant, on the lookout for a more nurturing, collaborative environment, where she could make a difference for others but take care of her own needs as well. Soon enough, very soon in fact, the ideal job appeared on the horizon, and she was back in the saddle, this time as the head of HR for a global engineering company, one whose CEO would prove visionary and committed to fostering and building a team—a place where Carolyn's soul could build a home.

Carolyn's rehearsal period was not without its anxious moments, and she hasn't completely discarded her tendency to over-function, to worry too much, or to be frightened by the demon of fear. But in her journey through the rupture, release, and retreat stages, she learned an invaluable life skill, one that, in addition to listening in for the nuance of soul, is key to successful self-renewal for anyone on the path: *self-observation*. If any of the practices in part two of this book serve their true purpose, it is just that: to help us stop the robotic motions of the ego, to get present and centered, and to shift our perspective to one of witness, becoming a student of self—with compassion and reverence.

Even in her new high-powered role as HR maven to the globe, Carolyn's ego sometimes takes over, the ghosts of the past come back to haunt her, and she freaks out with worry that she won't be able to "handle it all." But the recovery time, that elusive shift from forgetting—when the ego shouts, "be afraid, be very afraid"—to remembering—when the soul whispers, "just breathe, you're OK"—continues to get shorter and shorter. This is the true gift of transformation: learning to quickly, in a matter of moments, take a few long, deep breaths from the core, get centered, ground, and come home to our self.

Taking the Cake, and Eating It Too: Marie's Rehearsal

Given how ecstatically and randomly joyful Marie's life unfolded during her revival stage, it wouldn't have surprised me to see it go on for years. I mean, why not? Rediscovering her inner child, letting go of her identity as obedient follower, she might have saddled up the hobby horse and ridden off into the sunset. But life, as we all know, happens while we make other plans. In the midst of her play time, Marie was handed what might have been considered a death notice, or a gift from the universe: the "recommendation" that she take early retirement. Of course, I'm sure you'll be able to guess which way she viewed that poignant moment when she got called to the principal's office—or more accurately, down to see the head of human resources: She was both devastated *and* elated.

Initially, her fearful former identity reared its ugly head and she felt shocked and hurt. "I can't believe they would ask me to leave, Jeff. I've always been a loyal and dedicated worker. It just amazes me how cavalier corporations can be. I like my life as it is. I work hard when I need to, but thanks to my work with you, I now have time for dating, and dancing, and yoga and, well, as you would say, fun! Now I've got to go out and find a new job. Yuck!"

Of course, that was only half of the story. The nascent butterfly of Marie's metamorphosis was also thrilled at the prospect of unemployment, for now she could potentially take wing and fly free full time, at least for a while. So when I suggested to Marie that perhaps she could have both a new career and a lifestyle in which she could continue playing, she was intrigued and, no longer as caught up in her mind or her fear, savored the possibility. Marie's shift into the rehearsal stage was straightforward and like those of our other companions, without drama. (Word to the wise here: If there is drama in the midst of the shift from revival to rehearsal, it may not be time to commit; this particular shift, when it is right, will come naturally, with relative ease.)

Marie accepted the early retirement package, continued enjoying herself, and simply added "find work" to her "to play" list (that's how we decided to *reframe* her to-do list; I highly recommend it when in the revival stage). The goal remained elusive perhaps, but the intention was crystal clear: to find employment that would nurture her soul; that would honor her desire to learn, to create, to have fun, and to lead. Over the next several months Marie remained focused, disciplined, and committed to her personal practices of self-care.

With her newly forged alignment of head, heart, and body, she was pumped up with vitality, and managed to juggle more balls of possibility than people half her age. In the midst of her rehearsal stage, she trained to become a Reiki practitioner, became certified as an executive coach, and took a part-time job managing the office for a regional financial services firm. And she continued dating, dumping the old flame who, although great for a practice run, was clearly not up for the life-shifting game—on the playing field called "mastery"—that she had consciously embraced.

Marie is a great example of what I have come to believe is true for all of us: We can have our cake and eat it, too. But we have to learn, as with Carolyn, to be master observers of that old trickster, our ego, and steer clear of its attempts to run the show. We have to become adept at nurturing, honoring, and balancing the full complement of our internal systems—head, heart, and body—because living at the growing edge requires a level of vitality and that is antithetical to what is perhaps a busy, yet far from life-sustaining, culture.

Most of all, we have to shift our perspective, not just from ego to soul, but from *future to present*—to remember that time is short, *and* it is all we have.

Just as we must learn to revere ourselves, and tend to our dreams and desires, we need to reinvent our relationship with time, making it our friend. "I just don't have time, Jeff" is another conceit of the ego, one driven—here we go again—by fear.

"Time is all you've got, my dear," I will reply, so you have a choice. You can make it your enemy, gasping and grasping as it slips through your fingers, or you can befriend the moment, take a deep breath, and revel in now.

MAKING THE FIFTH SHIFT: TRACKING FAILURE

Far too often in our productivity-crazed culture, I see individuals who, even after downshifting in the wake of a major loss, will rise far too quickly from the ashes of depression or anxiety and feel compelled to get back on the same treadmill of activity that brought them down in the first place. Feeling revived and ready to commit, to a new job or new relationship, we may shift into the rehearsal stage ready to take on the world. But I must advise: Proceed with caution. The rehearsal stage *is* a time for renewed commitment, discipline, and practice. Yet, it is also the time for learning to live in the world in a new way, to bring the fledgling new story of our self, our new way of being out, into the world.

Unfortunately, if we are surrounded by a social circle or family that still views us in the old way, people who love us but who may not have witnessed, supported, or understood that we have changed, we can easily fall victim to repeating the past, just in a new guise. Far too often, we are admonished by well-meaning news anchors and career counselors to take the pink slip in stride, spruce up the résumé, get out and network, and nail down another job as soon as possible. Or in the wake of a painful breakup or divorce, good pals will chide us to "get back in the scene," to find a new playmate so as to avoid that dreadful in-between time called being alone.

Unfortunately, this well-intentioned counsel emanates from within a culture of busy-ness that abhors the vacuum of repose and receptivity. In fact, the push to perform, or what I will call the *curse* of achievement, whether emanating from the gut in the form of guilt (and the relentless VOJ) or from the drive to accelerate the pace of change, is once again driven by fear. This time it is a fear with which we are all too familiar: fear of failure. Yet, the truth is something we all know deep in our hearts, but rarely live as if it were true: *There is no such thing as failure.* There is only learning, growing, falling down, and getting up again—over and over.

Life-Shifting Reflection Step

If, after reading this chapter and taking the diagnostic exam, you discover that you are in the rehearsal stage in a particular domain of your life, *be careful*. The key signpost of making the shift from revival to rehearsal is commitment, which will be exciting, energizing, and inspiring, especially to your newly forming story of self. But, even though the commitments you make at this time may require that you focus, practice, and, God forbid, *work*, keep the tool set for transforming fear handy, even if you don't think you need it. Be vigilant and observant of self, and on your guard for two prominent danger signs on the road to realization: (1) attachment to a result; and (2) thinking the route to your destination is a straight line (you may miss some wonderful detours along the way!). Here are some questions for you to reflect on:

1. What is the experience of yourself that you are trying to create by making a commitment?

2. How defined, limited, and specific are your intentions? Can you expand them?

3. Why do you care about your vision or goal? What do you *value* about its achievement?

4. Can you relax and give yourself permission to enjoy the process?

5. Can you grasp the truth, in the moment, that you have all the time in the world?

{ Chapter Six }

THE REALIZATION:
DON'T HOLD ON TO YOUR HAT

"Wisdom means listening to the still, small voice, the whisper that can be easily lost in the whirlwind of busyness, expectations, and conventions of the world. . . ."

—JEAN M. BLOMQUIST

One day Carolyn sauntered into my office and rather coyly said, "You know, Jeff, I understand that you would want to have six stages in your life cycle of renewal, and that you would want to tie up the package of six R's in a nice, neat bow, but here's the thing I don't get: If we have been doing our work properly, according to your instructions, why is the realization stage a separate stage? If I learn to live in the moment, to live in delight and not dread, won't I end up being 'realized' all along the way?" Wise woman, Carolyn. She makes a great point. It is certainly true that what I am calling "realization," that sense of having *arrived*, being vital and awake to the inherent *joy of now*, is always available to us, at any moment. That said, there is a reason why I give the realization stage its rightful place in the journey as the culminating point—a destination, as it were—along the trajectory of transformation. Far too often, in our rush to tote up success, nail the achievements, and garner the accolades, we once again miss the moment that counts, of celebration.

Success, like happiness, is an elusive and problematic concept in the Western culture. Far too often, even when the degree is conferred, the book published, revenue targets hit, or the marriage consummated, we let the moment, the amazing experience of completion, graduation, or culmination, just slip by, for the most part, unnoticed. I remember well my initial reaction when my dear friends, who had supported me through the arduous travails of earning a PhD at the ripe age of forty-three (yes, you can reinvent yourself at any age!), suggested that I throw a party and celebrate. "It's no big deal," I said to myself and them. "I don't want to be boastful, or self-congratulatory. Besides, I need to put this newfound credential to work and pay back those loans." Of course, they were having none of my humble protestations and proceeded to gather a splendid gaggle of friends and family for a dinner in honor of my achievement. It was a beautiful evening and a great teaching moment for me.

In our reciprocal expressions of gratitude for my hard work and their unwavering support (many of them had participated in my doctoral research), I realized that my achievement of a long-held dream not only deserved to be honored by a ritual of completion, but also that the real blessing of my doctoral education was more profound, if unacknowledged: the gift of community. The revelation in that rite of passage, for me, was realizing that although I had piloted the vehicle of self down the bumpy road to becoming a doctor, I had not been alone on the journey; it was my fellow passengers who made the whole enterprise worthwhile.

HONORING THE MOMENT(S) OF REALIZATION

The realization stage represents another key shift in the energy of transformation: It shows up when the fledgling yet prepped and potent new story of self is received and embraced, finally and unequivocally, by the outside world. It is a sweet moment, as the flow of internal and external dialogue of who we know ourselves to be overlaps, and the voice of the soul we have been nurturing through revival and rehearsal stages finally gets heard. It is a time for acknowledgment, celebration, and most of all gratitude—to self and others—for humans are not solitary beasts, and rarely do we become fully or even partially realized, in any domain of our lives, without help.

Success, however, in the form of graduate degrees, job promotions, bonus payouts, or the *New York Times* best-seller list, is a wily trickster, especially in a culture steeped in a puritanical work ethic and addicted to material rewards. Far too often, success is sought after through striving, struggling, and steamrolling the competition, as we try to "separate ourselves from the pack" and "come out on top." In this dog-eat-dog approach to life, we may garner the accolade yet totally miss the realization stage altogether, skipping right from rehearsal mode—to rupture. In fact, I have seen far too many highly successful clients, of corporate and even artistic bent, arrive in my office burnt to a crisp with overheated, overwrought rehearsal stages, individuals who, despite their best intentions, fail to stop and smell success, let alone roses.

Paul Pearsall, a psychologist and best-selling author whose work I greatly admire, wrote a book that describes the pathological dynamic in which we literally bypass the moment or moments of realization, getting caught up in what he aptly calls "Toxic Success." In his book of the same name, he describes the symptom—and just as I explained in chapter three of part one, success itself can be a symptom of fear—eloquently:

> *Most of the very successful persons I have met are [always] looking for something more or fearfully consumed by trying to sustain and protect their success. . . . Competition, in modern life, shows up as a nagging hum of "you can do it, keep going, you can win, you can do better" that raises our blood pressure, lowers our immunity, sends us to the pharmacy and takes our attention away from those we say we love and the life we say we want. The victory virus has become pandemic.*

Realization, as wisely described by my client Carolyn, is the felt experience of oneness, interconnectedness, and delight in being alive. It is that part of the dance with change in which our story of self literally dissolves into the ocean of consciousness, and it is always available to us, every moment. It may not be something that we, as mere humans, can cling to or grasp permanently but it can be realized, experienced, and embraced in myriad manifestations: a graduate degree, a book published, a moonlit stroll on the beach, or a hug.

On the other hand, realization is, from what I have seen in my twenty years of counseling individuals, the most elusive, denigrated, and misappropriated part of our lives. Fear of success, in all its craven and cryptic forms, seems destined, at least in our culture, to show up and knock us off the realization train, and instead puts the machinery of self in overdrive, win/lose, or "what's next" traffic patterns, in which we circle the airport but never land the plane, relax, breathe, and take in the view.

The most important reason I deigned to devote an entire chapter to this culminating transitional stage that I call realization is so that when you have embraced a new story of self, and discarded an identity that no longer serves, you will stand up and *take notice*, honoring and celebrating the change. These moments, which are always fleeting yet profound, are glossed over in our culture, or played out in entertainment forums that exalt the individual; we revere the hero, the Academy Award winner, and then cut short the acceptance speech because it's only the statue, the smile, and the Versace outfit that count. This fast-food approach to celebrating achievement is a travesty, making a mockery of our soul's work in the world. True moments of realization, of recognizing our full complement of skills and talents, and honoring both our contribution and the treasure trove of support we receive from loved ones, are what give life meaning.

A CAR, A CAREER, AND A COMMUNITY: HAL'S REALIZATION

As he picked me up in his brand-new Mercedes Benz A900 or some such snazzy moniker, I could not only smell that new-car aroma, I could also sense that the energy in Hal had once again shifted. He was relaxed, grounded, and even quieter than I remembered him, without a slight hint of that anxious edge that had been his calling card. Wanting to celebrate his new Web site, his new business plan, his new apartment (a luxury high-rise with a terrace overlooking the Hudson River, on which he could daily meditate, breathing in the energy of the sun and water), Hal was in rare form. Fully enveloped in his newfound identity of empowerment, and acknowledging himself—and me—for all our hard work together, he was a picture-perfect postcard of realization.

There was something else too, something more profound and noteworthy about Hal's return to the corporate arena than his new story of self, as a leader, self-made man, and entrepreneur. For when I expected us to reminisce about his past legacy as lackey to the lords of commerce, or to wax on about how he had escaped from the clutches of Mom and finally built himself a life, he demurred. Instead, rather uncharacteristically, he proclaimed his desire to celebrate with me an added bonus, something that he had only recently recognized, received, and fully embraced: *being part of a community*.

When I first met Hal one of his most consistent complaints was that he was alone in the world, that he lacked a life partner, or the right business partner, or the right organization, a place where he could find a home and hang his hat. Now, just a few short years later, he had found business partners, joined his condominium board of directors, become much more engaged if circumspect on the dating scene, and become active in his yacht club. On hearing about his reinvigorated social life, I said to him, "Haha, I guess you weren't really looking to hang up that hat, Hal. It strikes me that you wound up tossing it in the air and letting it take you on quite a ride! You should be very proud *of you*." The new story of Hal, as member, teammate, and soul mate to his business associates, fellow sailors, and even his long line of ex-girlfriends, is not about being oppressed, or playing second fiddle, or even playing solo, it is about *belonging*—and a long way from alone.

WOMEN RULE! CAROLYN'S REALIZATION

The irony was not lost on me that it was Carolyn, not Hal or Marie, who in a poignant moment of recognition noted that realization is an experience available to all of us, at any moment. Given her history of staying in the background as production support to the performance of others, she hardly noticed when the curtain got pulled back, she was handed the baton, and she found herself center stage. Not without a flood of worry, and a retrenchment into fear mode, Carolyn was genuinely surprised when as a board member for a global and diverse association of female executives, she was asked to give a keynote speech on, of all things, leadership. "I'm sure it is a mistake, Jeff," she would fretfully remark. "I'm just a wife, mom, and worker bee, trying to put food on the table and hold myself and my family together. Not sure that I have anything to say about women's roles in the world."

Content perhaps to be in rehearsal mode forever, Carolyn had to be gently chided to see the truth of who she has come to be: She is a role model, an exemplar par excellence for a world sorely in need of new voices of leadership, women who are not only breaking through the glass ceiling, but tearing down the walls of a collective story of patriarchy—and competition, win/lose, power over others—that has dearly outworn its useful life, in spite of its remarkable achievements in science and technology. So when she stepped up to the podium and told her story, of how a young woman who carried the burden of the world on her shoulders had broken down, and broken apart, only to rise from the ashes to stand before her peers, powerful women all, and declare a new story for her self and the world—a story of compassion, collaboration, interconnection, and unity—it was a revelation. Carolyn's moment of realization and now ongoing day-to-day experience of herself, as one among many, with a voice *that counts,* is a gift of huge proportions, not only to herself, but to the world.

A LONG COMMUTE TO THE YURT: MARIE'S REALIZATION

By now, Marie's story of being the compliant, obedient serf to the dictates of a surfeit of authority figures was a distant memory, for even while she ardently rehearsed for her new roles as healer, coach, and business manager, she kept the playful energy alive, detached from any need to set a specific goal of global domination. With a new portfolio career that kept her busy offering Reiki sessions, mentoring apprentices, and running circles around not just three, but a whole office full of headstrong, testosterone-fueled financial managers, Marie had learned to track herself, ever vigilant when the voice of judgment (fear)—of not being focused, not working hard enough, *not being good enough*—would emerge and attempt to shout down her soul. Remaining committed to the practices—yoga, meditation, and dancing—that keep the voice of her soul singing louder than the VOJ, she struck me as permanently affixed in the simultaneous throes of revival, rehearsal, and in moments of clarity, minus the muddle-in-the-middle, realization.

Yet, it turns out that even without setting a clear, distinct goal, once an individual like Marie is clear on the path, and committed to not only remake her story of self but also to have it expressed in the world, something else, what we might call divine intervention, intercedes—and that's again why I believe there is a true stage in the cycle for the full, embodied, emotional, physical, and mental experience of realization. Even when we may be happy, or at the very least content and open and receptive to life's ups and downs, our very magnetism, what I would perhaps presumptively call the energy of love, breaks us open to another level of receiving, offering us unexpected gifts.

As you might have by now intuited, the package that arrived on Marie's doorstep, clearly marked "realization," was a man. And not just any man. A powerful, awake, and sturdy partner showed up, one who was ready to join Marie in the playground of life. Today, Marie and this amazing light of a man travel between their yurt (a large round Native American–style geodesic home) in the wilds of Maine and her Wall Street hangout in the bowels of Manhattan. It is a long commute, but one that gives Marie plenty of time to write, not only her dreams, but her ongoing memoir of a life reborn.

Marie, as I like to say, is my proof in the pudding, that no matter what age, no matter what background, no matter what type you are—head, heart, or body—you can truly shift your life and rewrite your story. Marie's newborn identity has taken her to places beyond her wildest dreams, and ever vigilant to the bite of her past, the sting of her ego's fears, and the swirling swill of her chatterbox cerebellum, she marks the advent of the realization stage, full bore, by celebrating every day. With rituals, rites, and every variety of communal gathering imaginable, she has embraced her partner's family (which, by the way, is of an entirely different background from hers), brought him into her large and cacophonous familial fold, and made permeable all the boundaries that, in our typically "siloed" culture, would keep work, family, hobby, career, and self separate and aloof. There is only one rule that Marie holds dear: to finally, utterly, for the first time, be true to herself.

MAKING THE SIXTH SHIFT: TRACKING THE SHADOW OF SUCCESS

In the midst of our celebration dinner, Hal, like Carolyn, came forth with a profound, and not unexpected question, one that I feel certain many of you are asking right now: "OK, Jeff, I'm curious about this 'realization' thing. If we do the work of letting go and stay vigilant to the voice of fear through each stage of your cycle, why does the realization stage ever have to end? Can't we just hang out here, consider our work complete, and run our flag up the pole called 'enlightened'? After that last margarita, I'm feeling pretty darn realized . . . why would I want to let *that* go?"

"Hah," I chortled, thinking to myself how interesting it is that Carolyn and Hal, not cerebral Marie, are the ones to bombard me with the tough questions as we reach the end of our story. "I wish it were that simple, Hal, but you and I both know that the cycle of renewal is just that, a cycle. Your pinnacle period of realization, no matter how sweet, will come to an end soon enough. Something or someone will come along to disrupt your flight pattern and take you off course, delaying your imminent departure to the land of enlightenment. How many times have we witnessed, to our delight and dread, on the six o'clock news, another spiritual or political leader getting taken down from their lofty perch of sanctity by dastardly backroom, bathroom—and chat room—deeds that humble even the holiest of holy. It's called growing and learning, and if you don't become awake to the inevitability of the cycle, the universe gladly, and painfully, reminds you."

Not sure that Hal was very pleased with my answer, nor may you be. But the reality is that his desire to hold tight to success, no matter how grounded and present he may be, is a conceit of that well-worn story of the dictator, rising from the ash heap of our collective and personal ego's conditioning. In our simple and inevitable desire to hold on to the joy of realization, we spoil the meal, for our egos are alive and well, and only too willing to reemerge in new guises— of fear, and clinging—in their feeble attempts to hold on, even to the moment called "now." At this vulnerable juncture, even in the midst of partaking of the fine meal of realization, we must savor, but not linger, on our just dessert.

REVISITING RECONCILIATION

Here is the terrible, terrific truth: We cannot stay in a place we might call "fully realized." Doubt me on this one? Then think about this: Our friend

Philippe Petit can no longer dance across a wire slung between the twin tow-ers, not only because he is no longer the same Petit, but because *the towers are no longer there.* How's that for a reminder of the inevitability of change?

No, we cannot remain forever in realization, but we can express, expand, and envelop ourselves in the miracle of metamorphosis by practicing the two key hallmarks of shadow work: *acceptance* (of self, other, and the inevitability of change) and *humility*. I highly recommend that if you are in the realization stage, in any domain of your life, that you go back and revisit the tool of rec-onciliation. You may be surprised to find that it is easier now to acknowledge your strengths, to access your dark side, and to connect with the two sides of your essential nature: fear and love.

With a sense of gratitude for all your hard work, and the support of oth-ers who have propped you up along the way, take stock now of how your strengths, even the newly nascent narrative of self, which you have been ardently rehearsing, may become *a liability*. Practice staying awake to the paradox of human development: that our emergent identities cannot walk down the street in the sunlight without being followed by shadow. Literally and metaphorically, no matter how hard we might try to escape: It is always there, always attached to us, always ready to push us over the edge into the next rupture of self. And this is a good thing.

As I have stated all along in this book, fear, in its many guises and symp-toms, is a gift from our soul, for it operates as the wake-up call that it is time to move on, time to change, and time to grow. The journey toward fully real-izing our potential as human beings is a constant, recurring, back-and-forth dynamic between our ego's attempt to clarify, understand, and *know the way,* and a soul that has other plans for us—plans to take us up to the edge and fling us off into the abyss—so we can soar.

Life-Shifting Action/Reflection Step:
Holy Wholeness: Making a Mandala

If, after reading this chapter or taking the diagnostic exam, you find yourself in the realization stage of any domain of your life, congratulations! You have arrived. Take time to celebrate, honor, and recognize yourself for expanding, breaking through the "box" of your identity, and welcome your new sense of self.

The action step I recommend at this juncture is a beautiful gift you can give yourself in honor of your growth and movement toward wholeness. By taking time to meditate on your journey, and draw, paint, or collage a mandala, you create a mirror image of who you are today and an image that may point you places where you need to continue to work the edge of your fears and integrate your shadow.

The word "mandala" comes from the classical Indian language of Sanskrit and loosely translated means "circle." It is a universal symbol for wholeness utilized in the East, especially Tibet, to signify the complex interrelationship between the recurring incarnations of human beings and the ever-evolving path of the universe. It is also used by Jungian psychologists to aid individuals in accessing their deepest dreams, fears, and potential. The mandala can be seen as a model for the organizational structure of life itself—a cosmic diagram that connects us to the infinite, reminding us that the world extends both beyond and within our bodies, hearts, and minds.

Instructions: Take a blank piece of paper and draw a large circle. Using whatever tools you feel called to express yourself with—paint, crayons, pen, or collage—meditate for a few moments on your deepest questions about life, fear, love, and self. Allow time to just ruminate, reflect, and dream. There is no "answer" to arrive at, just as there is no right way to experience "realization." Be in the moment. Take time to just play with the images that arise in you and place them in whatever fashion feels appropriate inside the circle. You may want to draw a cross of straight lines within the circle to signify the four quadrants of wholeness—but this is not necessary.

When you have completed your first practice with making a mandala, you may want to practice imaginal dialogue with the image. A wonderful way to track your journey through the entire cycle of transformation—and to stalk your fears and your ego—is to embark on the next cycle by doing a series of mandalas along the way. Your mandala is a mirror reflection of your inner self, a doorway to the soul. It is an evolving, expanding, sometimes demanding, always revealing, reflection of the everlasting dance between ego and soul.

CRUISE CONTROL: GUIDELINES FOR LIFE-SHIFTING MASTERY

"Time changes everything except something within us which is always surprised at change."

—THOMAS HARDY

In bringing our journey together to a conclusion, I want to speak briefly on the subject of mastery. Not enlightenment, mind you, but mastery. By now I'm sure you have gleaned that although I believe that our path toward fulfillment of our potential as humans is a spiritual journey, I am suspect of the goal of enlightenment, or of the attainment of any form of final release, or dissolution of the self. Transcendence may be a marvelous, if momentary, peak experience, available to all of us as we journey through the hills and valleys of life, but, like capturing a hummingbird in midflight, if we hold on too tight, we set ourselves up for disappointment.

THREE PRINCIPLES FOR SAFE DRIVING

On the other hand, I do believe that by consistently applying the principles and practices outlined in this book, by customizing a life-shifting program to your own personal learning style, you can become masterful at *shifting*, at remaking yourself anew with less pain, more joy, and greater ease. Having enumerated the key steps and stages many times in the pages before, I won't repeat them here, but I do want to offer three final principles that may help you drive the vehicle of self safely through life's twists and turns:

1. Self-renewal is for everyone, at any age.
2. The cycle of renewal is not linear or static.
3. The process of reinventing your identity is not time dependent.

Regarding the first principle, I have to say, straight out, that I don't place much stock in midlife crises. It may be true that the three major case studies in this book involve individuals who hit a wall of fear and upheaval near a half-way point in the journey of their lives, but that has more to do with my belief in the power of their unique stories than any conscious desire to focus on a particular age bracket. I'm always wary of books and theorists who delineate stages of life as a linear, developmental process. It is true that we are different at age forty or fifty than we were at twenty, as I pointed out in chapter one, but by earmarking the ravages of fear and change as impacting the midlifers to a greater degree than others, we make two major blunders.

First, we minimize the sting of fear and accelerate the onset of anxiety, depression, and other painful symptoms during earlier transitions in life. Dismissing the importance of reexamining, discarding, and rewriting your personal narrative at the delicate coming-of-age periods—in your first intimate relationships, or your first career moves—may be great for selling books to baby boomers, but it does a disservice to the troubles of younger folks. My hope is that by learning to utilize the tools of life-shifting—with examples like Ellen and Peter and Mike—earlier in life, we may grow a middle-age population less in need of the pharmaceutical fix, more able to remain awake, aware, and amenable to change when, as it likely will, the shift hits the fan in later years.

Second, by only addressing the so-called special needs of midlifers, we reinforce the myth that life at sixty and beyond should be focused on retirement, winding down, and heading out to pasture, or at best, the golf club. Nothing could be further from the truth. My most vibrant, uplifting, and inspirational clients have often been those amazing individuals who refuse to toe the cultural line, who retain their youthful vitality and enthusiasm for life—and change—into their seventies and beyond. The upheavals and losses that inevitably occur as we age are no more or less frightful and potentially devastating to our sense of self-worth than our midcareer detours into divorce or unemployment. Yet we tend to dismiss the very possibility of renewal at later ages, forgetting that the energy, creativity, and passion of the divine child is alive in everyone, at any age, but it needs to be nourished, honored, and most of all, simply noticed.

My next principle for life-shifting mastery requests that you keep in mind that the process of self-renewal is not linear or static; i.e., you could end up in more than one stage at the same time! My six-stage model of change and the six tools for transforming fear are simply a road map and set of mechanic's tools just like ones you might carry in your glove compartment as you set out on a road trip. The nature of the trip itself, whether over rough terrain, backwoods, or superhighways, will be different depending on the particular territory of self that you traverse.

If you are focused on your career identity, the tools may help as you face down the terrors of downsizing, unemployment, or the tumult of voluntarily stepping off the corporate ladder. If you are experiencing upheaval in your relationships or your family dynamic, then you may discover that you are in a different stage on the road map in these domains. As a client who recently got married and lost her job *at the same time* reminded me, it can be daunting to toggle simultaneously between two unique travel itineraries. Nevertheless, the map and tool set are universally applicable, designed to give you permission to be *where you really are* along the route no matter how complex the multiple byways and highways of your journey may be.

The third principle, and to my mind, the most important, reminds us that there is no typical or standard length of time one must spend in any stage or even in any full cycle of self-renewal. We are all, every minute, being remade anew, and when clients ask me about stories like those of Hal, Carolyn, and Marie, wondering, "Does it have to take years to reinvent myself?" I gently give my now-expected response: "That depends." The key to being a master at life-shifting is to step back and reevaluate where you are, how you feel, and what you are doing, at each stage, not shortening the trip or trying to rush the process, but at the same time not becoming self-indulgent with your ego and allowing life to slip through your grasp. There is plenty of time *and* time is of the essence. Move through periods of transition, and transformation, with alacrity, agility, and patience. It is OK to wear a watch, just don't look at it every minute!

CLOSING THE LOOP: MY CYCLE(S) OF SELF-RENEWAL

To provide a bit of context for how self-renewal may unfold in a minute, or over a lifetime, I would like to travel full circle back to my personal story and share two examples that have taught me one thing for sure: The cycle and the shifts *happen*, sometimes so quickly, in a matter of days or weeks, that we may be shocked at just how fast we really can change. Likewise, as my leadership development colleagues like to say when working with teams, "norming, forming, storming, and reforming" your deepest beliefs and identifications—heeding your soul's call *to become*—is never finished. It is, in essence, the story of your life.

If you remember, in a moment of raw, unadulterated rupture—feeling totally out of alignment—I decided rather haphazardly to take up yoga. As I indicated in the introduction, my meeting with my wise teacher, Sadie, and my early forays into "downward dog" were painful and embarrassing. But it was also true that once I became facile in facing off with my fear—and recognized that fear was afoot at all—I actually went through the entire cycle of reinventing my relationship with my body, and my identity, at least in regard to yoga, in about five weeks.

Like yesterday, I remember the day I hit the wall of my ego, both literally and metaphorically. It occurred when Sadie decided that anyone, and I mean anyone, could learn to do what is considered one of the most challenging and advanced moves in yoga practice: a handstand. My first attempts to unfold my body upside down, arms outstretched, with a wall as backup, were disasters of the highest order. I have strong arms, and could push myself upside down well enough, but straightening my back, pulling in my butt, keeping my feet *off* the wall? Impossible.

The definitive story that I told myself was this: I am not a yogi. I will never be a yogi. I am not designed to go upside down, even for a few seconds. Hang from a bar perhaps, stand on my head, perhaps, but stand up on my hands and stroll around, *never*. My ego was so heartily attached to this story that when it came time for Sadie, as soul guide, to push me up against the edge of that psychic and physical box, I resisted mightily. I cursed (under my breath) her and all the flexible flyer felines who were dancing on their hands all around me. For days I stubbornly refused to let go of this story—of limitation, comfort, and arrogance—until one day, while simmering with frustration, my toes clinging to the wall, I collapsed in a heap, hit my head smack on the floor, curled up in a ball, and thought to myself, "That's it, I'm out of here."

I wasn't particularly hurt, just humiliated, so I took my tears of self-pity out on the sidewalk where no one, least of all, Sadie, would see. Yet, something else occurred in that singular moment of vanity and victimhood: As I walked down the street sniffling in self-pity, I glanced in a store window and saw my own reflection. What I saw was laughable: a grown man pouting like a child who had had his favorite toy stolen. I couldn't help but laugh. "Silly, silly man," I thought. "Just let it go. So what if you can't do a handstand at forty-five. Is that really a big deal?"

You know the rest of the story. Once I let go of my attachment to getting it right and my fear of doing it wrong, as well as my story of not being able to do it at all—and just decided to have fun, do whatever I could, and play—it was not three weeks later that I found myself in midair, upside down, holding steady for—OK, truth here—twenty seconds. A miracle occurred on Thirty-Fourth Street, as I had broken my own record of two seconds tenfold. Soon I would be redefining my self as a fledgling, albeit floundering yogi. Later, after making a commitment to a regular practice, and a powerful, if occasionally anxiety-producing, rehearsal stage, I was honored by Sadie with the receipt of my certification as a yoga instructor. If someone as handicapped as yours truly can reinvent their relationship with their body, and with their story, in a matter of weeks, you can easily become a master life-shifter—perhaps even a teacher of life-shifting to others—in short order. *It*, that grand two-lettered symbol for all the greatness in you that has yet to be revealed, is in you.

What is also true is that the struggle to carve out an identity with depth and resonance for our souls, a truly *meaningful me*, may take years. Consider, if you will, another part of my story. If you remember, my very first "rupture" of identity took place when I was seven years old, when my parents announced to me, in the form of a book (books can change your life!), that I was adopted. It took me many years to release the pain of the story of being abandoned, to move through the fear of being found out, supposedly, as unwanted and unloved, finally releasing the burden of shame and setting forth on the search for my true roots. Yet, even after that pinnacle period of realization, which I celebrated by having both my mothers, genetic and adoptive, with me at my PhD graduation ceremony, I find that I am still not done reinventing my relationship with that aspect of identity we call "family."

For many years I would look around at friends and acquaintances who have large, close, and expansive families, and be envious, attached to my story that even though I was blessed to have a great adoptive mother, I am still the survivor of a fractured family system. Only recently have I come, once again, to break apart this vestigial narrative of woe, and take up the revival stage with a new playmate: a younger brother. A recalibration of my identity of huge proportions, I have had to let go of my "only child" syndrome and welcome the newest truth on the landscape of self, that I have had a younger sibling all along, it just took us forty years to meet. The familial story of self may evolve, die, and be reborn, continuously, for life.

WE ARE ALL ORPHANS

Listening deeply and with compassion to my friends and clients who have stories of family fragmentation that make mine look like a walk in the park, I am constantly reminded that perhaps the one journey of self-renewal that does take a lifetime is the one we make with our families of origin. I think there is a way in which we all, in times of fear and breakdown, feel like orphans. We yearn for that *other* family, the one across the street that never fights; the one that is always loving and supporting, where we can hole up and bask in the light of unconditional love. But that fantasy is our downfall, for it is born of envy, fueled by our ego's need to complain, control, and hold intact a deeply forged story of fear—that we might not be lovable, or good enough.

Ultimately, there comes a time when you must leave off the search for belonging in your particular family constellation and look inward, peering into your own heart for an answer to the deepest questions of identity: Who am I? Where do I belong? And it is here, in the inner family circle, where you will not only discover a whole cast of loving characters just waiting to greet you, but something else too: an inner voice, *the voice of your soul*, whose raison d'être is to remind you of two simple truths. First, that you are never truly alone (loneliness is an emotional state, and a sign of the rupture stage, not a state of being); you always belong in a universe that is overflowing with potential playmates, in the form of life-shifters who, just like you, are longing to connect. Second, and most important, is that the source of salvation, a bottomless, bountiful wellspring of nurturing, is always available to you, just by turning the dial on your internal car radio to the VOR—and listening in for those top three hits of all time: self-acceptance, self-acknowledgment, and self-compassion.

THE SHIFTING SEASONS OF LIFE

Sitting here in the Hudson River valley, overlooking my crackling creek and the Catskill Mountains beyond, I watch wistfully as the leaves dry up, detach from their mighty oak and maple mothers, and in sunlit sparks of gold, orange, and yellow, float off in the wind. Autumn has arrived and the death of another remarkable year is imminent. Fitting, that nature herself would remind us, each day, each season, without fail, that life is fleeting, cyclical, and in a state of constant change, which if we are truly honest with ourselves, is both bad and good news. Bad news, because it is sad to watch the leaves fall, sad to feel time slip by, sad to know the only outcome that is certain: All things end. But good news as well, to know that spring will come once again. If we are more aware that it is in the nature of things to be reborn, remade, and rewritten anew, perhaps we may learn to face into winds of change with a bit more lightness, and go with the flow.

It is also timely to note, during this age of technological advances and upheavals, that there is another form of leaf that is drying up, and supposedly passing away: the "leaves" of books. Many of my close pals have asked me, "Why would you want to write a book now, Jeff? No one reads them anymore, the publishing industry is in upheaval (rupture?), and the book itself is dying out, being replaced with video, text messaging, and all sorts of instant communications." Well, I reflect back in response, this may very well be true. The death knell of the book, at least in forms we have come to know and love, may have rung. Although, I do believe that, as a lover of books, I'm hardly alone and that even in some high-tech digitized form, we will always love stories and desire that they be told.

In any case, just as I advised you to avoid setting hard and fast goals during the rehearsal and realization stages of your life's journey, I have not been particularly motivated by the goal of "writing a book." What drives me and inspires me even in the midst of the possible demise of the very product that I have worked to produce is my desire to create a *new conversation* about fear and change. My intention has been to help people reinvent their relationship with fear, to recalibrate their view of change, and to reenvision ways of *seeing through* themselves, from ego to soul.

If just one person reads this book and wakes up to the possibility that being anxious or depressed at times when change is afoot is *normal,* and that he or she may not need to medicate or focus solely on alleviating the pain, instead choosing to tune in to the symptom as a signal, a symbolic language speaking to him or her from deep within, then what form this work ultimately evolves into—book, video, workshop, or tweet—doesn't matter. I have done what my soul compelled and there is only one thing left to do: surrender these "leaves" to the universe.

ACKNOWLEDGMENTS

Looking back on the learning and healing journey that ultimately led to the creation of this book, I can't help but smile as I think of the idealistic and somewhat cavalier attitude with which I began the project. I naively believed that writing a book was a solo enterprise. Nothing could be further from the truth. Of course, in the final weeks, I did hole up at my country home and scribble away, interrupted only by a hungry cat, scene-stealing visits from the bountiful deer, and gentle chiding from my editor that I could "make that deadline." And yet, I was far from alone. As I stand on the cusp of the "realization" stage of this process, I am deeply humbled, and eternally grateful to the many partners, friends, teachers, and clients who have touched, influenced, and helped to shape every word in this document.

I began this project with a partner-in-crime, my dear friend and muse par excellence, Judy Fox, who is the breath of fresh air that I turn to whenever my flames of inspiration dim. Judy is a unique individual. A deeply insightful teacher, healer, and creative spirit, she moves effortlessly between the seemingly opposing worlds of expert/counselor and student/practitioner. Many of the themes and practices in this book have been co-created with her over omelets in our favorite diner in Larchmont, New York. Her guiding hand and loving soul lies behind much of the process that comprises the Life-Shifting Program.

It would be difficult to enumerate all the teachers, spirit guides, and mentors who have played a part in making this book a reality, but I have been so blessed by the right teacher showing up at just the right time that I must attempt to acknowledge at least a partial list. In the introduction, I note three of my most influential teachers, Carl Jung, S. N. Goenka, and Sadie Nardini, but there have been many others, whose wisdom and insight form the foundation stones of any artful edifice that I might claim as my own. Tom and Flame Lutes, whose powerful group process is poignantly called "Stalking the Truth," have been role models for me for over a decade. They are responsible for teaching me, among many things, the importance of honoring and integrating the body into any personal work that hopes to result in lasting transformation.

Other key mentors on my path have been Robert Forman, CEO of the Forge Institute for Trans-traditional Wisdom; Rev. Diane Berke, founder of the One Spirit Interfaith Alliance; Malidoma Somé; Toni Stone of Wonder Works Studio in Fairfax, Vermont; David Frechter; Pema Chödrön; Margaret Wheatley; David Whyte; and my inspiring professors of depth psychology, Mary Watkins and Helene Shulman Lorenz at the Pacifica Graduate Institute.

Then there are many amazing clients, coaches, friends and colleagues, with whom I have often played both student and teacher, some of whom have found their way into this book. Without their stories, their willingness to *shift*, their commitment to their own growth, and their unwavering support, this book would not have been possible. With a bow of gratitude, I salute Marion Robinson, Colette Gardner, Harry Kobritz, Scott Seale, Steven Hess, Steve Miller, Robert Smith, David Jacobs, Frank Gibney, Xavier Roux, Florence Magne, Lisa Sussman, Lisa Tener, Kathy Calabrese, Gabriele Ganswindt, Hudson Talbott, Kenneth Karpel, Ira Rosenblum, Steve Mendelsohn, and Yannick Claareboudt.

And then there are close friends, loved ones I turned to when the writing journey seemed endless, even tiresome, and I felt that deep yearning for a hug, to be heard, and to belong. The list begins with my dear pal, Gary Drake, the one person who despite his own health and life challenges, has always been available to deeply listen and support me through both the highs and lows of this writing journey. He is also a talented writer in his own right, and I hope that I can return the favor of supporting him as he evolves towards his dream of seeing his name in print. He has great wisdom to share in a world that sorely needs voices like his.

My soulmate and friend for life, Barbara Phillips, was also crucial to the healing foundations of this book, for as the very first person with whom I shared my story of being adopted, she was the loving catalyst that spurred me on the quest to find my birth family. Thank you, Barbara, for always making me feel safe.

My other dear partner-in-life has been Justin Chen, M.D., whose love and support saw me through the early stages of crafting the phrase, "life-shifting," into a process, a program, and now a book. On his way to becoming the kind of psychiatrist that the world sorely needs now more than ever, Justin is intellectually exceptional but also willing to listen to his heart and be true to his soul—and the souls of his patients. I feel honored to be a collaborator with him in keeping the importance of emotional healing alive in the midst of the overly bio-mechanical medical regime of our time.

Crucial to my success as a writer, executive coach, and psychotherapist have been other long-standing partners: Pascal Scemama, M.D. who rescued me from unemployment and set forth with me on the path of entrepreneur-ship; and Julie and Morgan McKeown, whose professional and personal partnership at their executive coaching firm, *CorBusiness*, was responsible for much of the real-world experience that led this book to shift from dream to reality. I am grateful to Morgan, especially, for introducing me to an amazing array of senior executives at Fortune 100 companies, whose willingness to change and grow as leaders, in spite of the fiscal and political pressures to perform—and conform—inspires my unyielding optimism about the future of corporate America.

To my wonderful agent, Malaga Baldi, whose persistence and calm, even during the darkest moments of the economic recession, kept my enthusiasm for this project alive. I am forever grateful. Likewise, true blessing arrived in the midst of the worst economic downturn in seventy years, when the universe provided me with not only the perfect publishing team at GPP, but Lara Asher, editor extraordinaire. Without Lara's unwavering support and adept handling of all the ins-and-outs of the publishing process, not to mention her deft skills as an editor, this book would never have seen the light of day.

Finally, my eternal thanks to my birth mother Toni, and, posthumously, my adoptive mother, Lucille, who passed away just weeks after I signed the contract for *Shift*. She would have been thrilled to see this project unfold, for she was unwavering in her support and love for me, no matter how far from a linear path her perpetually wayward son roamed. Having two mothers might be viewed as double indemnity by some, but I feel truly blessed. Together, they have provided me with just the right combination of nature and nurture, such that any gifts readers receive from reading this book may be directly attributed, not to me, but to them.

Sources

Ablow, Keith, M.D. *Living the Truth: Transform Your Life through the Power of Insight and Honesty.* New York, NY: Little Brown & Company, 2007.

Attwood, Janet and Chris. *The Passion Test: The Effortless Path to Discovering Your Life's Purpose.* New York, NY: Penguin Plume, 2008.

Chödrön, Pema. *The Places That Scare You: A Guide to Fearlessness in Difficult Times.* Boston, MA: Shambhala Publications, 2001.

Chopra, Deepak. *Re-inventing the Body, Resurrecting the Soul: How to Create a New You.* New York, NY: Harmony Books, 2009.

Corbett, Lionell. *The Religious Function of the Psyche.* London, UK: Routledge, 1996.

Cornell, Ann Weiser, Ph.D. *The Power of Focusing: A Practical Guide to Emotional Self-Healing.* Oakland, CA: New Harbinger Publications, 1996.

Gendlin, Eugene T., Ph.D. *Focusing.* New York, NY: Bantam Dell, 1981.

Goswami, Amit. *The Visionary Window: A Quantum Physicist's Guide to Enlightenment.* Wheaton, IL: Quest Books, 2000.

Heckler, Richard Strozzi. *The Anatomy of Change: A Way to Move Through Life's Transitions.* Berkeley, CA: North Atlantic Books, 1993.

Jeffers, Susan, Ph.D. *Feel the Fear and . . . Do It Anyway.* New York, NY: Ballantine Books, 1996.

Jung, Carl, and Jaffé, Aniela (ed.), Winston, Clara (trans.), Winston, Richard (trans.), *Memories, Dreams, Reflections.* New York, NY: Random House, 1989.

Katie, Byron and Mitchell, Stephen. *Loving What Is: Four Questions That Can Change Your Life.* New York, NY: Three Rivers Press, 2002.

Lorenz, Helene Shulman, Ph.D. *Living at the Edge of Chaos: Complex Systems in Culture and Psyche.* Zurich: Daimon Verlag, 1997.

Nardini, Sadie. *Road Trip Guide to the Soul: A 9-Step Guide to Reaching Your Inner Self and Revolutionizing Your Life.* Hoboken, NJ: John Wiley & Sons, 2008.

Orloff, Judith, M.D. *Emotional Freedom: Liberate Yourself from Negative Emotions and Transform Your Life.* New York, NY: Harmony Books, 2009.

Pearsall, Paul, Ph.D. *Toxic Success: How to Stop Striving and Start Thriving.* Maui, HI: Inner Ocean Publishing, 2002.

Peck, M. Scott. *The Road Less Traveled: A New Psychology of Love, Traditional Values and Spiritual Growth.* New York, NY: Touchstone, 2003.

Somé, Malidoma Patrice, Ph.D. *The Healing Wisdom of Africa.* New York, NY: Penguin Putnam, 1998.

Stone, Toni. *Discovering Prosperity: Principles to Open Understanding.* Fairfax, VT: Wonderworks.org, 2007.

Tolle, Eckhardt. *The Power of Now: A Guide to Spiritual Enlightenment.* Novato, CA: New World Publishing, 1999.

Watkins, Mary, Ph.D. *Invisible Guests: The Development of Imaginal Dialogues.* Woodstock, CT: Spring Publications, 2000.

Wheatley, Margaret J. *Finding Our Way: Leadership for an Uncertain Time.* San Francisco, CA: Berrett-Koehler, 2005.

Whyte, David. *Fire in the Earth.* Langley, WA: Many Rivers Press, 1997.

_____. *The Heart Aroused: Poetry and the Preservation of the Soul in Corporate America.* New York, NY: Currency Doubleday, 1994.

Wilkinson, Margaret. *Coming into Mind: The Mind-Brain Relationship: A Clinical Jungian Perspective.* New York, NY: Routledge, 2006.

INDEX

employment and, 9
fear symptoms and change of, 46–47
grief and death of, 186–87
nature of, 9–11, 19–20, 153
quantum physics and, 11–13
sense of, 6–7
soul conflict with, 6, 16, 19, 70
story of, 12–13, 27, 156–57, 220, 268
vitality and, 33–36
wounds as components of, 8–9
illness
medical profession perception of, 41, 45
reframing exercises using, 159–60
as reinvention opportunity, 50–52
social support benefits, 96
stress, 52–55
as symptoms of needed change, 39–40, 146, 164
symptoms *vs.* cause of, 45–50
imaginal (inner) dialogues
dreams as, 14–15, 118–22, 213–15, 219
fear awareness using, 128–29
negative self-talk, 42, 100
with realization mandalas, 264
as self-support, 97–102
inadequacy, 83, 246–47
individuation, theory of, 16, 66
intention, 31–32
intuition, 43, 161
isolation, 96

Jeffers, Susan, 246
judgment, voice of (VOJ), 84, 101, 102–4, 118
Jung, Carl
Active Imagination practices, 118, 122
divine child energy, 246
dream studies and unconscious, 14–15, 118
happiness addiction, 71
individuation, theory of, 16, 66
inner support, 99
personality "shadows," 169, 170

personality traits as energy domains, 111

Katie, Byron, 69
Keller, Helen, 73

language, power of, 12–13
life
metaphors for, 250
nature of, 5–6, 24, 64, 65, 66, 67, 74, 181
road maps of, 74, 77–80
listening, 18, 40, 99–100
loneliness, 82, 270
Loving What Is (Katie), 69
Lutes, Flame, 134
Lutes, Tom, 21, 134

mandala exercises, 264
material wealth, 21, 69–72, 73–74, 188
meditation, 42, 132–35, 136, 218
Memories, Dreams, Reflections (Jung), 14
Mess in the Middle, The (Stone), 226–27
midlife crises, 265–66
mirroring, 89
monkey mind, 40
moving energy exercises, 134, 137–39
Myers-Briggs Type tests, 111

neuroscience, 16–17, 132–33, 201

One Spirit Interfaith Church, 157–58
orphan metaphors, 269–70
Oz, Mehmet, 33

pain, 159–60, 197
paralysis, fear of, 82–83
parents, as fear factors, 91–92, 102–3, 126–27, 213–15
passions, 71–72
Passion Test, The (Attwood and Attwood), 71
Pearsall, Paul, 257–58
Peck, M. Scott, 55, 58
personality, 111–16, 169–75. *See also* ego; identity

ABOUT THE AUTHOR

Jeffrey W. Hull, PhD, is a Jungian psychotherapist, executive/life coach, and author widely recognized as a pioneer in the fields of performance and life coaching for executives. His clients range from individuals to multinational Fortune 500 corporations. He has been profiled in the *New York Times* and *Investors Business Daily*, and he has appeared on national television programs such as *Good Morning America*. He lives in New York City and in the Hudson River Valley. For more information and inspiration, visit www.life-shifting.com.